Ethnonationalism

D0165573

Ethnonationalism

THE QUEST FOR UNDERSTANDING

Walker Connor

PRINCETON UNIVERSITY PRESS

PRINCETON, NEW JERSEY

Copyright © 1994 by Princeton University Press
Published by Princeton University Press, 41 William Street,
Princeton, New Jersey 08540
In the United Kingdom: Princeton University Press,
Chichester, West Sussex

All Rights Reserved

Connor, Walker, 1926–
Ethnonationalism : the quest for understanding /
Walker Connor.
p. cm.
Includes bibliographical references and index.
ISBN 0-691-08784-9 (cloth : alk. paper)
ISBN0-691-02563-0 (pbk. : alk. paper)
1. Nationalism. 2. Ethnic relations—Political aspects.
3. Ethnicity—Political aspects. 4. Ethnic groups—
Political activity. 5. National characteristics—Political
aspects. 6. World politics I. Title.
JC311.C644   1994   323.1'1—dc20   93-17829

This book has been composed in Adobe Palatino

Princeton University Press books are printed on acid-free paper
and meet the guidelines for permanence and durability of the
Committee on Production Guidelines for Book Longevity
of the Council on Library Resources

Printed in the United States of America

3   5   7   9   10   8   6   4

This book is dedicated to

—in order of appearance—

PETER, JOAN, AND DANIEL

Remember the sequoias . . .

CONTENTS

LIST OF FIGURES AND TABLES

FIGURES

TABLES

INTRODUCTION

A LIKELY first response to the title of this book, *Ethnonationalism*, is "What is it and how does it differ from just plain *nationalism?*" The answer is that there is no difference if nationalism is used in its pristine sense. Unfortunately, this is rarely the case. As will be discussed in chapter 2 and more fully in chapter 4, slipshod use of the key terms, nation and nationalism, is more the rule than the exception, even in works purportedly dealing with nationalism. As used throughout this book, nation connotes a group of people who believe they are ancestrally related. Nationalism connotes identification with and loyalty to one's nation as just defined. It does *not* refer to loyalty to one's country. Admittedly then, ethnonationalism has an inner redundancy, and it is used solely to avoid any misunderstanding concerning our focus. Throughout this work, nationalism and ethnonationalism are treated as synonyms.

The body of this book consists of nine essays whose publication dates span a quarter-century. The interest of Princeton University Press in publishing such a collection was first raised by Sanford Thatcher nearly twenty years ago. Although excited by the prospect, I allowed myself to be sidetracked by a series of other projects. My interest in publishing a collection on nationalism persisted, however, and several articles that I produced during the 1970s and 1980s were written with an eye to their inclusion. As a result, when Gail Ullman of Princeton University Press raised anew the question of whether I would be interested in publishing a series of my articles on nationalism, I had several more from which to select.

Gail Ullman suggested I select articles that "would focus primarily on the theoretical issues involved in studying nationalism." Consonant with this advice, it is the study of nationalism, and not the politics of nationalism, which forms the interconnecting theme of the various chapters. This is not to say that the political consequences of ethnonationalism are ignored. Indeed, contrasting the literature on political development with *actual political developments* is a major element of the critique of scholarship in Part 1 of this book. Nevertheless, had the title of this book been *The Politics of Ethnonationalism*, a completely different selection of writings would have been made.

All of the articles are reproduced essentially as they first appeared. The political map underwent numerous significant changes since the earliest piece was published in 1967, of course. The number of independent states grew by nearly 50 percent, from approximately 120 to 180. Overseas colonial empires continued to dissolve. The overland, multinational empire, which had been formed by the Russian czars and ruled over by Marxist-Leninists during its last seven decades, decomposed into fifteen separate "republics." Two states that had been created at the end of World War I under the banner of self-determination of nations, Czechoslovakia and Yugoslavia, also sundered along ethnonational lines. The Bengalis of Eastern Pakistan seceded to create their own state. Cyprus underwent a de facto division into Greek and Turkish components. The two Germanies were reunited as were the two Vietnams. Ethnonationally inspired struggles continued to proliferate. But on balance, all these developments appear to support rather than challenge the general analytical framework presented in the following chapters. In those relatively few instances where it was believed necessary to update the material, asterisks, highlights, and brackets have been used to alert the reader.

Deletions have been almost entirely restricted to unnecessary duplications. Because each article was designed to stand alone, some groundwork (such as the author's definition of nation) had to be presented on more than one occasion. In addition, particularly insightful and elegantly written citations from Ernest Barker, Rupert Emerson, Carleton Hayes, Hans Kohn, and the like, were also used in more than one piece. In a very few instances, such repetitious material has been knowingly retained for the sake of emphasis. Hopefully, however, duplication has been cut to a tolerable level.

The ordering of the articles was dictated by the desire for continuity of theme. Neither the year of writing nor the year of publication was a consideration. However, both dates will be given for each article, so that the reader will be able to differentiate foresight from hindsight. A personal experience may help to explain why I consider it important for the reader to be able to do so. In the 1960s, I had occasion to reread the *Essays on Nationalism* which Carleton Hayes had published forty years earlier (1926). What truly amazed me was that Hayes's analysis of trends in European politics (including a warning of future trouble between ethnonational groups within Belgium and Switzerland and a discussion of what he termed "the budding little nationalisms" of Icelanders, Basques, Catalans, Belorussians, and others) had all been borne out by developments in post–World War II Europe, although even post–World War II scholars had been unable to anticipate them. A hindsight analysis by Hayes, written in the 1960s, could not have so indelibly impressed upon me the realization that his profound regard for the vitality and stamina of ethnonational sentiments was not in the least exaggerated. Because of this encounter with the Hayes of the 1920s, my own subsequent work has reflected a strong respect for the influence that ethnonationalism exerts on human perceptions and behavior. It is my hope that a few of my earlier pieces, read from the vantage point of the 1990s, may help to generate among others a similar respect for the power and influence of the ethnonational factor.

The schema of this work is as follows: Part 1 reviews how various scholars have perceived ethnonationalism and its political consequences. It begins (chapter 1) with a multigenerational debate among some of Britain's most esteemed nineteenth- and early twentieth-century scholars concerning the viability and desirability of the multinational state; and it measures the accuracy of their conclusions against the yardstick of actual political developments. Chapter 2 notes that the school of thought called "nation-building," which dominated the literature on political development in the post–World War II United States, totally ignored or vastly underestimated the significance of nationalism; and it suggests a number of reasons therefor. Chapter 3, written when evidence of ethnonationally inspired unrest had become so widespread as to attract the attention of large numbers of scholars, notes that the resulting explosion of the literature on nationalism evidences little concord concerning (1) the nature of ethnonational identity and (2) how or even whether ethnic heterogeneity can be peacefully accommodated.

Part 2 examines four impedimenta to improving scholarship on ethnonationalism: terminological confusion (chapter 4), a tendency to perceive homogeneity even where heterogeneity thrives (chapter 5), an unwarranted tendency to seek explanation for ethnic conflict in economic differentials (chapter 6), and lack of historical perspective (chapter 7).

The thrust of Part 3 might also be classified within the category of impedimenta to the study of nationalism. But here we are not concerned with correctable deficiencies or tendencies on the part of some analysts. Rather, we are concerned with problems of analysis arising from the very nature of ethnonational identity. As explained in chapter 8, the national bond is subconscious and emotional rather than conscious and rational in its inspiration. As such, it is capable of overcoming a welter of contrary fact (chapter 9). Overall then, Part 3 is concerned with inherent limitations of rational inquiry into the realm of group identity.

PART ONE

Ethnonationalism and Scholars

Chapter One

THE BRITISH INTELLECTUAL TRADITION

The following article ("Self-Determination: The New Phase") was written in 1966. It is my earliest published piece on nationalism, and I beg the reader's indulgence for the use of *culture group* as a substitute for *nation* in its first few pages. As noted in the text, I was resolutely trying to avoid "that labyrinthine question, 'What constitutes a nation?' " I would shortly come to realize that avoidance was impossible (see below, chapters 2 and 4), and I would henceforth certainly not consider "culture group" a worthy substitute.

The subtitle ("The New Phase") is important, for a main goal of the piece was to draw attention to the then generally unrecognized fact that national movements were surfacing all over the globe. A handy vehicle for presenting the matter was found in a British intellectual debate concerning the survivability of the multination state. At least to this author, the debate had two interesting sidelights. One was its long-running character. Eighty years elapsed between its initiation by John Stuart Mill and the contribution of Alfred Cobban during World War II. By contrast, interest today in the works of a scholar of nationalism seldom survives her/his demise; perhaps this helps account for a current catchphrase within academic circles: "Every generation must reinvent the wheel." The second sidelight arises from its normative theme: the contributors to the debate are divided over whether it is the nation-state or the multination state that represents (in Hegel's words) "the march of God in the world." There is more than a whiff of vanity in the debate, an unstated but implicit assumption that whoever presents the best case for or against the multinational state will control its destiny. References to the actual experiences of states are few and often misconceived. Overall then, the debate evidences an exaggerated notion of the importance of the intellectual and a somewhat poor knowledge of the real world.

Self-Determination: The New Phase[*]

CAN TWO OR MORE self-differentiating culture groups coexist within a single political structure? The question may well seem clearly settled by the overwhelming factual evidence of contemporary international politics, for it is indeed a truism that political and ethnic borders seldom coincide. Thus, the very existence of a host of multinational states, including such a time-tested example as the Soviet Union, would appear to document an affirmative answer. On the other hand, a recent spate of political unrest within such geographically diverse and historically unrelated states as, inter alia, Canada, Guyana, India, Uganda, Belgium, the Sudan, Burma [Myanmar], Yugoslavia, Cyprus, Rwanda, the United Kingdom, and Iraq, focuses attention on the common root cause of intrastate yet international conflict and again brings into question the assumptions of the multinational state.

These assumptions were never seriously challenged until the rise of *popular* national consciousness, and the issue is therefore of relatively recent origin. As Sir Ernest Barker noted:

> The self-consciousness of nations is a product of the nineteenth century. This is a matter of the first importance. Nations were already there; they had indeed been there for centuries. But it is not the things which are simply 'there' that matter in human life. What really and finally matters is the thing which is apprehended as an idea, and, as an idea, is vested with emotion until it becomes a cause and a spring of action. In the world of action apprehended ideas are alone electrical; and a nation must be an idea as well as a fact before it can become a dynamic force.[1]

Barker here provides us with the means of avoiding the labyrinthine question, "What constitutes a nation?" In the final analysis, the coincidence of the customary tangible attributes of nationality, such as common language or religion, is not determinative. The prime requisite is subjective and consists of the self-identification of people with a group—its past, its present, and, what is most important, its destiny.

What lent political force to the growth of national consciousness was

[*] Published in "Self-Determination: The New Phase," *World Politics* 20 (October 1967): 20–53. Copyright © 1967 Johns Hopkins University Press. Reprinted with permission of Johns Hopkins University Press.

the ancillary doctrine that political self-expression was a necessary concomitant of cultural consciousness, a doctrine that seriously challenged, perhaps even totally denied, the legitimacy of the multistate structure. There is general agreement that the first indications of this concept of the right of nations to political self-expression can be detected in the fruits of the first Polish partition, and more evidently in the American and French revolutions. Denied by the Congress of Vienna and the Holy Alliance, national consciousness throve on adversity, spreading throughout Europe and Latin America during the nineteenth century.[2] Although the peace settlements that followed World War I honored the concept more in the breach than in application, the numerous wartime and postwar public espousals of the doctrine by leading statesmen of the Allied Powers accorded to it a recognition of validity that would henceforth prove difficult to ignore or deny. The doctrine, by this time expressed in the phrase "self-determination of nations," was clearly never intended by Wilson and other contemporary advocates to have universal application. Rather, it was intended by them to apply solely to areas formerly under the sovereignty of the defeated powers.[3] However, the principle had been consistently stated in the broadest of terms,[4] and it could therefore be cited with equal validity by any group desirous of repudiating foreign rule.[5] The doctrine thereafter became both a catalyst and a defense for independence movements throughout the world and was instrumental in the post–World War II recession of European power from Africa and Asia.

There was, however, a unique feature to the African and Asian independence movements. Although they had been conducted in the name of self-determination of nations, they were, in fact, demands for political independence not in accord with ethnic distributions, but along the essentially happenstance borders that delimited either the sovereignty or the administrative zones of former colonial powers. This fact combined with the incredibly complex ethnic map of Africa and Asia to create, in the name of self-determination of nations, a host of multinational states.[6] Now, in turn, these new political structures, along with some of the older European states, are the targets of growing demands that self-determination be carried a further step toward its natural conclusion. And the leaders of these new states, though recent espousers of national self-determination, are now perforce the defenders of multinationalism.

Multinationalism has had both its detractors and supporters among scholars. Although criticism of the logical bases of traditional political borders was inseparable from Locke's and Jefferson's insistence that government must rest upon the consent of the governed, it is in the writings of John Stuart Mill that the issue is first clearly posed in terms of nationality. His remarks, published in 1861 in *Considerations on Representative Government*, ignited a controversy among British scholars which was ultimately to include such notables as Lord Acton, Ernest Barker, and Alfred Cobban.

Mill maintained that "it is in general a necessary condition of free institutions that the boundaries of government should coincide in the main with those of nationality."[7] This conclusion was predicated upon his fear of despotic government, for he believed that a multinational population would invite authoritarianism by lending itself to a divide-and-rule technique. He feared that the mutual antipathies and jealousies of the nationalities would prove greater than any distrust of governmental power. Mill was particularly concerned about the possible impact that multinationalism might have upon the army. Convinced that a major deterrent to despotism was the common bond of nationality between army personnel and the public at large, he foresaw the danger that a despot of a multinational state might employ troops of one ethnic strain against his subjects of another. According to Mill, in such event the soldiers "will have no more scruple mowing them down, and no more desire to ask the reason why, than they would have in doing the same thing against declared enemies."[8]

Mill's analysis spurred a strong rebuttal in an article published during the following year by Lord Acton.[9] The contrast between the two men's antithetical conclusions is the more remarkable because of the identity of goals. Acton, as Mill, desired foremost to prevent absolutism, but he envisaged the homogeneous population advocated by Mill as the natural ally of authoritarianism. In an argument not dissimilar to that advanced by Madison in *Federalist Paper No. 10* (if economic and geographic diversity be replaced by distinctions of nationality), Acton contended: "The presence of different nations under the same sovereignty . . . provides against the servility which flourishes under the shadow of a single authority, by balancing interests, multiplying associations and giving to the subject the restraint and support of a combined opinion."[10] He added: "That intolerance of social freedom which is natural to absolutism is sure to find a corrective in the national diversities, which no other force could so efficiently provide. The coexistence of several nations under the same State is a test as well as the best security of its freedom."[11]

In addition to recognizing its antidespotic function, Acton also supported the multinational state as the necessary vehicle of civilization. It was only within the larger crucible of the heterogeneous state that separate nations would interact, amiably compete, and contribute to the progress of one another. Small homogeneous states were therefore viewed as "impediments to the progress of society, which depends on the mixture of races under the same government."[12] The word "mixture" should not be taken too literally, however, for Acton was certainly not making a case for assimilation. What he desired was stringent cultural autonomy. Although a state within which no mixture of nationalities occurred was described as "imperfect," a state that attempted to neutralize or absorb divergent cultures thereby, Acton maintained, "destroys its own vitality" and is "decrepit."[13]

Acton's analysis was criticized, in turn, by Ernest Barker, who found it wanting on pragmatic grounds. With the advantage of the knowledge provided by an additional sixty-five years of political history, Barker characterized Lord Acton's defense of the multinational state as abstract and controverted by facts. "But even in 1860," he contended, "it might have been perceived that in a multi-national State the government either pits each nation against the rest to secure its own absolutism [as maintained by Mill], or allows itself to become the organ of one of the nations for the suppression or oppression of others."[14] Barker acknowledged that history provided examples of autocratic states that were composed of a number of nations, but he held that an unassimilated democratic state tended to dissolve into as many democracies as there were nationalities. This tendency, combined with what Barker perceived as a seemingly inexorable movement toward assimilation brought on by the rise of such forces as public school systems, mass communication facilities, and the need for a common statewide tongue, caused Barker to predict a worldwide "scheme of political organization in which each nation is also a State, and each State is also a nation."[15]

The redressing of the scholarly balance on the issue was undertaken by Alfred Cobban during World War II. Cobban unequivocally aligned himself with Lord Acton, holding that the nationally heterogeneous state "must re-enter the political canon, from which, as Acton many years ago declared, it should never have been dispelled."[16] He shared Acton's sentiment that the nation-state had no logical relationship to freedom and noted that "the most prevalent solutions of the national problem in a world of competing nationalisms . . . are likely to be expulsion, massacre, or economic attrition."[17]

Despite his preference for multinationalism, however, Cobban recognized that the concept of the nation-state was growing in influence. But he vehemently denied that this development was necessary. Taking exception to Barker's contention that history proved that only autocratic states could remain multinational, Cobban enumerated a number of contemporary states that he held to be working examples of multinational democracies, and he felt compelled to the vastly different conclusion that in most instances political and ethnic borders could not possibly be made to coincide.[18] Looking to the future, Cobban correctly anticipated the subsequent withdrawal of European political domination from most of Africa and Asia, and he expressed his belief that the popular misconception of a necessary link between political and ethnic borders would be particularly inapplicable and pernicious on these continents. Consistent with Acton's proposals, he favored for these areas transgroup political structures within which tribal and cultural sentiments would enjoy autonomy.

Aside from the more philosophic question of what ought to be the incidence of identity between nations and sovereign political entities, there remain two questions, the answers to which are intrinsic to the conclusions of each of the foregoing authorities, and both of which can be subjected to empirical investigation. The first involves the potentiality of the multination state to survive as an effective political form. Is it essentially an anachronism, albeit a tenacious one, whose death knell sounded with the first indications of popular national consciousness? The second question involves the relationship between the nation-state, on the one hand, and democratic principles and institutions on the other. Is it the single-nation state or the multination state that manifests the greater adherence to democracy? Political developments since World War II may well indicate the appropriate answers to these questions, for although only two decades have elapsed since the publication of Cobban's study, an unprecedented quantity of pertinent data has emerged from that period. The number of states has multiplied, global research and reportorial coverage have been greatly expanded, and the forces of political change have accelerated. Moreover, the post–World War II experiences of multination states follow a remarkably uniform pattern, thus furnishing more definite answers to these questions. The pattern is particularly evident in relation to the question involving the potential for survival of the multination state.

As earlier noted, the policy of politically dividing Africa and Asia along the former political and administrative lines of empire created a large number of transcultural states. If the movement for political separatism had given evidence of culminating at this point, the faith in the sustaining power of the multination form, which was shared by Acton and Cobban, would appear vindicated. But the overwhelming weight of evidence indicates that the movement is still far from completion.

Consider Asia: Reports persist that the Chinese Communist government is turning the Turkic peoples of Sinkiang Province into a minority by promoting an intensive migration of Chinese into the province in order to ensure the region's allegiance to Peking. Moreover, earlier Ti-

betan resistance to Chinese rule has led to the continuous military occupation of that region since 1959. On Taiwan there are rumblings of
dissatisfaction on the part of the indigenous population, who tend to
look upon the ruling group of mainland expatriates as aliens. Despite
Indonesia's recent preoccupation with the question of internal communism, it should not be forgotten that regionalism underlay the rebellion
waged between 1958 and 1961 and that common awareness of cultural
distinctions remains a source of resistance to rule from Djakarta.[19] In
the case of Vietnam, the intra-Vietnamese (Annamese) struggles have
tended to obscure an active "self-determination" movement on the part
of tribal hill peoples who populate more than half of the country's territory. Popularly but mistakenly grouped under the single designation
"Montagnards," they have made evident, by a number of open revolts
against Vietnamese rule and by the creation of a liberation front, that
the internal political problems of Vietnam would not terminate even
with the highly unlikely creation of a government acceptable to all the
ethnic Vietnamese.[20] In Laos, the confused and many-sided civil war
has in no small part been due to the absence of transcultural identification with the Laotian state on the part of the diverse population.[21] In
Thailand, the effectiveness of Bangkok's writ diminishes rapidly when
one leaves the culturally compatible Chao Phraya Valley for the Lao-
speaking northeast, for the Karen-populated hills of the west, or for the
Malay- and Chinese-populated regions of the Malay Peninsula. In
neighboring Malaysia, cohesion suffers from the antagonisms between
Malays and a strong Chinese minority, antagonisms that have already
led to the expulsion of Singapore from the Federation.[22] In the case of
Burma [Myanmar], it has been estimated that Rangoon controls only
half of its territory; the remaining territory is populated by dissident,
non-Burmese groups such as Shans, Kachins, Karens, Chins, and
Mons.[23] Within East Pakistan, the inhabitants have long voiced strong
dissatisfaction with their political ties to the peoples of West Pakistan
from whom they are differentiable on practically every basis other than
religion.* In Ceylon [Sri Lanka], state unity has been frustrated by the
intense rivalry between Sinhalese and Tamils which has periodically
manifested itself in riots. Indian history has been even more often
marred by eruptions of violence caused by the dissatisfaction of linguistic and cultural groups, and major governmental concessions concerning the delineating of provincial borders and the recognition of
several languages as "official" have been the price of a return to order.

---

* Stress between East and West Pakistan heightened during subsequent years,
and East Pakistan (aided by Indian troops) became the independent state of
Bangladesh in 1971.

In India's eastern areas, Naga and Mizo tribesmen are in open rebellion against rule by New Delhi. Iraq is riven by the Kurdish movement for self-determination, a problem that cannot be dissociated from the continuation of Kurdish territory into neighboring Iran and Turkey. Perhaps the most publicized failure of multinationalism since World War II involves an Asian and a non-Asian people on Cyprus; the only noteworthy interlude to the communal warfare there between Greek and Turk coincided with the ill-fated attempt at transnational government in the period 1960–1963.*

Sub-Sahara Africa's short history of broad-scale independence has also provided a number of challenges to the concept of the multiculture state. Indeed, there is very little evidence of the existence of supratribal allegiance to the new political entities that have been created south of the Sahara, and much contrary evidence, such as the entire anarchic history of the Congo [Zaire]. The rejection of transnation principles has been particularly pronounced in situations coinvolving "Europeans" and "Africans." Antagonisms between a white, ruling minority and a black majority within the southern tier of states and territories are one manifestation of the relative weakness of transracial sentiments; the pursuit of "Africanization" (the replacement of non-blacks by blacks in all endeavors as rapidly as possible) throughout much of the remaining area of sub-Sahara Africa is another. Nor has the presence of "Europeans" been a necessary prerequisite for racial tensions. Thus, the now rather lengthy insurrection waged by the negroid peoples of southern Sudan against the politically dominant Arabs of the northern sector, the overthrow and expulsion of the ruling Arab minority on Zanzibar in early 1964, the very bloody confrontations within Rwanda between the formerly dominant Watusi and the Bahutu from 1959 to 1963, sporadic genocidal conflicts between the same two peoples for political control of neighboring Burundi, the revolt during 1966 of the important Buganda tribe against the centralization of rule in Uganda, the Somali irredentist movements in Ethiopia and northeastern Kenya, and the general resentment of East Coast blacks toward settlers of Asian ancestry are all cases in which consciousness of race (in the minimal sense of readily visible distinctions) has proved antithetical to the concept of the

---

* Turmoil between the two peoples, fueled in no small measure by the governments of Greece and Turkey, continued to mount. In 1974, following the intervention of Turkey's armed forces, the ethnic map was radically redrawn and a de facto division of the island into two separate political entities occurred: a Turkish Republic of Northern Cyprus wherein Turks accounted for 99 percent of the population and an overwhelmingly Greek entity, covering the southern two-thirds of the island and retaining the designation of the Republic of Cyprus.

multination state. Although less apparent a source of intrastate dissension than either tribalism or race, a third cultural division that seriously affects a number of states is that between the coastal and riverine people, who were most influenced by European ways and institutions during the period of colonialism, and the more isolated people of the interior. This bifurcation helps to explain, for example, the demise of the Mali Federation brought about by the withdrawal of Senegal in 1960, as well as the animosity between the Hausas and Ibos which threatens the survival of Nigeria.[*] Yet a fourth division of Africa, which cuts across state lines and which appears to be growing in political significance, is that between Islamic and non-Islamic cultures. This distinction is perhaps the most important factor in an Eritrean movement for independence from Christian Ethiopia, and it is also a contributing element in Somali irredentism within Ethiopia and Kenya, in attitudes toward political independence within French Somaliland [Djibouti], and in the internal strife of both Nigeria and the Sudan.

The most warranted conclusion to be drawn from a review of recent developments throughout Africa and Asia would therefore appear to be that the concept of self-determination has proved more powerful than could be appreciated from the vantage point of the 1940s. If the evidence were limited to these two continents, a demurrer could be made on the ground that analysis had been limited to societies in which political institutions are in an inchoate and therefore ephemeral and inconclusive stage; it could be contended that analysis of long-range trends should logically give greater weight to the time-tested, modern states of Europe and of regions politically dominated by people of European background. However, the recent history of multinationalism in such cases does not differ appreciably from the Afro-Asian experience. This becomes particularly evident when one examines the subsequent history of those states that were deemed successful examples of multinationalism by Mill, Acton, Barker, and Cobban. The purpose of such examination is not to sit in hindsight judgment of their observations, but to illustrate the acceleration of cultural-political consciousness, for cultural tensions have surfaced even where competent observers could not detect them at earlier points in history.

Events have already furnished conclusive answers to the fate of Acton's major examples, the Austro-Hungarian and the British empires. Of the former, Barker has noted: "Unfortunately they tried to unite a territory which, if one may use a geological term, was full of 'faults'; and they inevitably failed. A nation can only be made by a State

---

[*] Between the writing and the publication of this article, the Ibos attempted to secede, leading to a three-year struggle involving an estimated one million casualties.

if the population on which it works already possesses some homogeneity. The mixture of Magyar, German, and Slav was too rebellious to the
potter's hand."[24] Barker's commentary would apply with equal validity to the British Empire, for whether in a particular region the impetus
for independence was indigenous or came from Britain, whether or not
the new state opted for membership within the loose structure of the
British Commonwealth, the basic cause of the disintegration of empire
was the refusal of people to accept political rule by those deemed aliens.

But what of those "Western" multinational states that are still in existence? As previously noted, Alfred Cobban took exception to Barker's
assertion that history indicated that democratic, multination states
could not survive. His empirical case on this point rested essentially
upon the examples of Great Britain, South Africa, Canada, Belgium,
and Switzerland.[25]

The inclusion of Britain as an example of multinationalism is puz-
zling; although Barker also acknowledged Britain to be an exception to
his rule, it is an exception that cannot go unchallenged. Both Barker
and Cobban had the transnationalism of the Scots and Welsh in mind,
but the view of most authorities holds that the self-identification of
these people with London is the product of assimilation rather than of
the continuing coexistence of prospering cultures. Indeed, authorities
have customarily emphasized the remarkable homogeneity of Britain's
major island.[26] Moreover, when this homogeneity was challenged by
the postwar influx of immigrants from the West Indies and southern
Asia, the result was racial friction and the passage of restrictive immigration legislation, antithetical to the concept of multinationalism. And
in Northern Ireland, the attempts by the Catholic minority to express
through the electoral process their long-standing discontent with political rule by a religiously and culturally distinct people, as well as the
attempts of the moderate government to move toward equalization of
opportunity for the minority, resulted in a series of violent reactions
during 1966.[27]

As to the example of South Africa, it is assumed that this state would
not have been included by Cobban could the subsequent governmental
adherence to the policy of apartheid been prophesied. If, on the other
hand, Cobban was referring solely to the relations between the two
white minorities—Briton and Boer—it must be noted that fundamental
differences of attitude persist, even though currently suffused by the
overriding issue of black-white relations.[28] The political outcome of the
cultural division between Englishmen and Boer therefore awaits a
more normal environment.

The examples of Canada and Belgium are more instructive because of the elongated period during which two distinct cultures have survived within their borders on an apparently harmonious basis. Thus, Cobban wrote that French and British Canadians "have achieved a common political nationality without abandoning their characteristic cultural differences."[29] Tracing the unity of Canada back almost two hundred years to the French and Indian Wars, he credits its success to the wisdom of the British peace terms under which demands for compulsory anglicization were eschewed in favor of guarantees of cultural autonomy to the French community.[30] Similarly, with regard to Belgium, Mill, although the proponent of the nation-state, acknowledged more than a century ago the existence of a common national consciousness shared by the Flemings and Walloons; and Cobban, as late as 1944, could detect "no reason at all" for believing that cultural consciousness would lead to the disintegration of the state.[31] The contrast between these observations and recent events is striking. Contemporary relations between the two Belgian groups have been characterized more by street violence and demands for strict separation than by harmony. The breadth and fervor of the "Flanders for the Flemish" movement have been illustrated by broadly supported demands that French-speaking faculty members and students of Louvain University be forced to leave Flanders for Wallonia and by Flemish insistence on legislation that would preclude desirous Flemish parents from "denationalizing" their offspring by sending them to French schools.[32] Canada, meanwhile, has been troubled by (1) separatist movements, (2) the insistence of the culturally French province of Quebec for increased independence of the central government and a greater share of governmental revenues, (3) demands for a balancing of opportunities between French and non-French people, (4) resistance to a governmental requirement that civil servants be bilingual, and (5) even by a question of the degree to which the traditional flag (since replaced) did and should symbolize the hegemony of "Anglo" culture.

Cobban's final example, Switzerland, is the most commonly employed illustration of a multinational "going concern." Here again, mid–nineteenth- and mid–twentieth-century assessments are in accord, for Mill perceived a powerful sentiment of Swiss nationality which "went beyond different races, different languages, and different religions,"[33] and Acton, after noting the ethnological division of the population into French, Italian, and German components, concluded that "no nationality has the slightest claim upon them, except the purely political nationality of Switzerland."[34] It is tempting to pass over Switzerland as a rule-proving exception attributable to the peculiarities of its size, location, topography, and special historical circumstances. And, admittedly, Swiss unity does not appear as seriously challenged by cultural cleavage as does that of Canada and Belgium. Nevertheless, the assertion that the subnationalities do not have the "slightest claim" upon the allegiance of the Swiss populace cannot be accepted as a valid characterization of the situation. It should be remembered that, as a result of Swiss neutrality, allegiance to Switzerland has not been severely tested against ethnic ties to Germany, France, or Italy. While the reasons for Swiss neutrality are multifold, there is reason to speculate upon the degree of adherence that the central government could have expected had it elected to enter the Franco-Prussian War or either of the world wars. In each instance, even a policy of impartiality was threatened by considerable sympathy for France or Germany, particular preference following linguistic-cultural lines.[35] Vastly more significant, however, is the evidence that Switzerland has not been immune to the growing intrastate tensions that have recently plagued other multinational states. In Bern, the only canton with a substantial French-speaking minority (more than 5 percent, less than 50 percent), there has been an active secessionist movement in recent years, despite the fact that the boundaries of this canton were fixed more than 150 years ago.[36*]

In addition to the foregoing states, Cobban also referred to the Soviet Union as an example of successful multinationalism. Although aware that Barker's analysis differentiated between "autocratic" and "democratic" states, Cobban felt the inclusion justified because the Soviet Union was, in his opinion, at least more democratic and yet more cohesive than had been the tsarist regimes. No matter where one places the Soviet Union on the democratic-authoritarian spectrum, however, it cannot be accepted as an exemplar of cultural cooperation. Authorities may disagree on the level of assimilation that has been attained within the Soviet Union, but it is generally held that the Soviet government has steadfastly followed a policy of russification. It is difficult to assess actual results because the government has purposefully tolerated the continued use of minority languages, while simultaneously eroding the wellsprings of the minority cultures, such as the Islamic religion. Thus, through a number of devices—some coercive, others seductive— the Soviet Union has moved toward assimilation while maintaining the most superficial guise of cultural autonomy.[37] Moreover, authorities anticipate an acceleration of the russification program which will include the denigration of non-Russian languages.[38] Such a move would be consonant both with Lenin's prerevolutionary plan that a short pe-

---

* The pressure for a separate French-speaking canton continued for more than another decade, concluding with the division of the Bern canton into French-speaking and German-speaking components on 1 January 1979.

riod of linguistic autonomy would be followed by the establishment of a single state language and with the statement in the new party program that "full-scale communist construction constitutes a new stage in the development of national relations in which the nations will draw still closer together until complete unity is achieved."[39] But a compelling reason for governmental acceleration of the assimilation process may well be the continuing discordant impact of culture-group orientation. Thus, a number of Latvian notables were accused in 1961 of fanning local nationalist sentiments. In a similar vein, the First Secretary of the Central Committee of the Uzbekistan Communist party was quoted in *Pravda* in early 1963: "There is no ground—either social or political or economic—for nationalism in our land. But we cannot forget that vestiges of it are still tenacious among a certain segment of politically immature people . . . [and are] always ready to break out to the surface."[40] The government also felt constrained to censure nationalist groups in the Ukraine during the spring of 1966.[41] Assuming that the Soviet Union would prefer to conceal such problems for both internal and external reasons, the few such official acknowledgments of the existence of nationalistic attitudes are probably indicative of what the government conceives to be a problem of serious magnitude. At the minimum, it can be said that Soviet policy-makers have not yet solved "the minority problem."

The elusiveness of a solution is illustrated by contrasting the experiences of two other nondemocratic European states, Yugoslavia and Spain. Following the Soviet example, the Yugoslavian government has paid at least limited homage to the concept of cultural autonomy. Thus, the ostensible form of government is a federation of six ethnically delineated republics and two autonomous areas, and the use of diverse languages and alphabets is permitted. However, Yugoslavia has not been as successful as the Soviet Union in preventing the public airing of intercultural enmity. The prevalence of ethnic tensions became a major issue in the mid-1966 purge of Vice President Rankovic and his followers. This group was accused of "Great Serbian chauvinism," thereby intensifying the hostility that Croatians, Slovenes, Albanians (Shiptars), Macedonians, and other minority peoples felt toward the dominant Serbs. Even a year prior to these disclosures, the government had been forced to suppress a Croatian Liberation Movement, the average age of whose members, most of whom could not have remembered a pre-Tito regime, indicates that the movement represents a resurgence rather than a vestige of Croatian aspirations for independence. It is evident, then, that the Yugoslav policy of granting limited autonomy to culture groups has not furthered the cause of unity.

Franco's response to cultural division was enforced homogeneity.

Although the Catalan and Basque minorities had enjoyed a short period of linguistic autonomy under the Spanish Republic, Franco ordered that only the Spanish language was to be taught in the schools and used by the communications media. However, despite three decades of implementation, the policy continued to meet strong resistance, and the government has recently retreated from its earlier position and become more permissive toward the use of minority tongues. Thus, the Spanish attempt at forceful eradication of minority cultures failed.

Additional evidence of European failure to accommodate multinationalism within a single state might include the often-expressed dissatisfaction of the German-speaking people of the Italian Tyrol, the strained relations between Romanians and the Magyars of Romanian Transylvania,[42] and the reappearance of the "Macedonian question," which involves minorities within Albania, Bulgaria, Greece, and Yugoslavia.[43] It is also pertinent to note that "European" Australia and New Zealand have determinedly resisted multinationalism. Although seriously underpopulated, both countries maintain barriers against the influx of non-Caucasoids while proffering a variety of allurements to the more readily assimilable people of northwestern Europe.

European experience, therefore, only tends to confirm a broad-scale trend toward political consciousness along lines of nationality. If the desires of nationalities were controlling, the second part of Ernest Barker's prediction of a global political division "in which each nation is also a State, and Each State is also a nation" would therefore rapidly be approaching realization. Yet, as indicated, seldom do political and ethnic borders coincide.

The principal reason for the wide gap between anticipation and realization in matters involving self-determination is the universal tendency of governments to render decisions upon the implicit assumption of the need to preserve the entire political unit. As against a claim of the right of self-determination, the government proclaims the right to stamp out rebellion and the duty to prevent secession. What is a self-evident truth to those desiring independence is treason to those in custody of the government. This polarization in the attitudes of the "ins" and the "outs" toward self-determination is most evident in the about-face of those former proponents of self-determination who led successful independence movements. As earlier noted, the African and Asian leaders who once castigated European domination as violative of the right of self-determination are not now prepared to recognize such a right on the part of their own minorities.[44]

A survey of multinational states does not indicate that any particular form of government has solved this dichotomy between the need for unity and the fissiparous impact of ethnic consciousness. It will be remembered that Ernest Barker was willing to concede that nondemocratic governments might impede the rise of political consciousness among ethnic groups. Yet despite great variations in the form and effectiveness of their respective governments, most of the Afro-Asian states that are troubled by ethnic tensions are clearly not democratic. Nor, as we have noted, are nondemocratic states such as the Soviet Union, Romania, Yugoslavia, and Spain free of such problems. The inability of authoritarian governments to cope successfully with multinationalism must therefore be considered still another testament to the increasing power of ethnic aspirations, for it indicates that the immunity believed to be enjoyed by authoritarian governments four decades ago is no longer effective.

The prevalence of ethnic dissonance within so many authoritarian systems must be considered significant because authoritarianism does enjoy real advantages in combating nationalist movements. Among the more formidable weapons at the disposal of such governments are a clandestine reporting apparatus and the ability to intern leaders for long periods without bringing formal charges. Control of communications is also important, for, if effective, it permits the government to cut the leadership off from possible domestic and foreign support. Such a government, if it acknowledges at all the presence of a self-determination movement, will typically describe it as the activity of a few provocateurs or malcontents. In such cases, evaluation of the actual situation is difficult, perhaps impossible. The problem of assessing ethnic movements within the Soviet Union has already been touched upon, but it should be noted that a number of movements elsewhere were excluded from earlier consideration because of the unavailability of dependable data. How strong, for example, is the Kashmiri desire for independence? How strong the movement within India for a Dravidistan? Tamilstan? Sikhistan? How much support is there within West Pakistan or, for that matter, within Afghanistan for an independent Pushtunistan? In southwestern Iran for an independent Arabistan? In eastern Turkey for an independent Armenian state? In eastern Ethiopia for an independent Eritrea? In northwestern Algeria for Berber independence? In each of these instances, and the list could be greatly expanded, it is known that an ethnic movement does, in fact, exist, but lack of information prevents a valid assessment of its strength. However, it is safe to conclude that the political consciousness of various ethnic groups is even much more prevalent than we can document.

This trend obviously conflicts with the widely held opinion that nationalism has proved too parochial for the modern age and that its zenith is now well passed. This position has been lent credence by the postwar proliferation of multistate organizations, which ranged, in their original aims, from limited military or economic cooperation to complete unification. However, although the goals of a transstate organization may be contrary to national aspirations, they need not be so. One factor will be the degree of integration that is anticipated. There is nothing in military or economic cooperation that is inconsistent with extreme national consciousness, when the results of such cooperation are viewed as beneficial to the national interest. But the nearer one moves toward the erection of a multinational state, the sharper becomes the conflict between the organization and nationalism. For example, de Gaulle's nationalism does not blind him to the economic advantages that might flow to the French from regional economic cooperation under the EEC, but it explains his resistance to any proposed transfer of the decision-making power away from the individual states. Similarly, he supports limited military cooperation, but refuses to accept a position of national dependence concerning any aspect of military strategy. In short, there is nothing intrinsically incompatible between the growth of national consciousness and organizations of such limited goals as the European or Latin American Free Trade Associations. Significant, however, is the fact that in the case of those organizations whose goals have most clearly conflicted with nationalism, it is the organization that has been forced to retreat. The EEC structure remains, but few are still optimistic about its supranational objectives. Similarly, the amazingly short-lived "Sino-Soviet bloc" foundered on the incompatibility of Chinese and Soviet national aspirations. Subsequent attempts by the Soviet Union to perpetuate the monolithic nature of the geographically more limited Eastern European multinational structure (including the Council for Mutual Economic Assistance and the Warsaw Pact) have experienced a series of major setbacks due to the rising nationalism of the Poles, Romanians, Czechs, Bulgars, and other East European peoples. In interstate relations, as within the typical multinational state, the centrifugal forces of national aspirations are proving more powerful than the centripetal forces of transnationalism.

There is, moreover, considerable reason to expect a further proliferation of self-determination movements. For most people, ethnic consciousness still lies in the future. National consciousness presupposes an awareness of other culture-groups, but, to a majority of the world's population, the meaningful world still ends with the village.[45] If the past and present are instructive, it can be expected that cultural and political consciousness will spread with increased communications and that the ethnic hodgepodges that are Asia and Africa will produce a host of new demands for the redrawing of political borders.

Should such demands for self-determination be met? The question can be viewed within two distinct contexts: the one, moral; the other, practical. If the question means whether each nationality, simply because it is a self-distinguishing culture-group, has a right to self-rule, then the question defies a provable conclusion. Axioms, such as "the right of self-determination," appear as moral imperatives until countered with opposing maxims. As earlier indicated, a "principle" of self-determination can be countered by other "principles," such as the right of states to preserve themselves, to protect their territorial integrity, to maintain internal order, to legislate against treasonable acts, and so forth. If, on the other hand, the question is intended to ask whether it is reasonable or even possible to grant statehood to each nation, it is doubtful that even those who are most sympathetic to the principle of self-determination would answer in the affirmative. Mill and Barker, for example, were both prepared to acknowledge the impracticality of self-determination in the case of two or more groups who were so geographically intermingled as to preclude a clear-cut geographic separation. Another possible objection to self-determination is that the people in question are not prepared for self-rule. Other critics have raised the issue of minimum standards, maintaining that self-determination should be denied when the group is too small, or the territory too limited, or the possibility of maintaining a viable economy too remote.

The interesting point is that such practical considerations have seldom had much influence upon ethnic aspirations. Even the absence of a clear geographic base has not necessarily prevented self-determination movements from arising. In the case of the Greeks and Turks on Cyprus and that of the Hindus and Moslems in British India, there was a high degree of geographic suffusion of the two cultures, but this intermingling did not prevent intergroup violence in the first instance and actual partition in the second.* So, too, the proposition that lack of readiness for self-rule is a legitimate bar to immediate independence: although accepted by Mill and later institutionalized in the mandate system of the League of Nations and the trusteeship system of the United Nations, this principle has been increasingly depicted as predicated upon bias and, consequently, is decreasingly heard in public debates concerning independence. With regard to the criteria of size, it is again instructive to turn to Cobban in order to illustrate how self-determination has altered international affairs over the past two decades. In the course of emphasizing the impracticality of granting independence to each small nation, Cobban raised, as a *reductio ad absurdum*, the spec-

---

* As earlier noted, Cyprus—following large population transfers between north and south—would also undergo a de facto partition.

ter of granting independence to Malta and Iceland. The fact that these areas have been granted statehood and that they have been joined in this successful endeavor by such other tiny entities as Gambia, the Maldive Islands, Barbados, Trinidad-Tobago, and Western Samoa again illustrates that practical considerations are not apt to prove a match for the emotional power of self-determination in those cases in which the sentiments of the national group are decisive.

But are the sentiments of a national group apt to prove decisive? The last stages of the colonial era have produced a number of instances in which a realistic Britain and France took the initiative in ceding independence to overseas territories. Nevertheless, as Rupert Emerson has noted, history clearly establishes that governments are not apt to grant self-determination, and that cases in which it has been granted are rare indeed.[46] But history also clearly indicates that the refusal to grant self-determination hardly eradicates the problem. The peacemakers of 1920 may have thought that they could dictate the proper limits of self-determination in Eastern Europe, stopping short of balkanization, but ferment for a furtherance of the self-determination principle plagues the area a half-century later. The appeal and the power of self-determination are quite independent of considerations of what a government ought to do or what it is apt to do. It is granted that the governments of multination states will continue to resist the minorities' requests for independence, but, in such cases, it is also expected that the states' existence will be increasingly challenged by secessionist-minded groups.

A quite natural response to this challenge is assimilation. If the coexistence of differing cultures appears incompatible with continued unity and yet partition is deemed unthinkable, policies to further homogeneity would seem to be in prospect. Moreover, this negative, albeit compelling, reason for instituting a policy of assimilation may be joined by positive considerations, in that marked heterogeneity represents an impediment to the statewide social and economic integration demanded by the modern state. This is particularly evident when linguistic differences are present. Certainly the Soviet Union must find a multiplicity of languages an efficiency-sapping nuisance, requiring countless oral and written translations of orders, blueprints, directions for the use of machinery, and so forth. So, too, a tendency for people to identify themselves with a particular culture and territory must constitute a most serious impediment to the mobility of labor. Aside, then, from the need to combat the divisiveness that springs from ethnic factionalism, the demands of modernization also exert pressure upon the government to eradicate its multinational character.

It would be a mistake, however, to underestimate the resistance to assimilation which governments can be expected to encounter. A number of governments have discovered belatedly that the enmity of groups toward acculturation represented a more formidable adversary than had been contemplated. Thus, the Indian and Pakistani governments have both been forced to backtrack on their plans for a single, official language; and Franco, by discarding many features of his assimilation program, has confessed failure to overcome Basque and Catalan resistance. On the other hand, the example of the American "melting pot" is often employed to illustrate that the assimilation of diverse cultures can be accomplished within a relatively short time. But it is highly questionable whether the experience of the United States is germane elsewhere.[47] A number of important factors peculiar to United States history point up by their very presence some of the major hindrances to assimilation that are faced by other states. For example, the American policy of conquest eliminated the indigenous people as cultural competitors; the pattern of early settlement created a dominant, almost exclusive Anglo-Saxon culture; upon this firmly entrenched cultural base, representatives of other cultures, on their own initiative,[48] were periodically added in relatively small numbers. As a result, ethnic problems in the United States have not been primarily characterized by minorities resisting assimilation, but rather by the unwillingness of the dominant group to permit assimilation at the tempo desired by the minorities. Dealing with a proportionally small number of people who have voluntarily left their homeland to enter an existent cultural-political structure within which acceptance of the mores and language is a sine qua non of success is one matter; treating the relations between two large and neighboring ethnic groups, each possessing impressive title to its respective territory, is something quite different. The second situation more closely characterizes Canada, Belgium, and, for that matter, most of the ethnic problems to which reference has been made.

The continuous spread of modern communication and transportation facilities, as well as statewide social institutions such as public school systems, can be expected to have a great influence upon programs of assimilation. But can the nature of that influence be predicted? It is a truism that centralized communications and increased contacts help to dissolve regional cultural distinctions within a state such as the United States. Yet, if one is dealing not with minor variations of the same culture, but with two quite distinct and self-differentiating cultures, are not increased contacts between the two apt to increase antagonisms? Improvements over the last two decades in what was an already effective transportation and communications network within Belgium have not been accompanied by improved relations between the Walloon and Flemish people. And in the less modern states, we have noted that cultural consciousness precedes political consciousness, and that cultural consciousness presupposes an awareness of other cultures. Is it not possible, then, that increased awareness of alien cultures on the part of the Baluchi people who inhabit either side of the Pakistani-Iranian border will result in Baluchistan's becoming a slogan rather than just the name of a geographic area?[*]

The obvious point is that assimilation is even more of a natural foe to self-determination than is the multination state. The growing emotional power of ethnic consciousness, which threatens the multination state, also casts serious doubt upon the probable success of assimilation programs. Nonetheless, partly in resistance to the divisiveness of growing national consciousness and partly in response to the demands of modernization, an increased emphasis upon assimilation appears in prospect. As a consequence, the multination state faces a dual threat, consisting of demands for self-determination from below and governmental programs of assimilation from above.

Contemporary political forces, therefore, clearly move in the direction of that second part of Barker's prophecy that envisages a world order in which "each State is also a nation." However, the first part of his prophecy, holding that "each nation is also a State," is clearly not upheld by the present political division of either the Arab world or the Spanish-speaking region of Latin America. The conclusion appears to be that diversity of cultures tends to preclude political unity but that sameness of culture does not preclude political division.

On the other question that divided Mill, Acton, Barker, and Cobban—whether heterogeneity promotes authoritarianism or democracy—postwar developments indicate a link between multinationalism and pressure for nondemocratic actions. This is not to say that one can predict the form of government simply by the degree of cultural homogeneity within a state. Most of the governments of the multinational states merit, on balance, characterization as authoritarian. But so, too, did the prewar governments of highly homogeneous Germany and Japan, as well as the present governments of most Arab states. It is evident, then, that there are many factors that combine in a varying and unpredictable mixture to determine form of government. However, the aforementioned tendency of governments to stress their political and territorial integrity has not been conducive to democratic responses to the growing problem of cultural-political consciousness.

[*] Although intended at the time as an essentially rhetorical question, Baluchi movements for greater independence from both countries soon surfaced.

There is a logical relationship between the *self*-determination of nations and the democratic concept that popular opinion should determine political allegiance. It is therefore ironic that while so many governments pay lip-service to self-determination, the instances in which a government has permitted a democratic process to decide a question of self-determination within its own territory are rare indeed.[49] The general position of African governments with respect to Rhodesia during 1965 and 1966 offers a striking illustration of this inconsistency. Motivated by the pragmatic desire to rid Africa of "white rule," they insisted that British cession of independence, prior to the instituting of popular government, would be a travesty of the self-determination principle. Yet, at the same time, these governments were not prepared to permit the popular will to determine the political allegiance of ethnic segments of their own population.

The natural repugnance of governments toward democratic solutions to questions involving the political allegiance of minorities has been underlined by instances of the refusal to grant plebiscites despite prior promises. India, for example, has suffered years of international embarrassment rather than honor its promises concerning a vote for the Kashmiri. Similarly, there were those who suspected that Sukarno never intended to hold a plebiscite in West Irian (the former Netherlands New Guinea), even though his promise to this effect was a basic condition of the UN's support for the Indonesian takeover in 1963. The subsequent abortive Communist coup brought into power a moderate group who were disposed to disagree with the major planks of Sukarno's domestic and foreign policies; but it was, nonetheless, under the authority of this group that the pledge for a plebiscite was in fact renounced during late 1966. It seems clear that governments believe that questions involving the political allegiance of groups residing within the sovereign territory are much too important to be left to popular opinion.

The methods by which governments have combated national movements have, in the main, been coercive. Where expedient, governments have shown little hesitancy in conducting military campaigns against such movements. Present or recent cases in point include Algeria (the Berbers), Burma [Myanmar], Burundi, mainland China (Tibet), the Congo [Zaire], Cyprus, India (Mizos, Nagas), Indonesia, Iraq, Nigeria, Rwanda, South Vietnam (the "Montagnards"), and Uganda. Moreover, as indicated earlier, the leaders of self-determination movements have seldom been accorded the legal safeguards that would be deemed minimal to meet democratic requirements. Often their only choices have been to live in exile, as do the Dalai Lama and many of the leaders of the Formosan movement, or, like Khan Abdul Ghaffar Khan (an advocate of an independent state of Pushtunistan within present Pakistan), to be committed periodically to long terms of imprisonment without legal process. Viewing self-determination movements as threats to survival, governments have tended to react violently and to justify the cruelest of treatment accorded to implicated leaders by branding them as rebels or traitors and therefore something worse than criminals. Admirably suited to such attitudes are the emergency acts and detention acts authorizing, in the broadest and most ambiguous terms, the internment without due process of law of persons acting in a manner inimical to the interests of the state. Such laws are extremely common in multination states and, in some cases, are found even within countries whose political system is ostensibly democratic.[50] Whether or not such responses are justified, either in general or in a particular instance, is not at issue; the point is that multination states have tended to become less democratic in response to the growing threat of nationalistic movements.

.   .   .

Political developments since World War II clearly establish that national consciousness is not on the wane as a political force, but is quite definitely in the ascendancy. Its force is currently being felt throughout sub-Sahara Africa and Asia, as ethnic consciousness demands political recognition, in place of the present political division that reflects colonial patterns. Moreover, the influence of nationalism is expected to increase greatly throughout these continents as the multitude of ethnic groups, many of whom are not yet cognizant of their identity, further acquire national awareness. The multination states of Europe and of areas settled by Europeans are also experiencing an increase in nationalistic orientations.

No multinational structure has been immune to this surge of nationalism. Authoritarian and democratic, Communist and non-Communist societies have been similarly affected. Nor does the postwar proliferation of transstate organizations and blocs repudiate the influence of nationalism; indeed, recent interstate developments further attest to the increasing tendency to think in nationalistic terms.

No government of a multination state has found the solution to the dilemma posed by the goal of state unity on the one hand and the centrifugal tendencies of growing national consciousness on the other. Motivated both by the desire to prevent partition and by the demands of modernization, such governments can be expected to resist nationalistic movements, with coercive methods if need be, while concurrently promoting assimilation.

The outcome of such programs is unpredictable, but the proven tenacity and emotional power of nationalism make this abstraction a most formidable opponent. In any event, that pernicious and perhaps unrealistic principle termed "self-determination of nations" is far from spent as a significant force in international politics.

NOTES

1. Ernest Barker, *National Character and the Factors in Its Formation* (London, 1927), 173.

2. Lord Acton believed that 1831 was the "watershed" year. He considered revolutionary movements prior to that date to be based upon either rival imperial claims or the refusal of people to be misgoverned by strangers. He noted that prior to 1831, Turks, Dutch, or Russians were resisted not as "usurpers" but as oppressors, "because they misgoverned, not because they were of a different race." John E. E. Dalberg-Acton, *The History of Freedom and Other Essays* (London, 1907), 284.

3. See Sarah Wambaugh, *Plebiscites Since the World War*, vol. 1 (Washington, D.C., 1933), 488.

4. See, for example, Wilson's speech before the League to Enforce Peace on 27 May 1916: "We believe these fundamental things: First, that every people has a right to choose the sovereignty under which they shall live . . ." Quoted in Wambaugh, *Plebiscites*, 4.

5. Wilson was later to admit to the Senate Foreign Relations Committee his amazement and chagrin at the large number of requests for support of independence movements. Excerpts from his testimony are cited in Alfred Cobban, *National Self-Determination* (Chicago, 1949), 21.

6. Although Europe is similarly afflicted, most of its present political borders are not the result of fulfilled "self-determination" demands.

7. John Stuart Mill, *Considerations on Representative Government* (New York, 1873), 313.

8. Ibid., 311. Similar fears concerning the ethnic composition of the army played a major role in Nigerian events during 1966.

9. Entitled "Nationality," it was published in *Home and Foreign Review* in July 1862 and is reprinted in Acton, *History of Freedom*, 270–300.

10. Ibid., 289.

11. Ibid., 290.

12. Ibid.

13. Ibid., 298.

14. Barker, *National Character*, 16.

15. Ibid., 125–26.

16. Cobban, *National Self-Determination*, 62.

17. Ibid., 73.

18. Ibid., 62, 63.

19. See, for example, George Kahin et al., *Major Governments of Asia*, 2d ed. (Ithaca, 1963), 674.

20. The name of the liberation front is FULRO, the French acronym for the United Front for the Liberation of Oppressed Races. For references to two of the more important revolts of the tribesmen, see the *New York Times*, 21 September 1964 and 20 December 1965.

21. For a description of the various ethnic strains and their relations, see Frank LeBar et al., *Laos* (New Haven, 1960).

22. For a report that Sarawak may also attempt to withdraw from the Federation because of ethnic considerations, see the *New York Times*, 17 November 1966.

23. Robert McCabe, "When China Spits, We Swim," *New York Times Magazine*, 27 February 1966, 48.

24. Barker, *National Character*, 123.

25. Cobban, *National Self-Determination*, 63.

26. See, for example, Gwendolen Carter et al., *Major Foreign Powers*, 3d ed. (New York, 1957), 7–8. The degree of assimilation is evidenced by the fact that only a minority of Welshmen and an insignificant number of Scotsmen are able to converse in their original languages, and all but a handful of these are fluent also in English. In both regions there have been recent nationalist movements whose goals range from minor alterations in administrative forms and school curricula to total independence. However, these movements are not considered to pose a serious challenge to "British nationalism," and, in any event, are more a manifestation of a resurgence of nationalist particularism than of cooperative multinationalism.

27. J. H. Huizinga, "Captain O'Neil and the Anti-Papist," *The Reporter* (New York), 20 October 1966, 43–44.

28. Paul Fordham, *The Geography of African Affairs* (Baltimore, 1965), 207.

29. Cobban, *National Self-Determination*, 60.

30. Ibid., 79.

31. Mill, *Considerations on Representative Government*, 308; Cobban, *National Self-Determination*, 144.

32. See, for example, the *New York Times*, 9 October and 30 October 1966.

33. Mill, *Considerations on Representative Government*, 308.

34. Acton, "Nationality," 294–95.

35. George Codding, Jr., *The Federal Government of Switzerland* (Boston, 1961), 154 ff.

36. Ibid., 39. See also the article in the *New York Times*, 19 March 1966, which describes the sentencing of secessionists for terrorism, together with the judge's admission of a general climate of political tension.

37. For a historical account of this process as applied to the Turkic peoples of the USSR, see Michael Rywkin, "Central Asia and the Price of Sovietization," *Problems of Communism* 13 (January–February 1964): 7–15. For a more general treatment of russification, see also the articles by Richard Pipes and Hugh Seton-Watson in the same issue.

38. This was the consensus at a conference of specialists held at Brandeis University in the fall of 1965, as reported in the *New York Times*, 31 October 1965.

39. Quoted by Richard Pipes, "The Forces of Nationalism," *Problems of Communism* 13, (January–February 1964): 4.

40. Ibid., 5.

41. *New York Times*, 16 April and 20 April 1966.

42. Ibid., 5 February 1966.

43. Ibid., 18 September 1966.

44. For a penetrating treatment of this phenomenon, see Rupert Emerson, *Self-Determination Revisited in the Era of Decolonialization* (Cambridge, Mass., 1964), esp. 28.

45. A 1962 UNESCO survey estimated that 70 percent of the world's population is essentially unaware of happenings beyond the village. See also Emerson, *Self-Determination Revisited*, 36.

46. Emerson, *Self-Determination Revisited*, 63–64.

47. Recent studies have even questioned the degree of melting that has occurred within the American pot. See, for example, Nathan Glazer and Daniel Moynihan, *Beyond the Melting Pot* (Cambridge, Mass., 1963).

48. The major exception was the African slave.

49. The actions of France and the United Kingdom with respect to their overseas territories, after it became evident that the days of empire were numbered, are not considered true exceptions to this statement.

50. Typical is a so-called Security Bill passed by the government of Guyana in late 1966 and obviously intended by the politically dominant blacks to restrict the activities of the East Indian segment of the population. Under its terms, the prime minister is empowered to intern without trial, for eighteen months, anyone he believes has acted or will act "in any manner prejudicial to the public safety or public order or the defense of Guyana." *New York Times*, 9 December 1966.

Within India, Kashmiri leaders have been periodically interned by the Indian government under an "emergency" measure. Moreover, in 1963, essentially in response to a Dravidistan movement, the Indian government passed the Sixteenth Amendment to the Constitution which sought to "prevent the fissiparous, secessionist tendency in the country engendered by regional and linguistic loyalties and to preserve the unity, sovereignty, and territorial integrity" of the Indian union. Cited in Robert L. Hardgrove, Jr., "The DMK and the Politics of Tamil Nationalism," *Pacific Affairs* 37 (Winter 1964–65): 397.

Chapter Two

AMERICAN SCHOLARSHIP IN THE
POST–WORLD WAR II ERA

The following article is an expanded version of a paper presented at the Seventh World Congress of the International Sociological Association, held at Varna, Bulgaria, in September 1970. The so-called Cold War was in full flower, and the fact that Bulgaria was part of the Soviet Union's sphere of influence guaranteed a heavy representation of academicians from the Marxist-Leninist states. Even my very few, bland references to growing ethnic antagonisms within the Soviet Union were vehemently criticized.

The focus of the paper, however, had nothing to do with the Soviet Union. It was a criticism of the school of thought called "nation-building" that dominated the literature on political development, particularly within the United States. The near total disregard of ethnonationalism that characterized the school, which numbered so many leading political scientists of the time, still astonishes. Again we encounter that divorce between intellectual theory and the real world.

Nation-Building or Nation-Destroying?*

SCHOLARS ASSOCIATED with theories of "nation-building" have tended either to ignore the question of ethnic diversity or to treat the matter of ethnic identity superficially as merely one of a number of minor imped- iments to effective state-integration. To the degree that ethnic identity is given recognition, it is apt to be as a somewhat unimportant and ephemeral nuisance that will unquestionably give way to a common identity uniting all inhabitants of the state, regardless of ethnic heri- tage, as modern communication and transportation networks link the state's various parts more closely. Both tendencies are at sharp vari- ance with the facts, and have contributed to the undue optimism that has characterized so much of the literature on "nation-building."

It is not difficult to substantiate the charge that the leading theoreti- cians of "nation-building" have tended to slight, if not totally ignore, problems associated with ethnic diversity. A consultation of the table of contents and indices of books on "nation-building" will quickly con- vince the doubtful that the matter is seldom acknowledged, much less accorded serious consideration.[1] In order to be justified, such omissions must be occasioned either by the fact that most states are ethnically homogeneous or that ethnic diversity poses no serious problems to integration.

The former possibility is readily eliminated by reference to the actual ethnic composition of contemporary states. The remarkable lack of co- incidence that exists between ethnic and political borders is indicated by the following statistics. Of a total of 132 contemporary states, only 12 (9.1 percent) can be described as essentially homogeneous from an ethnic viewpoint. An additional 25 states (18.9 percent of the sample) contain an ethnic group accounting for more than 90 percent of the state's total population, and in still another 25 states the largest element accounts for between 75 and 89 percent of the population. But in 31 states (23.5 percent of the total), the largest ethnic element represents only 50 to 74 percent of the population, and in 39 cases (29.5 percent of all states) the largest group fails to account for even half of the state's

* Published in Walker Connor, "Nation-Building or Nation-Destroying?" *World Politics* 24 (April 1972): 319–55. Copyright © 1972 Johns Hopkins University Press. Reprinted with permission of Johns Hopkins University Press.

population. Moreover, this portrait of ethnic diversity becomes more vivid when the number of distinct ethnic groups within states is considered. In some instances, the number of groups within a state runs into the hundreds, and in 53 states (40.2 percent of the total), the population is divided into more than *five* significant groups.[2] Clearly, then, the problem of ethnic diversity is far too ubiquitous to be ignored by the serious scholar of "nation-building," unless he subscribes to the position that ethnic diversity is not a matter for serious concern.

The validity of this position apparently also rests upon one of two propositions. Either loyalty to the ethnic group is self-evidently compatible with loyalty to the state, or, as mentioned earlier, ethnic identification will prove to be of short duration, withering away as modernization progresses. More consideration will be later given to the matter of the two loyalties (i.e., to the ethnic group and to the state), but clearly the two are not naturally harmonious. One need only reflect on the ultimate political dissection of what was once known as the Habsburg Empire, or contemplate the single most important challenge to the political survival of Belgium, Canada, Cyprus, Guyana, Kenya, Nigeria, the Sudan, Yugoslavia, and a number of other multiethnic states. The theoretician of "nation-building" may well contemplate some proposal that he believes will reduce the matter of competing loyalties to manageable proportions (such as confederalism or cultural autonomy); but, if so, his proposal is an important element in his model and should occupy a prominent place in his writing.[3]

As to the assumption that ethnic identity will wither away as the processes collectively known as modernization occur, it is probable that those who hold this premise have been influenced, directly or indirectly, by the writings of Karl Deutsch. It is debatable, however, whether such an opinion concerning the future of ethnic identity can be properly inferred from his works. His perception of the intereffects of what he calls "social mobilization" and of assimilation (i.e., "nation-building," so far as identity is concerned) is not always clear and appears to have undergone significant fluctuations. But given the magnitude of his influence, a closer scrutiny of his works appears warranted in order to define and evaluate more clearly his conclusions concerning the significance that ethnic identity possesses for "nation-building."

Deutsch's most famous work, *Nationalism and Social Communication*,[4] illustrates the problem of defining his position with precision. On the one hand, this work contains a few passing acknowledgments that increasing contacts between culturally diverse people *might* increase antagonisms.[5] On the other hand, there are several passages that might lead the reader to conclude that Deutsch was convinced that modernization, in the form of increases in urbanization, industrialization, schooling, communication and transportation facilities, and so on, would lead to assimilation. Even the development and extensive discussion of the concept of social mobilization, in a book ostensibly dedicated to the analytical study of nationalism, implied an important relationship between the two. Moreover, it was in a chapter entitled "National Assimilation or Differentiation: Some Quantitative Relationships" that Deutsch discussed the factors that determined, in his view, the rate of social mobilization. Then, after discussing the rates of mobilization and of assimilation separately, he strongly intimated a causal or reinforcing interrelationship:

> Thus far we have treated all the rates of change as completely independent from each other. . . . However, we already know empirically that the rate of assimilation among a population that has been uprooted and mobilized—such as immigrants coming to America—is usually considerably higher than the rate of assimilation among the secluded populations of villages close to the soil. . . . Probably the theoretical investigation of these quantitative aspects of the merging or splitting of nations could be carried still further. One reason to stop here might be that we know now what statistical information is worth looking for, but that there seems little point in going further until more of the relevant statistics have been collected.[6]

Later, in summarizing the same chapter, Deutsch noted:

> A decisive factor in national assimilation or differentiation was found to be the process of social mobilization which accompanies the growth of markets, industries, and towns, and eventually of literacy and mass communication. The trends in the underlying process of social mobilization could do much to decide whether existing national trends in particular countries would be continued or reversed.[7]

In the following chapter, Deutsch discussed the rate of assimilation in terms of six balances of both quantitative and qualitative factors and then restated what he conceived to be the relationship between the rates of mobilization and assimilation.

> Assimilation among people firmly rooted in their own communities and their native setting usually proceeds far more slowly than it would among the mobilized population, but it does proceed even though it may take many generations. . . . Any more general quantitative comparison between the relatively high assimilation speeds among mobilized persons and the considerably lower assimilation speeds among the underlying population remains to be worked out. Likewise to be worked out would have to be the *mutual interaction* of the different rates of change which thus far have been discussed as if they were wholly independent of each other.[8]

Such citations would appear to justify the interpretation that Deutsch felt that modernization, by socially mobilizing large segments of the population, would increase both the likelihood and the tempo of their assimilation. Such a conclusion was lent further credence by Deutsch's optimistic view that the matter of assimilating diverse ethnic groups is subjectable to social engineering. Concluding a discussion of the role of the policy-maker, he noted: "Too often men have viewed language and nationality superficially as an accident, or accepted them submissively as fate. In fact they are neither accident nor fate, but the outcome of a discernible process; and as soon as we begin to make the process visible, we are beginning to change it."[9]

By 1961, Deutsch's view of the relationship between social mobilization and assimilation appeared to have undergone a fundamental change. Mobilization was now seen as being apt to have the opposite effect upon assimilation.

> Other things assumed equal, the stage of rapid social mobilization may be expected, therefore, to promote the consolidation of states whose peoples already share the same language, culture, and major social institutions; while the same process may tend to strain or destroy the unity of states whose population is already divided into several groups with different languages or cultures or basic ways of life.[10]

The practical consequences of this altered view, in terms of what it portended for the survival of that preponderant number of nonindustrialized states which are multiethnic, was blunted, however, by Deutsch's immediate addendum that all things, in any event, are not equal. More specifically, he contended that ethnic identity would prove no match for the power of self-interest.

> In the last analysis, however, the problem of the scale of states goes beyond the effects of language, culture, or institutions, important as all these are. In the period of rapid social mobilization, the acceptable scale of a political unit will tend to depend eventually upon its performance. . . . At bottom, the popular acceptance of a government in a period of social mobilization is most of all a matter of its responsiveness to the felt needs of its population.[11]

An essay written by Professor Deutsch two years later indicated a swing back to his earlier position. In a return to his earlier optimism concerning the impact of modernization upon ethnicity, he chided unnamed authors for maintaining that ethnic divisions constituted a long-run challenge to "nation-building."

> Tribes, we know from European history, can change their language and culture; they can absorb other tribes; and large tribes come into existence

through federation or mergers of smaller tribes or through their conquest and absorption by a larger one.

In contrast to this picture of plasticity and change, many writings on African and Asian politics still seem to treat tribes as fixed and unlikely to change in any significant way during the next decades. Yet in contemporary Asia and Africa, the rates of cultural and ethnic change, although still low, are likely to be faster than they were in early medieval Europe. . . . Research is needed to establish more reliable figures, but it seems likely from the experience of ethnic minorities in other parts of the world that the process of partial modernization will draw many of the most gifted and energetic individuals into the cities or the growing sectors of the economy away from their former minority or tribal groups, leaving these traditional groups weaker, more stagnant, and easier to govern.[12]

Later in the essay, Deutsch specified four stages by which he anticipated assimilation would take place:

Open or latent resistance to political amalgamation into a common national state; minimal integration to the point of passive compliance with the orders of such an amalgamated government; deeper political integration to the point of active support for such a common state but with continuing ethnic or cultural group cohesion and diversity; and, finally, the coincidence of political amalgamation and integration with the assimilation of all groups to a common language and culture—these could be the main stages on the way from tribes to nation. Since a nation is not an animal or vegetable organism, its evolution need not go through any fixed sequence of these steps. . . . Yet the most frequent sequence in modern Asia and Africa may well be the one sketched above. How long might it take for tribes or other ethnic groups in a developing country to pass through some such sequence of stages? We do not know, but European history offers at least a few suggestions."[13]

In sharp contrast to this optimistic prediction concerning the fate of the new states of Africa and Asia are the views expressed by Deutsch in his most recent work on nationalism,[14] views which more closely approximate those expressed in his 1961 article. As in that article, and unlike the position he took in the still earlier *Nationalism and Social Communication*, Deutsch now treated assimilation and mobilization as two causally isolated processes.[15] The only relationship between the two that was discussed is chronological, that is, the question of which antedates the other:

The decisive factor in such situations is the balance between the two processes that we have been discussing. If assimilation stays ahead of mobilization or keeps abreast of it, the government is likely to remain stable, and eventually everybody will be integrated into one people. . . . On the other hand, where mobilization is fast and assimilation is slow the opposite happens.[16]

Although this position echoed that expressed by Deutsch in 1961,[17] he no longer contended that the logical consequences of this analysis could be avoided by increasing state services and benefits. The result is a note of pessimism not detected in his 1961 analysis, and one that seems to be diametrically opposed to his unequivocal optimism of 1963:

> We have seen that the more gradually the process of social mobilization moves, the more time there is for social and national assimilation to work. Conversely, the more social mobilization is postponed, the more quickly its various aspects—language, monetization, mass audience, literacy, voting, urbanization, industrialization—must eventually be achieved. But when all of these developments have to be crowded into the lifetime of one or two generations, the chances for assimilation to work are much smaller. The likelihood is much greater that people will be precipitated into politics with their old languages, their old outlook on the world and their old tribal loyalties still largely unchanged; and it becomes far more difficult to have them think of themselves as members of one new nation. It took centuries to make Englishmen and Frenchmen. How are the variegated tribal groups to become Tanzanians, Zambians, or Malawians in one generation?[18]

If Deutsch's most recent analysis of the interrelationship between social mobilization and assimilation is accepted, that is, if it is granted that the connection between the two is in no way causal but purely chronological, then it is difficult to perceive what predictive value the concept of social mobilization holds for the "nation-builder." To say, "if assimilation stays ahead of mobilization or keeps abreast of it . . . eventually everybody will be integrated into one people" is in fact to say very little. If assimilation progresses, then clearly assimilation will be achieved.[19] And to add, as Deutsch does, "where mobilization is fast and assimilation is slow, the opposite happens," is not to furnish the state planner with a guide for action, but is to deny that the matter is subjectable to social engineering. If assimilation, in those cases where and when it can be achieved, is a lengthy process requiring generations, and if Professor Deutsch is not recommending that the states of the Third World be immunized from modernization (and in the preceding quotation he states that such an immunization is impossible), then what is left is the conclusion that where assimilation has not yet been achieved, it is highly unlikely to be.

Professor Deutsch's most recent book therefore provides no brief for those who assume that ethnicity will wane as modernization progresses. The opposite is the case. On the other hand, some of his earlier comments, and particularly those in which he propounded four stages of assimilative growth, could indeed be cited as supporting this school of thought. Regardless of the interpretation one places upon Deutsch, however, the doctrine that modernization dissolves ethnic loyalties can be challenged on purely empirical grounds.

If the processes that comprise modernization led to a lessening of ethnic consciousness in favor of identification with the state, then the number of states troubled by ethnic disharmony would be on the decrease. To the contrary, however, a global survey illustrates that ethnic consciousness is definitely in the ascendancy as a political force, and that state borders, as presently delimited, are being increasingly challenged by this trend.[20] And, what is of greater significance, multiethnic states at all levels of modernity have been afflicted. Particularly instructive in this regard is the large proportion of states within the technologically and economically advanced region of Western Europe that have recently been troubled by ethnic unrest. Examples include (1) the problems of Spain with the anti-Castilian activities of the Basques, the Catalans, and on a lesser level, the Galicians; (2) the animosity indicated by the Swiss toward foreign migrant workers, and the demands of the French-speaking peoples of Berne for political separation from the German-speaking element; (3) the South Tyroleans' dissatisfaction with Italian rule, currently muffled by recent concessions on the part of the Italian government; (4) evidence of Breton unhappiness with continued French rule; (5) the resurgence of Scottish and Welsh nationalism, the conflict in Northern Ireland, and the wide-scale popularity of anti-immigrant sentiments epitomized in the figure of Enoch Powell—all within the United Kingdom; and (6) the bitter rivalry of the Walloon and Flemish peoples within Belgium. Outside of Europe, the challenge to the concept of a single Canada represented by the Franco-Canadian movements and the existence of black separatist movements within the United States also bear testimony that even the combination of a lengthy history as a state and a high degree of technological and economic integration does not guarantee immunity against ethnic particularism.

That social mobilization need not lead to a transfer of primary allegiance from the ethnic group to the state is therefore clear. Can we go beyond this to posit an inverse correlation between modernization and the level of ethnic dissonance within multiethnic states? Admittedly, there is a danger of countering the assumption that the processes of modernization lead to cultural assimilation with an opposing iron law of political disintegration which contends that modernization results, of necessity, in increasing demands for ethnic separation. We still do not have sufficient data to justify such an unequivocal contention. Nonetheless, the substantial body of data which is available supports the proposition that material increases in what Deutsch termed social communication and mobilization *tend* to increase cultural awareness and to exacerbate interethnic conflict. Again, the large and growing number of ethnic separatist movements can be cited for substantiation.

There are many statesmen and scholars, however, who would protest this macroanalytical approach because the data cited for support contain a number of former colonies. The inclusion of former dependencies in a list purporting to substantiate a correlation between modernization and ethnicity is improper, they would contend, because ethnic consciousness was deliberately kept alive and encouraged by the colonial overseers as an element in a policy of divide-and-rule. The prevalence of ethnic consciousness and antagonism in these territories is therefore held to be the product of the artificial stimuli of colonial policy. Otherwise, ethnicity would not constitute a serious problem for the new states.

The validity of such a conviction can be tested by contrasting the experience of former colonies with that of industrially retarded, multiethnic states that did not undergo a significant period as a colony. No important distinctions are discernible on this basis. Consider, for example, the cases of Ethiopia and Thailand, both of which have enjoyed very lengthy histories as independent states.[21] Diverse ethnic elements were able to coexist for a lengthy period within each of these states because the states were poorly integrated, and the ethnic minorities therefore had little contact, with either the (mostly theoretic) state governments or with each other. Until very recent times, then, the situation of the minorities in these states was not unlike the situation of ethnic groups within colonies where the colonial power practiced that very common colonial policy of ruling through the leadership of the various ethnic groups. In all such cases, the conflict between alien rule and the ethnic group's determination to preserve its lifeways was minimized. The governments of the underdeveloped states may well have long desired to make their rule effective throughout their entire territory, but advances in communications and transportation were necessary before a governmental presence could become a pervasive reality in the remote territories of the minorities.

As a result of this new presence, resentment of foreign rule has become an important political force for the first time. In addition, quite aside from the question of who rules, there is the matter of cultural self-preservation. An unintegrated state poses no serious threat to the lifeways of the various ethnic groups. But improvements in the quality and quantity of communication and transportation media progressively curtail the cultural isolation in which an ethnic group could formerly cloak its cultural chasteness from the perverting influences of other cultures within the same state. The reaction to such curtailment is very apt to be one of xenophobic hostility.

Advances in communications and transportation tend also to increase the cultural awareness of the minorities by making their members more aware of the distinctions between themselves and others. The impact is twofold. Not only does the individual become more aware of alien ethnic groups; he also becomes more aware of those who share his identity. Thus, the transistor radio has not only made the formerly isolated, Lao-speaking villager of northeast Thailand aware of linguistic and other cultural distinctions between himself and the politically dominant Siamese-speaking element to the west; it has also made him much more aware of his cultural affinity with the Lao who live in other villages throughout northeast Thailand and across the Mekong River in western Laos.[22] Intraethnic as well as interethnic communications thus play a major role in the creation of ethnic consciousness.

As an end result of these processes, Thailand is today faced with separatist movements on the part of the hill tribes in the north, the Lao in the northeast, and the Malays in the south.[23] Similarly, as a result of growing self-awareness by minorities and an increasing presence of the central government, the state of Ethiopia, despite its three-thousand-year history, is also currently faced with a number of ethnic separatist movements.[24] Other underdeveloped, multiethnic states without a history of colonialism indicate a similar pattern.[25] The colonial and noncolonial patterns are not significantly different.

Another challenge to the contention that modernization tends to exacerbate ethnic tensions may also be anticipated. As was noted earlier, the recent upsurge in ethnic conflict within the more industrialized, multiethnic states of Europe and North America seriously challenges the contention that modernization dissipates ethnic consciousness. But does not this upsurge also run counter to the assertion that modernization increases ethnic consciousness? Given the fact that the Industrial Revolution was introduced into each of these states more than a century ago, should not the high-tide mark of ethnic consciousness have appeared long ago? Part of the answer may be found in what Marxists term "The Law of the Transformation of Quantity into Quality," a paraphrase of which might read "enough of a quantitative difference makes a qualitative difference." The processes of modernization prior to World War II did not necessitate or bring about the same measure of international contacts as have developments in the postwar period. With fewer and poorer roads, far fewer and less efficient private cars, local radio rather than statewide television as the primary channel of nonwritten mass communications, lower levels of education and of knowledge of events beyond one's own experience, and lower general income levels that kept people close to home, ethnic complacency could be maintained: Brittany's culture appeared safe from French encroachment, Edinburgh felt remote and isolated from London, most Walloons and Flemings seldom came into contact (including artificial contact through media such as television) with members of the other group. In short, the situation of ethnic groups within these states was not totally dissimilar from that which was described earlier with regard to nonindustrialized societies.[26] The difference was only one of degree until that point was reached at which a qualitative change occurred. However, the point at which a significant number of people perceived that the cumulative impact of the quantitative increases in the intensity of intergroup contacts now constituted a threat to their ethnicity represented, in political terms, a qualitative transformation.

Perhaps an even more important factor in explaining the recent upsurge of militant ethnic consciousness in advanced as well as less advanced states involves not the nature or density of the communications media, but the message. Although the expression "self-determination of nations" can be traced to 1865,[27] it did not receive great attention until its endorsement by a number of world-renowned statesmen during the World War I era. Moreover, by their failure after the war to apply this doctrine to the multiethnic empires of Belgium, Britain, France, the Netherlands, Portugal, and Spain, the statesmen indicated that they did not consider self-determination an axiom of universal validity. Not until after World War II was the doctrine officially endorsed by an organization aspiring to global jurisdiction.[28] It is therefore of very recent vintage. But despite its short history, it has been widely publicized and elevated to the status of a self-evident truth. Today, lip service is paid to it by political leaders of the most diverse persuasions. Admittedly, the doctrine has often been misapplied, having been regularly invoked in support of all movements aimed at dissolving a political allegiance, regardless of the basis for secession. But in its pristine form, the doctrine makes ethnicity the ultimate measure of political legitimacy, by holding that any self-differentiating people, simply because it *is* a people, has the right, should it so desire, to rule itself. In recent years, with its wide acceptance as a universal truth, the doctrine has induced minorities in Europe and North America, as well as in Africa, Asia, and Latin America, to question the validity of present political borders. It has therefore been more than a justification for ethnic movements: it has been a catalyst for them. The spreading of effective communications has had an evident impact upon ethnic consciousness, but the full impact of the communications media did not precede the message of self-determination.

Still another element contributing to the upsurge in ethnic consciousness is the evident change in the global political environment, which makes it much more unlikely that a militarily weak polity will be annexed by a larger power. During the age of colonialism, the probability of that eventuality was sometimes so great as to encourage independent units to seek the status of a protectorate in order to be able to select rule by the lesser evil. By contrast, a number of relatively recent developments, including what is termed the nuclear stalemate, cause independence to appear as a more enduring prospect for even the weakest of units. Thus, a favorable environment, the generating and justifying principle of self-determination, an expanding list of successful precedents, and a growing awareness of all these factors because of increased communications, are all involved.

A summary of our findings thus far would consist of the following points. The preponderant number of states are multiethnic. Ethnic consciousness has been definitely increasing, not decreasing, in recent years. No particular classification of multiethnic states has proven immune to the fissiparous impact of ethnicity: authoritarian and democratic; federative and unitary; Asian, African, American, and European states have all been afflicted. Form of government and geography have clearly not been determinative. Nor has the level of economic development. But the accompaniments of economic development—increased social mobilization and communication—appear to have increased ethnic tensions and to be conducive to separatist demands. Despite all this, leading theoreticians of "nation-building" have tended to ignore or slight the problems associated with ethnicity.

If we turn to an analysis of the reasons for this wide gap between theory and reality, twelve overlapping and interrelated possibilities offer themselves.

(1) CONFUSING INTERUTILIZATION OF THE KEY TERMS,
NATION AND STATE:

It may appear whimsical to begin with the often picayune matter of semantics. It is very doubtful, however, that any discipline has been more plagued by the improper utilization of its key terms than has international relations. Anthropologists often bemoan the nebulosity underlying the concept of race—an ambiguity which has been reflected

in many unscientific theories, which, in turn, have required time-con-
suming repudiations. But, though the concept of race is a matter of
great significance to anthropology, it is not the key concept, that being
man. By contrast, the concept of the state and of man's relationship to
the state are at the heart of international relations. Yet, despite their key
roles, both of these concepts are shrouded in ambiguity because of
careless use of terms.

Consider first the concept of the state and the manner in which it is
commonly treated as synonymous with the vastly different concept of
the nation. The League of Nations, the United Nations, and, indeed, the
expression *international relations* are but a few of the many available
illustrations of the fact that statesmen and scholars are inclined to the
indiscriminate interuse of the two concepts.[29] Why this confusion in
terminology has been perpetuated is difficult to explain, for authorities
are certainly well aware of the distinctions between the state and the
nation. Thus, a dictionary designed for the student of global politics
defines the state as "a legal concept describing a social group that occu-
pies a defined territory and is organized under common political institutions and an effective government."[30] By contrast, a nation is defined
as "a social group which shares a common ideology, common institutions and customs, and a sense of homogeneity." It carefully adds: "A
nation may comprise part of a state, be coterminous with a state, or
extend beyond the borders of a single state." Writers of textbooks and
monographs in international relations generally also detail these same
distinctions between state and nation. Unfortunately, however, these
same writers are then apt to revert to the indiscriminate interutilization
of the two terms.[31]

It is probable that the tendency to equate the two expressions developed as alternative shorthand substitutes for the hyphenate, *nation-
state*. This term is also supposed to have a precise meaning, referring to
a situation in which the borders of the nation approximate those of the
state. We have noted that, technically speaking, less than 10 percent of
all states would qualify as essentially homogeneous. But authorities
nevertheless tend to refer to all states as nation-states.[32]

The confusion wrought by the misuse of these terms has long ham-
pered the study of many aspects of interstate relations, but it has especially impeded the understanding of nationalism. More particularly,
loyalty to the nation has often been confused with loyalty to the state.
Again, this confusion has been reflected in, and largely caused by, inappropriate terminology.

The definitions of state and nation quoted above make clear that
what we have thus far been calling self-differentiating ethnic groups
are in fact nations. Loyalty to the ethnic group, therefore, should logi-

cally be called nationalism. But nationalism, as commonly employed, refers to loyalty to the state (or to the word *nation*, when the latter has been incorrectly substituted for state).[33] Thus, the same dictionary whose precise definitions of state and nation we have just cited defines *nationalism* as a mass emotion that "makes the *state* the ultimate focus of the individual's loyalty" (emphasis added). With the term *nationalism* thus preempted, scholars have felt compelled to offer a substitute to describe loyalty to the nation. Regionalism, parochialism, primordialism, communalism, ethnic complementarity, and tribalism are among those that have been advanced. Unfortunately, however, the perpetuation of the improper use of the word *nationalism* to refer to devotion to the state, while using other terms with different roots and with fundamentally different connotations to denote devotion to the nation, is hardly conducive to dissolving the confusion surrounding the two loyalties.[34] On the contrary, it is conducive to dangerously underestimating the magnetism and the staying power of ethnic identity, for those terms simply do not convey the aura of deeply felt, emotional commitment that nationalism does. Every schoolboy is made aware, for example, that the German and Celtic tribes of antiquity became obliterated in a higher identity; that regionalism within the United States or Germany has steadily receded in significance. By contrast with these vanquished forces, the schoolboy learns that nationalism is a vibrant force that has largely shaped the direction of global politics for the past two hundred years. But since nationalism is equated with loyalty to the state, the student has been preconditioned to perceive the state as the certain ultimate victor in any test of loyalties with these lower-form anachronisms that have been proven to be ephemeral.

If the nation-state were in fact the universal form of polity, the confusion would not be important. In those cases in which the nation and the state essentially coincide, the two loyalties mesh rather than compete. A common pitfall of scholarship, however, has been to equate the resulting emotional attachment to a nation-state with loyalty to the state alone. The study of nationalism in the late twentieth century has been heavily influenced by the experiences of Germany and Japan, perceived as illustrations of the extreme dedication that nationalism is able to evoke. The implication is that other states have the potential for evoking the same type of mass response, though, it is to be hoped, in a less fanatical form. Largely ignored is the fact that these two states are among the very few that are ethnically homogeneous.[35] As such, *Deutschland* and *Nippon* have been something far more profound to their populations than mere territorial-political units called states; they have been ethno-psychological inclinations called nations. To perceive German or Japanese nationalism as loyalty to the state is to miss the mark badly. It is also to distort beyond recognition the power to evoke loyalty to the state in the absence of a linking of state and nation in the popular psyche. With that linkage, the leaders can voice their appeals in terms of the state (*Deutschland*) or the nation (*volksdeutsch, Volkstum, Volksgenosse*) because the two trigger the same associations. The same is true for members of the politically dominant group in some multiethnic states. Thus, the Han Chinese are apt to view the state of China as the state of their particular nation, and are therefore susceptible to appeals either in the name of China or in the name of the Han Chinese people. But the notion of *China* evokes quite different associations, and therefore quite different responses, from Tibetans, Mongols, Uighurs, and other non-Han people. The confusing use of terminology has diverted scholars for some time from asking the key question: How many examples come to mind of a strong "state-nationalism" being manifested among a people who perceive their state and their nation as distinct entities?

The likelihood of contemporary scholars being diverted from the posing of this question would have been greatly reduced had the misnomer, "nation-building," not been adopted. Since most of the less developed states contain a number of nations, and since the transfer of primary allegiance from these nations to the state is generally considered the sine qua non of successful integration, the true goal is not "nation-building" but "nation-destroying." Would scholars have been less sanguine concerning the chances of success if proper terminology had been employed? Certainly they would have been less likely to ignore, or to dismiss lightly, the problem of ethnic identity, the true nationalism.[36]

(2) A MISUNDERSTANDING OF THE NATURE OF ETHNIC
NATIONALISM AND A RESULTING TENDENCY TO UNDERRATE
ITS EMOTIONAL POWER:

In its broadest implications, this reason for the failure of authorities to pay proper heed to ethnicity is the end product of all other reasons. If so understood, it is a statement of the problem rather than an explanation. However, as used here, it is intended to point to the tendency of scholars to perceive ethnic nationalism in terms of its overt manifestations rather than in terms of its essence. The essence of the nation is not tangible. It is psychological, a matter of attitude rather than of fact.

In accordance with an earlier quoted definition, we can describe the nation as a self-differentiating ethnic group. A prerequisite of nationhood is a popularly held awareness or belief that one's own group is unique in a most vital sense. In the absence of such a popularly held conviction, there is only an ethnic group. A distinct group may be very apparent to the anthropologist or even to the untrained observer, but without a realization of this fact on the part of a sizable percentage of its members, a nation does not exist.

Because the essence of the nation is a matter of attitude, the tangible manifestations of cultural distinctiveness are significant only to the degree that they contribute to the *sense* of uniqueness. Indeed, a sense of vital uniqueness can come about even in the absence of important, tangible cultural characteristics of a distinctive nature, as evidenced by the ethnopsychological experience of the American colonists, the Afrikaners, and the Taiwanese with regard to their former British, Dutch, and Han Chinese identities. Conversely, the concept of a single nation can transcend tangible cultural distinctions, such as the Catholic-Lutheran division within the German nation.[37]

Any nation can, of course, be described in terms of its particular amalgam of tangible characteristics, for example, in terms of the number of its members, their physical location, their religious and linguistic composition, and so forth. But one can so describe any human grouping, even such an unimportant categorization as the New Englander. By intuitively valuing that which they have in common with other Americans more than that which makes them unique, the New Englanders have self-relegated themselves to the status of a subnational element. By contrast, the Ibos clearly place greater importance on being Ibo than on being Nigerian. It is, therefore, the self-view of one's group, rather than the tangible characteristics, that is of essence in determining the existence or nonexistence of a nation.

The abstract essence of ethnic nationalism is often not perceived by the observer. There is an understandable propensity, when investigating a case of ethnic discord, to perceive the struggle in terms of its more readily discernible features. Thus, Ukrainian unrest is popularly reported as an attempt to preserve the Ukrainian language against Russian inroads; Belgium's major problem is also viewed as essentially linguistic; the Ethiopian-Eritrean, as well as the Northern Ireland conflict, is seen as religious; the Czech-Slovak, the West Pakistani-Bengali, and the Serb-Croat disputes are characterized as essentially matters of economic differentiation. Linguistic, religious, and economic distinctions between peoples are all easily discerned and, what is of at least equal moment, are easily conveyed to one's audience.

This propensity to perceive an ethnic division in terms of the more tangible differences between the groups is often supported by the statements and actions of those most involved. In their desire to assert their uniqueness, members of a group are apt to make rallying points of their more tangible and distinguishing institutions. Thus, the Ukrainians, as a method of asserting their non-Russian identity, wage their campaign for national survival largely in terms of their right to employ the Ukrainian, rather than the Russian, tongue in all oral and written matters. But would not the Ukrainian nation (that is, a popular consciousness of being Ukrainian) be likely to persist even if the language were totally replaced by Russian, just as the Irish nation has persisted after the virtual disappearance of Gaelic, despite pre-1920 slogans that described Gaelic and Irish identity as inseparable?[38] Is the language the essential element of the Ukrainian nation, or is it merely a minor element which has been elevated to *the symbol* of the nation in its struggle for continued viability? National identity may survive substantial alterations in language, religion, economic status, or any other tangible manifestation of its culture. Nevertheless, not only do those involved in an ethnic dispute tend to express their own national consciousness in terms of tangible symbols, but they also tend to express their aversion to the other nation in terms of ostensibly readily identifiable attributes. Seldom will a person acknowledge that he dislikes a member of another group simply because the latter is Chinese, Jewish, Ibo, Afro-American, Italian, or what have you. There is a very common compulsion to express what are fundamentally emotional responses to foreign stimuli (prejudices) in more "rational" terms. "They" are inclined to laziness (or aggressiveness), crime, having too many children, and, if a minority, to disloyalty. "They" are prejudiced toward us, haughty in their dealings, disparaging of our culture, determined to take unfair economic advantage, intent on forcing their culture and standards upon us, and relegating us to an inferior status.[39] Employment, crime, birth, income, emigration, life expectancy, and bilingual statistics of varying reliability and applicability are among the data commonly advanced as tangible evidence of such allegations. Thus is the "idea" made flesh.

As a result of the tendency for both participant and reporter to describe ethnopsychological phenomena in terms of tangible considerations, the true nature and power of ethnic feelings are not probed. Indeed, in many cases analysts fail to realize they are dealing with ethnic nationalism. Northern Ireland offers a contemporary case in point.

Strife in the northern six counties of Ireland has been treated almost exclusively as a religious conflict, a quaint echo of the intranational religious wars of a bygone age that saw Frenchmen pitted against Frenchmen, German against German, and so forth. To the degree that Northern Ireland's problem has not been viewed as religious, it has been treated as a civil rights struggle for political and economic reform. In fact, it is neither in its essence; rather, it is a struggle predicated upon fundamental differences in national identity. Contrary to the typical account, the people of Northern Ireland do not uniformly consider themselves Irish.[40] Indeed, a survey, conducted in 1968 by representatives of the University of Strathclyde, indicates that a majority do not. Although 43 percent of the respondents thought of themselves as being Irish, 29 percent considered themselves to be British, 21 percent Ulster, and the remaining 7 percent considered themselves to be of mixed, other, or uncertain nationality.[41]

Unfortunately, the survey failed to correlate national identity with the religion of the respondents, but it is safe to assume, on the basis of the ethnic and religious histories of the island, that there exists a close correlation between self-identification as Irish and adherence to Catholicism.[42] The important distinction, however, lies between those who consider themselves Irish, and those who either do not so consider themselves or are not so considered by the bulk of the Irish element. That the religious issue is largely extraneous helps to account for the fact that the consistent urging of tolerance by all but a handful of religious leaders has gone unheeded.[43] Indeed, with at least as much accuracy, the conflict could be described as one of surnames rather than religions. Despite some intermarriage, the family name remains a relatively reliable index to Irish heritage, as compared to English or Scottish.[44] It is for this reason that a surname is apt to trigger either a negative or positive response. One tragic manifestation of this phenomenon has been the tendency of militant Irishmen (described as Catholics) to be particularly aggressive toward Scottish units of the British forces sent from the island of Great Britain, because of the preponderance of Scottish names among Northern Ireland's non-Irish population.[45] In popular Irish perception, their local enemies and the Scottish troops are linked in their common foreignness and Scottishness.

To the knowledge of this writer, there has been only one account of the strife in Northern Ireland that has placed it in its proper context:

> In Ulster, especially, much of the tension dates to the 17th century. After yet another round of fighting the Irish Catholics, the British encouraged Englishmen and Scotsmen to settle in Northern Ireland and tame the natives. The native Catholics have hated these invading Protestants ever since—not only as Protestants but also as outsiders with different customs and greater privileges. Then as now, the friction was as much social as religious.[46]

If one substitutes *ethnic* or *nationalistic* for *social* in the last sentence, it is evident that the conflict in Northern Ireland is not very distinct in its primary cause from the struggle between Fleming and Walloon in Belgium, between *les Anglais* and *les Canadiens* in Canada, Lao and Thai in Thailand, Ibo and Hausa in Nigeria, or "Asian" and "African" in Guyana. But how different is the image of the nature, depth, and intractibility of Northern Ireland's problem raised by this analysis from the image raised by C. L. Sulzberger's statement that "they are all Irish and therefore love a fight: formidable men and easily stirred to passion. . . . All Irish, whether they favor Green or Orange, enjoy a fight."[47]

In summary, ethnic strife is too often superficially discerned as principally predicated upon language, religion, customs, economic inequity, or some other tangible element. But what is fundamentally involved in such a conflict is that divergence of basic identity which manifests itself in the "us-them" syndrome. And the ultimate answer to the question of whether a person is one of us, or one of them, seldom hinges on adherence to overt aspects of culture. This issue has been at the core of the Israeli Government's long and still unsuccessful attempt to define a Jew. For political and legal purposes, the government may demand adherence to one of the denominations of the Judaic faith as a test of Jewishness. But, as the government is well aware, there are many self-proclaimed agnostics, atheists, and converts to other faiths who are, in the most thorough and psychologically profound sense of the word, Jewish. And there are practicing members of the Judaic faith who are not ethnically Jewish. The Judaic faith has, of course, been an important element of Jewish nationalism, as, to a lesser degree, Catholicism and Irish nationalism are related. But an individual (or an entire national group) can shed all of the overt cultural manifestations customarily attributed to his ethnic group and yet maintain his fundamental identity as a member of that nation. Cultural assimilation need not mean psychological assimilation.

(3) AN UNWARRANTED EXAGGERATION OF THE INFLUENCE OF MATERIALISM UPON HUMAN AFFAIRS:

A number of authorities have noted a propensity on the part of American statesmen and scholars of the post–World War II era to assume that economic considerations represent the determining force in human affairs. Programs of foreign assistance, for example, have been promoted and defended on the ground that the economic status of a state correlates directly with its form of government, political stability, and aggressiveness.[48] Policy-makers in the United States have also attempted to defuse a number of highly charged interstate (and interethnic) conflicts by making cooperation between the adversaries a condition of material recompense (for example, the Jordan, Indus, and Mekong River projects). The Marshall Plan, Point Four, the Eisenhower Doctrine, and the Alliance for Progress could all be interpreted as attempts to alter attitudes by appealing to material self-interest.

This presumption that economic considerations constitute the primary force which shapes the basic ideas and attitudes of humans has had an evident impact upon much of the literature concerned with political integration. An ethnic minority, it is implicitly or explicitly held, will not secede from a state if its living standards are improving, both in real terms and relative to other segments of the state's population.[49] Such a prognosis again underestimates the power of ethnic feelings and ignores contrary evidence: With regard to the matter of economic inequity among groups, for example, there are a number of cases in which the ethnic consciousness of a minority and its animosity toward the dominant element became accentuated although the income gap between the group and the dominant element was being rapidly closed. The Flemish of Belgium and the Slovaks of Czechoslovakia are cases in point.[50] Indeed, there are even cases in which separatist movements exist despite the fact that the group from which they emanate is more advanced economically than is the politically dominant element. The Croatians and Slovenes of Yugoslavia and the Basques and Catalans of Spain exemplify this situation. As to the matter of real rather than comparative economic status, we have noted earlier that multiethnic states at all economic levels have been troubled by growing ethnic discord. Economic considerations may be an irritant that reinforces ethnic consciousness. And, as noted, those most involved in the conflict may present the issue in economic terms. But economic factors are likely to come in a poor second when competing with the emotionalism of ethnic nationalism. Numerous colonial ties were severed irrespective of whether or not they were economically beneficial to the colonial people. Separatists (whether Anguillan, Eritrean, Naga, or Welsh) are not apt to be dissuaded by the assertion that the nation is too small to comprise an economically viable unit.* There is a simple, yet profound message of the broadest applicability in the slogan, "Better a government run like hell by Filipinos than one run like heaven by Americans."

(4) UNQUESTIONED ACCEPTANCE OF THE ASSUMPTION THAT
GREATER CONTACTS AMONG GROUPS LEAD TO GREATER AWARENESS
OF WHAT GROUPS HAVE IN COMMON, RATHER THAN OF
WHAT MAKES THEM DISTINCT:

A number of authorities have also noted that American foreign policy is heavily influenced by an optimistic view of human affairs in which man is seen as essentially rational and possessed of good will, and therefore preordained to find reasonable answers to problems.[51] As applied to ethnicity, this optimism is manifest in the conviction that mis-

---

* Eritrea, a regional rather than an ethnic movement, should not have been included.

understandings among nations are due to lack of knowledge concerning each other. Greater contacts, it would follow, should lead to greater understanding and harmony. One manifestation of this belief is the person-to-person diplomacy that forms the rationale of the Peace Corps and official sanctioning of massive cultural and educational exchange programs. It is also evident in the lack of official concern that the presence of large numbers of Americans in a foreign state is apt to trigger a xenophobic response.[52] This view also probably helps to account for the slighting of ethnicity in works dealing with political integration. If greater contacts, brought about by more intensive communication and transportation networks, promote harmony, ethnic heterogeneity is not a matter worthy of serious consideration.

We have noted, however, that the contacts occasioned by modernization have in fact had the opposite tendency. The optimistic position fails to consider that, while the idea of being friends presupposes knowledge of each other, so does the idea of being rivals. Indeed, the self-awareness which is the sine qua non of the nation requires knowledge of nonmembers. The conception of being unique or different requires a referent, that is, the idea of "us" requires "them." Minimally, it may be asserted that increasing awareness of a second group is not certain to promote harmony and is at least as likely to produce, on balance, a negative response. With an empirical eye to the evidence of growing ethnic consciousness and discord, we can add that the latter is much more likely.

(5) IMPROPER ANALOGIZING FROM THE EXPERIENCE OF
THE UNITED STATES:

Many works on political integration contain direct reference to the successful assimilationist history of the United States as evidence that the basic identity of people can be rather easily transferred from the ethnic group to a larger grouping coterminous with the state.[53] It is probable, moreover, that the "melting pot" idea has had an unarticulated influence upon much larger numbers of scholars. If broad-scale assimilation could occur within the United States, practically without design, why not elsewhere? If an extremely diverse ethnic hodgepodge became quite naturally a single "American nation," one may well expect the same process to occur quite naturally elsewhere. The analogy is a dangerous one, however.

A denial of the pertinence of the American experience does *not* rest upon the recent surge of interest in ethnic matters within the United States. There has been a recent spate of monographs and articles clearly documenting that the melting process has not yet caught up with

the myth, and that pre-American national heritage remains an important index to neighborhood, voting patterns, associations, and so
forth.[54] Moreover, large numbers of people within the United States
who formerly played down their pre-American heritage have recently
been demonstrating a new pride in it. But these facts are not necessarily
germane to the study of ethnic nationalism. Nor do they materially
alter the fact that an impressively high level of assimilation has been
achieved within the United States. Total melting has not yet occurred
and may never occur, but it has made great strides and is progressing
on a significant scale. In addition, even if the upsurge in ethnic pride
should prove to be more than a vogue, it does not follow that the upsurge is a manifestation of ethnic nationalism. It was noted earlier that
the concept of a single nation does not preclude internal divisions.
Lesser "us-them" relationships can exist within a single nation, so long
as in any test of allegiance the larger "us" of the nation proves more
powerful than the divisive call of a particular region, religion, pre-
American ethnic heritage, or whatever. There is nothing necessarily
incompatible between stressing one's Italian or Polish cultural heritage
and "the American nation."

Black nationalism, by contrast, may directly challenge the larger
"us" of "the American nation." Although many diverse attitudes and
goals are cloaked under the single rubric of black nationalism, an essential element is its insistence that what has hitherto been known as
"the American nation" has in fact been a white nation. In refusing to
identify with "the American nation," and in postulating a rival black
nation, black nationalism constitutes a nationalism in the most correct
sense of the word.[55] This is so whether the nationalist advocates "two
nations, one state" or actual political separation. Black nationalism is
therefore a legitimate object of inquiry in the study of ethnicity as a
global phenomenon. But, as noted, assimilation among white Americans is not an appropriate model for situations elsewhere.

The key factor that differentiates the process of assimilation in the
United States is that the impetus for assimilation has come principally
from the unassimilated, not from the dominant group. The typical non-
African immigrant *voluntarily* left his cultural hearth and traveled a
substantial distance, in both a physical and a psychological sense, to
enter a different ethnopolitical environment which recognized no notable political or psychological relationship with his former homeland.
Moreover, in any one generation, he and other immigrants of his particular ethnicity were few in number relative to the dominant, Anglo-
Saxonized, American population. Although he may well have lived
(and his descendants may still live) in an ethnic ghetto where his native

language and customs lingered on, the ghetto was neither sufficiently large nor economically adequate to permit the fulfillment of his most ambitious aspirations, whether of an economic-, prestige-, or power-oriented nature. He was constantly aware of being part of a larger cultural entity that pervaded and shaped the ghetto in countless ways,[56] and he realized that cultural assimilation was necessary if the more obvious limits to his ambitions were to be pushed back. As a result of all this, ethnic problems within the United States have not been characterized primarily by the resistance of minorities to assimilation, but by the unwillingness or inability of the dominant group to permit assimilation at the rate desired by the unassimilated.

Elsewhere, the typical ethnic problem is reversed, with the pressure for assimilation popularly being viewed by the minority as originating with the dominant group. Consider the case of a French-Canadian living within the large, predominantly French Province of Quebec. He lives in an ethnic homeland, which has been continuously inhabited by Frenchmen since before the coming of *les Anglais* and which is laden with emotional overtones. English-speaking people and their culture are therefore seen as invaders, aliens in a French-Canadian land. Moreover, the French-Canadian community is sufficiently large to accommodate visionary success totally within the ethnic confines.[57] As a result, there is little to entice the individual to surrender his own culture, and much—in terms of the reinforcing quality of the forces and symbols of his environment—to cause him to resent and resist the intrusion of the outside culture. In contrast to the United States where assimilation has, on balance, been viewed by the minority as a voluntary act, anything that necessitates a degree of assimilation takes on an aura of either physical or psychological coercion.[58] The universality of this response has led to the rapid spread of the expression "cultural imperialism." And the response is self-generating, as it exacerbates ethnic sensibilities and causes what was considered innocent yesterday to be perceived as offensive today. Interethnic tensions are thereby magnified, and the pale hopes of assimilation made still more dim.

In sum, then, analogies drawn from the experience of the United States are apt to be specious. A proportionately small number of people who have voluntarily left their cultural milieu to enter an alien politico-cultural environment in which cultural assimilation is perceived positively as indispensable to success is one thing; a situation characterized by two or more large groups, each ensconced in a territory it considers its traditional homeland and cultural preserve, is something quite different. The second situation characterizes the overwhelming number of ethnic struggles.

(6) IMPROPER ANALOGIZING FROM THE FACT THAT
INCREASES IN COMMUNICATIONS AND TRANSPORTATION HELP TO
DISSOLVE CULTURAL DISTINCTIONS AMONG REGIONS WITHIN WHAT IS
FUNDAMENTALLY A ONE-CULTURE STATE, TO THE CONCLUSION THAT
THE SAME PROCESS WILL OCCUR IN SITUATIONS INVOLVING
TWO OR MORE DISTINCT CULTURES:

It is evident that increased contacts between regions of the United States have tended to weaken sectionalism. Countrywide media of communication (particularly television and motion pictures), the inter-regional movement of people, the geographic suffusion of industry and its products, and the increasing standardization of education have all tended to homogenize the United States. Among the more evident factors that attest to this trend are the fading of formerly clear election patterns along sectional lines (for instance, "the Solid South," or Republican northern New England) and the progressive elimination of sharp distinctions among local customs in matters such as dialect, humor, dress, and music. But if one is dealing not with variations of a single culture-group, but with distinct and self-differentiating culture groups, then increased contacts, as we have noted, tend to produce disharmony rather than harmony. Discord between the Basques and Castilians, the Czechs and Slovaks, the Russians and Ukrainians, the Walloons and Flemish, the Welsh and English, the French-speaking and English-speaking Canadians, and the Serbs and Croats has increased with increased contacts. The same development has been noted in the case of Thailand and of Ethiopia. Increased contacts tend to have one impact in a one-culture situation, and quite a different impact in a variegated culture area.[59]

(7) THE ASSUMPTION THAT ASSIMILATION IS A ONE-DIRECTIONAL PROCESS:

If assimilation is assumed to be irreversible, then any evidence of a move toward assimilation becomes an irrevocable gain and a basis for optimism. Thus, because the Scottish and Welsh people had undergone generations of acculturation, including almost total linguistic assimilation, and because the concept of a British national identity did indeed possess an important measure of meaning to the preponderant numbers of Scots and Welshmen, authorities were for years almost unanimous in their conviction that homogeneity of identity had once and for all been achieved.[60] The sudden upsurge in Scottish and Welsh nationalism during the 1960s illustrates, however, that assimilation may indeed be reversed so long as some glimmer of a separate ethnic identity persists.

(8) INTERPRETATION OF THE ABSENCE OF ETHNIC STRIFE AS EVIDENCE
OF THE PRESENCE OF A SINGLE NATION:

The existence of a single national consciousness that is shared by all segments of the population of a state *cannot* be deduced simply from the absence of overt ethnic conflict. Such a conclusion is always dangerous, for, just as the fervor with which ethnic nationalism is embraced and the form in which it is manifested can vary substantially among individuals, so too, can it fluctuate widely within a particular nation over time. Few would contend that German nationalism is dead, although it is obviously more subdued, and following different channels, than was the case in the 1930s. Periods in which nationalism takes on more passive forms may be followed by periods of militant nationalism and vice versa. In addition, the bilateral relations between ethnic groups, just as those between states, vary greatly. They may range along a continuum from a genocidal relationship to a symbiotic one. The fact that Canada and the United States have dwelt for generations alongside one another without warfare has not meant that they form a single state. So, too, the absence of hostilities between neighboring ethnic groups does not confirm a single transgroup identity. We have already noted that separate ethnic groups may coexist, at least for a time, within the same political structure. Influential factors include the degree of cultural self-awareness, the minority's perception of the nature and magnitude of the threat to the preservation of the group as a unique entity, and the reputation of the government for the relative ruthlessness with which it is apt to respond to "treasonable" acts. But coexistence—even when peaceful—should not be construed as proof of a single nation.

The error of misconstruing the absence of strife between ethnic groups as indicative of national unity has not been restricted to peaceful situations. Another common pitfall has been to impute a single national consciousness to militant movements whose ranks include members of different ethnic groups. Ethnic consciousness is not an automatic bar to cooperative, nor even to coordinated or integrated, activities against a mutually perceived enemy or in pursuit of a mutually desired goal. A number of ethnic groups can, and often do, march under the same banner and shout the same slogans. All too often, however, such a composite movement has been misidentified as a manifestation of a single, all-embracing nationalism. In the waning days of colonialism, for example, diverse segments of the population of British India were agreed upon the desirability of ridding the subcontinent of alien rule, and this movement for the eradication of British control was generally described as Indian nationalism (further subdivided into Indian and Moslem nationalism after 1930). It would have been more accurate to characterize the movement as a wartime alliance, similar in many respects to those entered into by states. Just as alliances among states tend to weaken as the threat recedes or the goal nears attainment, so too the period dating from the British announcement of intention to withdraw has been one of rather steady deterioration of the interethnic bonds within the successor states. Comparable multiethnic, anticolonial movements exist today in a few remaining colonies, such as Angola and Mozambique.* They also prevail in a number of postcolonial situations, as in Burma [Myanmar], northern Borneo, western New Guinea, and throughout the cordillera of Indochina. Any such multiethnic alliance is comprised of a number of national movements, but it is not itself coincidental with a single nation. The absence of ethnic discord between specified ethnic groups—whether manifested by passivity or by positive, cooperative action—cannot be assumed to be evidence of one national consciousness.

The tendency to see ethnic unity in the absence of overt ethnic discord has had an important impact upon theories of "nation-building." It helps to explain the very common habit of describing Western Europe as though it were composed of fully integrated states, which, as we have noted, most certainly is not the case. Western Europe is therefore held up as a model of something it is not, as proof that something can be achieved elsewhere that is in fact far from achieved there.[61] A second outgrowth of this tendency is to view outbreaks of ethnic nationalism on an ad hoc basis rather than as only one contemporary manifestation of a more enduring global phenomenon. An outbreak of ethnic hostilities in Malaysia, in Jamaica, in Burundi, in Spain, or in Canada is viewed as an isolated phenomenon, soon forgotten by most outside observers after a more peaceful relationship has been reinstituted. The ubiquity and significance of ethnic nationalism are therefore not fully appreciated.

(9) IMPROPER REGARD FOR THE FACTOR OF CHRONOLOGICAL TIME
AND INTERVENING EVENTS WHEN ANALOGIZING FROM ASSIMILATIONIST
EXPERIENCES PRIOR TO "THE AGE OF NATIONALISM":

In emphasizing the manner in which the nations of Western Europe and Eastern Asia were created from rather disparate ethnic materials, authorities have failed to consider that the fact that the models predate the nineteenth century may obviate their pertinence to the current

* Both Angola and Mozambique achieved independence in the mid-1970s.

scene. No examples of significant assimilation are offered which have taken place since the advent of the age of nationalism and the propagation of the principle of self-determination of nations.

By and large, those peoples who, prior to the nineteenth century, were seduced by the blandishments of another culture—those who became "them"—were not aware of belonging to a separate culture-group with its own proud traditions and myths. There was no keen competition for group allegiance. By contrast, peoples today are everywhere much more apt to be cognizant of their membership in a group with its own mythical genesis, its own customs and beliefs, and perhaps its own language, which *in toto* differentiate the group from all others and permit the typical individual to answer intuitively and unequivocally the question, "What are you?" The spontaneous response, "I am Luo" rather than Kenyan, or "Bengali" rather than Pakistani, does not bode well for the architect of a nation-state.

As we have noted, there are numerous reasons for this increase in ethnic consciousness since the early nineteenth century, among them the great increase in the frequency, scope, and type of interethnic and intraethnic group contacts. At least in terms of "assimilationist time" (the time required to produce full assimilation), the radio, telephone, train, motor vehicle, and aircraft are recent innovations, postdating the advent of the age of nationalism and its standard of ethnicity as the basis of political legitimacy. As noted, there is little evidence of modern communications destroying ethnic consciousness, and much evidence of their augmenting it. The movement prior to the nineteenth century appears to have been toward assimilation into a number of larger nations, but since that time the movement appears to be toward the freezing of existing ethnic groups. Examples from the other side of the watershed must therefore be approached most cautiously.

(10) IMPROPER REGARD FOR DURATIVE TIME BY FAILING TO CONSIDER
THAT ATTEMPTS TO TELESCOPE "ASSIMILATIONIST TIME," BY INCREASING THE
FREQUENCY AND SCOPE OF CONTACTS, MAY PRODUCE A NEGATIVE RESPONSE:

If the matter of chronological time could be overcome, there would remain the matter of durative time. As indicated by the resurgence of Scottish nationalism, the total assimilation of a large people predominating in a particular territory requires a period of long duration extending over several generations. To be successful, the process of assimilation must be a very gradual one, one that progresses almost without visibility and awareness.[62] Since the essence of national identity is psychological and involves self-acceptance, a greater intensity of contacts, whether by accident or design, will conceivably not only fail to speed up the process, but will prove to be counterproductive. By their very numbers, the Han Chinese furnish proof of being history's most successful assimilators; but the many people of riverine and coastal China were sinified only over many centuries. Programmed attempts since 1949 to speed up the process of sinifying the remaining minorities has led to increased ethnic consciousness and anti-Han resentment on the part of the minorities. So, too, the Soviet Union, despite more than a half-century of programmed assimilation, finds its "national question" not only unresolved but growing in intractability. Similarly, Franco's stepped-up attempt to eradicate Basque, Catalan, and Galician self-consciousness seems only to have magnified them. Rather than telescoping the process, more intensive contacts appear to generate a psychological rebuff. Variations in the tempo of contacts may determine whether a people moves slowly toward assimilation or rapidly toward ethnocentrism.

This relationship of assimilation to durative time casts serious doubt on whether the process of assimilation is subjectable to social engineering. Planning is more geared to action than to inaction, and more to a time span of one generation or less than to a multigenerational period. More important, however, is the fact that modernization largely dictates its own timetable. There is an inbuilt accelerator in the technological advances and other forces that causes a continuous "shrinking of the world" and the shrinking of its states as presently defined. The frequency and pervasiveness of intergroup contacts appear, therefore, to be fated to increase exponentially, regardless of the desire of the planner.

(11) CONFUSING SYMPTOMS WITH CAUSES:

Most of the theoretic writings on political integration, as noted earlier, have been characterized by an unwarranted degree of optimism. But as the newly formed states proved less cohesive than had been anticipated, explanations for their political disintegration have become increasingly common. Many of these explanations, however, confuse some of the symptoms and minor contributing elements of political decay with its primary cause.

For example, a paper dealing with political decay in sub-Sahara Africa[63] lists among its causes, in addition to colonialism and neocolonialism, (a) exaggerated notions of the actual power of the centralized government, (b) the weakening of "mass parties," (c) the lessening of political mobilization, (d) the reduction of the links between the state government and segments of the population, (e) inability of the state to satisfy the perceived needs of its human components, (f) the loss of charismatic aura earlier enjoyed by the key figure, and (g) a "praetorian impulse." The question of primary loyalty and, more particularly, of ethnic identity, is not listed. And, clearly, those factors which are listed do not constitute causes, but either symptoms [(a), (b), (d), (e), (f)] or minor elements applicable to only a few specific situations [(c) and (g)]. A giant step toward identifying the primary cause would be made by asking *why* the power of the central government proved to be exaggerated, *why* the "mass" parties proved unstable, *why* the government was not able to forge solid links with all segments of the population, and *why* the father-figures could not retain their popularity.

The prime cause of political disunity is the absence of a single psychological focus shared by all segments of the population. Admittedly, ethnic homogeneity is not in itself sufficient to guarantee such a consensus. The intraethnic Vietnamese struggle illustrates this point. But in the case of the multiethnic state, we have noted that, for most of the inhabitants, primary identity will not extend beyond the ethnic group. And all but a handful of the new states are multiethnic.

To illustrate the importance of ethnic consciousness as a barrier to the political integration of the multiethnic state, let us return to the example at hand. Surely ethnic nationalism is the single most momentous political fact of sub-Sahara Africa, and the fundamental identity that it posits goes far toward answering the questions we have posed. Earlier estimates of the strength of the central governments proved exaggerated because the loyalty of the people seldom extended beyond their own ethnic group. Indeed, considering sub-Sahara's short, postcolonial history, a remarkably large number of states (more than one-third) have already experienced ethnic fragmentation in its most flagrant form of civil war along ethnic lines.[64] Similarly, in most states the mass party has been primarily a means of masking ethnic rivalry; identification of the individual with the party has been missing.[65] As to the father-figures, they have tended to retain their position in the eyes of those who see them as ethnic leaders. Kenyatta still possesses charisma for the Kikuyu; his problem is with the Luo and other non-Kikuyu who see him as one of "them."[66]

It bears repeating that ethnic homogeneity is not by itself sufficient to guarantee a bond of unity so infrangible that it can withstand any and all fissiparous forces. The impact of institutions, economic opportunities, geography, literacy, urbanization, and a host of other factors may therefore be very germane to the study of the components of an efficacious identity. But the experience of multiethnic states, past and present, strongly suggests that the ethnic nation may well constitute the outer limits of that identity. If there are means of transferring primary identification and allegiance from the nation to the state, or if there are ways of satisfying national aspirations within a multiethnic state, these possibilities should certainly be explored. But the potent fissiparous force of ethnic particularism should not be obscured by ascribing its role of prime mover to its symptoms.

(12) THE PREDISPOSITIONS OF THE ANALYST:

The last in this list of possible contributing factors to the broadscale underassessment of the ramifications of ethnic nationalism is the most difficult to document: it involves the influence that the ideals of the analyst exert upon his perception. Given the multitude of overt manifestations of ethnic nationalism throughout Africa and Asia (as well as elsewhere), it is difficult to reconcile its total absence or cursory treatment in so many studies on development. Even *in toto*, the preceding eleven considerations do not satisfactorily account for this failure to recognize the significance of the ethnic factor. Eventually it is difficult to avoid the conclusion that the predispositions of the analyst are also involved; that the "nation-builder" passionately wishes the people of his academic purview well; that he is convinced that their ultimate well-being is tied to the vehicle of the state as presently constituted; and that his compassion has colored his perception so that he perceives those trends that he deems desirable as actually occurring, regardless of the factual situation. If the fact of ethnic nationalism is not compatible with his vision, it can thus be willed away. A related factor is the fear that ethnic nationalism will feed on publicity. In either case, the treatment calls for total disregard or cavalier dismissal of the undesired facts. Such an approach can be justified for the policy-maker, but not for the scholar.

NOTES

1. A representative sampling of the literature on integration theory might well include the following titles: Gabriel Almond and James S. Coleman, *The Politics of Developing Areas* (Princeton, 1960); Gabriel Almond and G. Bingham Powell, *Comparative Politics: A Developmental Approach* (Boston, 1966); Gabriel Almond and Sidney Verba, *The Civic Culture* (Boston, 1963); David Apter, *The Politics of Modernization* (Chicago, 1965); Willard A. Beling and George O. Totten, eds., *Developing Nations: Quest for a Model* (New York, 1970); (6) Karl W. Deutsch and William Foltz, eds., *Nation-Building* (New York, 1966); Jason Finkle and Richard Gable, eds., *Political Development and Social Change* (New York, 1966); (8) Philip E. Jacob and James V. Toscano, eds., *The Integration of Political Communities* (Philadelphia, 1964); Lucian Pye, ed., *Communications and Political Development* (Princeton, 1963); and Lucian Pye, *Aspects of Political Development* (Boston, 1966). The inclusion of five readers on the list, with an aggregate of well over fifty separate contributions, substantially broadens the sample.

None of these ten works dedicates a section, chapter, or major subheading to the matter of ethnic diversity. By contrast, the roles of the military, the bureaucracy, social classes, personality, industrialization, urbanization, and transaction flows and other modes of communication are common entries in tables of contents. In instances in which the tables of contents contain categories that might be expected to include a serious discourse on the ramifications of ethnicity—categories such as "internal legitimacy" or "national identity"—further investigation proved unrewarding.

The slighting of ethnicity is further evidenced by the indices. Six of the ten show not a single reference to ethnic groups, ethnicity, or minorities. Two make a single passing reference to ethnicity, and still another accords to all types of minorities less than two pages, limiting the discussion to their impact upon democracy. The tenth work, a collection of papers, represents only a partial exception. Discussion of the impediments that ethnicity, per se, poses to state-integration is limited to general comments in an introductory essay. Moreover, in this essay the author assumes that the matter is one of relatively short duration, in line with the second tendency described in this paper's introductory sentence.

It should be acknowledged that readers dealing with "nation-building" are apt to contain a few regional or country studies whose authors are well aware of the fissiparous impact of ethnic diversity therein. (In one of the above works, for example, a contribution on sub-Sahara Africa and another on Ceylon [Sri Lanka] clearly demonstrate such an awareness.) But the significant fact is that the issue of ethnic diversity is not perceived by the editors as one that transcends the particular case(s). If the format of a book, as reflected in both its table of contents and index, fails to recognize the problem of ethnicity as more than a local phenomenon, the user of the book is hardly likely to do so.

The above ten works, as noted, are believed to be representative. But two decidedly nonrepresentative titles should be noted: The concept of ethnicity pervades Rupert Emerson, *From Empire to Nation* (Boston, 1960); and an important segment of Charles W. Anderson et al., *Issues of Political Development* (Englewood Cliffs, 1967), is dedicated to a serious treatment of the issue.

2. The 132 units include all entities that were generally considered to be states as of 1 January 1971, with the exception of a few microunits such as Nauru and Western Samoa. However, East and West Germany, North and South Korea, and North and South Vietnam were treated as single entities in the belief that such treatment would minimize their distorting effects. It should not be assumed that the inclusion of all microunits would substantially alter the statistics in favor of homogeneity. In the case of Nauru, for example, despite a population of only 6,500, the largest ethnic element fails to constitute a majority.

3. See, for example, Arnold Rivkin, *Nation-Building in Africa* (New Brunswick, 1969). After reviewing a number of problems throughout Africa, many of which he readily acknowledges are essentially ethnic (see, e.g., 35–37, 195, 196, and 226), the author concludes (238): "Although the divided populations of Africa—of different tribes, ethnic origin (as the Watusi and Bahutu in Rwanda and Burundi), religions (Christian, Islamic, animistic, etc.), and historical background—pose serious and major problems for nation-building, compared to Latin American divisions, developed over centuries, and involving an intermixture of race, social structure, and economic status, they seem relatively

manageable and over time susceptible of solution." No further details concerning a solution are offered, however, and the reader is therefore asked to accept this optimistic forecast solely on faith.

One of the most perplexing illustrations of a failure to confront a problem of ethnic diversity is offered by Lucian Pye, *Politics, Personality, and Nation-Building: Burma's Search for Identity* (New Haven, 1962). Although the politically dominant Burmese have been involved in open ethnic warfare with that country's minorities almost uninterruptedly since that state achieved independence, and although this continuing struggle unquestionably represents that state's most visible and significant barrier to integration, a passing reference to some of the minorities is limited to a single page.

4. *Nationalism and Social Communication: An Inquiry into the Foundations of Nationality* (Cambridge, Mass.). The first edition was published in 1953, and the second, which contains no substantive changes, in 1966. All references to page numbers in this paper correspond to the second edition.

5. See, for example, 126: "Linguistically and culturally, then, members of each group are considered outsiders for the other. Yet technological and economic processes are forcing them together, into acute recognition of their differences and their common, mutual experience of strangeness, and more conspicuous differentiation and conflict may result."

6. Ibid., 152.

7. Ibid., 188.

8. Ibid., 162, 163; emphasis added.

9. Ibid., 164.

10. Karl Deutsch, "Social Mobilization and Political Development," *American Political Science Review* 55 (September 1961): 501.

11. Ibid. It may be instructive that Deutsch offered negative examples of this phenomenon (e.g., the secession of the United States and Ireland from Britain), but no examples of ethnic groups submerging their identity because of effective government.

12. Karl Deutsch, "Nation-Building and National Development: Some Issues for Political Research," in *Nation-Building*, ed. Deutsch and Foltz, 4–5.

13. Ibid., 8–9. It is worth noting that in discussing these prospective stages of assimilation, Deutsch cited several of his own works, including *Nationalism and Social Communication*, thereby indicating his feeling that that work was fully compatible with this view of the ultimate eradication of ethnic divisiveness.

14. Karl Deutsch, *Nationalism and Its Alternatives* (New York, 1969).

15. One indication of a change of attitude toward the problem of assimilation is that while it played a central role in *Nationalism and Social Communication*, the process of assimilation is allocated less than two pages in his most recent work and is treated in terms of its "dimensions" rather than its "components." See 25–27.

16. Deutsch, *Nationalism and Its Alternatives*, 27.

17. See above.

18. Deutsch, *Nationalism and Its Alternatives*, 73.

19. Another example of this tautology can be found in ibid., 68. Referring to earlier cases of national integration, Deutsch concludes that *"the combined proc-*

esses of social mobilization and assimilation eventually turned them into consolidated peoples and nations." If the italicized words are omitted, the statement is an evident truism in that it defines assimilation. Indeed, to the degree that social mobilization presupposes the industrial age and relatively modern transportation and communication networks, the statement as worded is false. The Chinese nation, and nearly all others, antedate the Industrial Revolution.

20. For a treatment of this trend as a global phenomenon, see chapter 1 in this volume.

21. It is assumed that Ethiopia's very short period of domination by Italy in the 1930s does not invalidate its use as an example of a state without a colonial history.

22. For a more complete discussion of the relationship of communications distance to physical distance, see chapter 5 in this volume.

23. For a fascinating account of how increased contacts have strengthened Lao identity, see Charles F. Keyes, "Ethnic Identity and Loyalty of Villagers in Northeast Thailand," *Asian Survey* 6 (July 1966): 362–69.

24. See the perspicacious comment concerning Ethiopia by a newspaper reporter: "Lack of communications helped hold this empire together. Now developing communications and the political awareness they encourage are straining its unity." (Frederich Hunter in the *Christian Science Monitor*, 8 January 1970.)

Problem areas include not just the rather recently acquired Eritrea, but also Bale and Gojam Provinces. See the *New York Times*, 1 April 1969.

25. Cases in point would include Afghanistan, Iran, and Liberia. Many of the Latin American states would also qualify. For a treatment of the latter, see Anderson et al., *Issues of Political Development*, 45–46. For more details on growing ethnic awareness in Thailand and South Asia, see Connor, "Ethnology and the Peace of South Asia," *World Politics* 22 (October 1969): 51–86.

26. One piece of evidence that there were substantial distinctions in the pervasiveness of pre– and post–World War II intergroup, intrastate contacts is offered by American regionalism. As will be noted below, regionalism, in contradistinction to ethnicity, does tend to evaporate in direct proportion to the intensity of interregional communication and transportation networks. Yet regionalism, as manifested in concepts like "states' rights" and in voting blocs and voting patterns, was still strong following World War II. The most enduring manifestation of American regionalism, "the Solid South," has shown symptoms of dying only in recent years.

27. The expression appeared as part of the Proclamation on the Polish Question, endorsed by the London Conference of the First International. The Proclamation noted "the need for annulling Russian influence in Europe, through enforcing the right of self-determination, and through the reconstituting of Poland upon democratic and social foundations." Cited in G. Stelkoff, *History of the First International* (New York, 1968), 85. For a reference to a still earlier use of the expression by Karl Marx in his *Herr Vogt*, see Stefan Possony, "Nationalism and the Ethnic Factor," *Orbis* 10 (Winter 1967): 1218.

28. United Nations Charter, art. I, par. 2.

29. *The Worldmark Encyclopedia of the Nations*, 3d ed. (New York, 1967), 1:254–57, lists fifty intergovernmental organizations whose names begin with *International*. Not one of them has anything to do with nations.

30. Jack C. Plano and Roy Olton, *The International Relations Dictionary* (New York, 1969).

31. See, for example, A.F.K. Organski, *World Politics*, 2d rev. ed. (New York, 1968), 12: "The story we are about to tell is a tale of nations. Nations are the major characters, and it is with their actions, their goals and plans, their power, their possessions, and their relations with each other that we shall be concerned." See also Deutsch, *Nationalism and Its Alternatives*, where, despite defining the word nation to mean a people (i.e., an ethnic group) in charge of a state (p. 19), the author refers to the multiethnic populations of Spain (p. 13), and of Belgium (p. 70), as nations. See, too, the concluding paragraph of Dankwart Rustow, *A World of Nations* (Washington, D.C., 1967), in which he notes that "more than 130 nations, real or so-called, will each make its contribution to the history of the late twentieth century." The author had earlier (e.g., p. 36) differentiated between state and nation. For evidence that studies dealing specifically with the problems that ethnic diversity poses for state integration are also not necessarily immune from improper interuse of terminology, see Donald Rothchild, "Ethnicity and Conflict Resolution," *World Politics* 22 (July 1970): 597–98 particularly. "First, in spite of the oft-used distinction between a fairly coercive domestic order and a fairly noncoercive international order, the jockeying for power of ethnic groups within states corresponds markedly to that of *nation* and *nation*. . . . New and more productive 'decades of development,' with their presumed attempts at re-allocation, may be as indispensable to the comity among ethnic groups within the state as they are among the nations of the world" (emphasis added). Examples abound of this tendency to use key terms improperly, so the authorities who are singled out in this and following footnotes are *not* selected because they have been unusually uncircumspect in their terminology. On the contrary, they have been selected, in part, because they are acknowledged scholars.

32. See, for example, Norman J. Paddleford and George A. Lincoln, *The Dynamics of International Politics*, 2d ed. (New York, 1967), 7: "The actors in the international political system are the independent nation-states." Or Louis J. Halle, *Civilization and Foreign Policy* (New York, 1952), 10: "A prime fact about the world is that it is largely composed of nation-states." And Elton Atwater et al., *World Tensions: Conflict and Accommodation* (New York, 1967), 16: "Since there are some 120 different nation-states in the world." Karl Deutsch also regularly refers to all states as nation-states. See, for example, *Nationalism and Its Alternatives*, 61, 125, and 176. For his description of the multiethnic states of Czechoslovakia, Rumania, and Yugoslavia as nation-states, see 62–63.

33. Meanwhile, expressions such as *statism* or *étatisme*, which should refer to loyalty to the state, have been assigned still other meanings that have little to do with loyalty of any sort.

34. See, for example, the section in Edward Shils, *Political Development in the New States* (The Hague, 1968), entitled "Parochialism, Nationality, and Nation-

alism," 32–33. As used therein, parochialism refers to loyalty to the ethnic group, and nationality and nationalism refer to identity with, and loyalty to, the state.

35. One manifestation has been the grouping of the *nationalism* of Japan and Germany during the 1930s and early 1940s with that of multiethnic Argentina, Italy, and Spain under the rubric of fascism, a doctrine positing the superiority of the corporate state.

36. See, for example, Rothchild, "Ethnicity and Conflict Resolution," 598. "Second, the interethnic confrontation raises questions about the unifying potential of nationalism. Although nationalism has effectively repulsed the claims of metropolitan hegemony in a number of crucial confrontations, it has still to demonstrate the ability to overcome 'primordial sentiments' and to foster a sense of common purpose." By equating nationalism with loyalty to the state, Rothchild is unwittingly criticizing nationalism for not being able to overcome itself. Nonetheless, if his pessimism persisted, his basic analysis concerning the relative strength of ethnic and state loyalty would be sound. However, he later criticizes the authors of a number of books dealing with ethnic problems for emphasizing the depth of the cleavages rather than the positive possibilities for "ethnic balancing." They represent "an all-too-general preoccupation with the nature of past cleavages and conflicts instead of with the evolving dimensions of the process of political integration" (p. 612). "They tell us more about the cleavages than about links, more about conflict than about cooperation and reciprocity. Their details are sharply delineated; however, the complete picture requires somewhat greater attention to adjustment, interrelatedness, adaptation, and exchange" (p. 615). One suspects that the author might have been more likely to question whether he was not asking for answers to the unanswerable if he had been aware that nationalism was on the side of state-disintegration rather than state-integration.

37. Since the concept of the nation does not preclude significant internal divisions, it actually embodies two important levels of attitudes. Relative to *intranational* distinctions and similarities, the stress, when need be, is upon those traits that unite; relative to distinctions and similarities among nations, the ultimate stress is upon those that divide.

38. Still other examples would include the resurgence of Scottish and Welsh nationalism even among those who are linguistically assimilated to English.

39. The pioneering efforts of the late Hadley Cantril in the study of the stereotype images that one group holds of another are of great pertinence and value to the study of ethnic nationalism. The value of the work of Cantril and of those scholars most influenced by him is lessened only slightly because the objects described are the populations of countries rather than ethnic groups. When asked to select those adjectives that best describe the people of another country, it is probable that the respondent envisages the politically dominant ethnic group of that state (e.g., British is perceived as English, South African as Afrikaner, Czechoslovakian as Czech, etc.). A more important limitation lies in the fact that the responses are not tabulated according to the ethnicity of the respondents. There is still another factor: the adjectives usually employed in such studies cannot adequately convey the depth of irrational hatred which may be

involved. Negative attributes, such as *backward, domineering, conceited*, and even *cruel*, are of a different order than are the unarticulated passions that can cause Cambodians to massacre huge numbers of unarmed Vietnamese civilians; Balinese, Javanese, and Malays to massacre Chinese; the Bahutu to massacre Watusi; the Hausa, the Ibo; or the Turks, the Armenians.

40. For an example of a typical account, see Linda Charlton's article in the *New York Times*, 15 August 1969, in which she describes the crisis as "Irishman against Irishman" and "Prods" (Protestants) against Catholics.

41. Richard Rose, *The United Kingdom as a Multinational State* (Glasgow, 1970), 10.

42. The religious composition is 35 percent Catholic, 29 percent Presbyterian (Church of Scotland), 24 percent Episcopal (Church of England), 10 percent other Protestant, and 2 percent other. Ibid., 13.

43. See the *New York Times*, 24 January 1971, for an account of a protest demonstration by Belfast women before a Catholic Bishop's house because he had given a sermon advising Catholics not to have anything to do with the outlawed Irish Republican Army.

44. A notable exception is Terrence O'Neill, the former, moderate prime minister. An awareness within Northern Ireland's political community that strong emotions are often associated with surnames caused his colleagues to presume that his name would prove a real asset in gaining the respect and trust of the Irish minority.

45. See the *New York Times*, 30 April 1970. See also the *New York Times* of two days earlier, where it was reported that order was restored in Belfast only after Scottish troops were replaced by English troops.

As is evident from the above-mentioned survey on national identification, the term Scotch-Irish is a misleading ethnic description. It simply refers to people whose Scottish ancestors emigrated to Ireland, but it need not indicate any Irish ancestry.

46. *Wall Street Journal*, 16 August 1969. A somewhat similar analysis appeared in the letter to the editor column of the *New York Times* on 12 July 1970, signed John C. Marley. "But the religious persuasions of the opposing elements are only incidental to the underlying political question, which is whether the six counties of Northern Ireland shall be ruled by a foreign power. The overwhelming majority of the Irish people, North and South, are united in their desire that the British get out of Ireland. The only exception to this view comes from a British ethnic group which constitutes a local majority, not in the entire six occupied counties, but in a small enclave within a thirty mile radius of Belfast."

47. *New York Times*, 10 July 1970.

48. For descriptions of this tendency, see Hans Morgenthau, "The American Tradition in Foreign Policy," in *Foreign Policy in World Politics*, ed. Roy C. Macridis, 3d ed. (Englewood Cliffs, 1967), 254, and Stanley Hoffman, *Gulliver's Troubles in the Setting of American Foreign Policy* (New York, 1968), 120–21.

49. As noted earlier, Karl Deutsch explicitly held this opinion in 1961.

50. Afro-Americans within the United States may offer a comparable case.

51. Particularly significant for the present discussion is the comment of Gab-

riel Almond: "This overt optimism is so compulsive an element in the American culture that factors which threaten it, such as failure . . . are pressed from the focus of attention and handled in perfunctory ways." *The American People and Foreign Policy* (New York, 1961), 50–51. See also Frederick Hartman, *The New Age of American Foreign Policy* (New York, 1970), 58.

52. Contrast, for example, the American practice of encouraging huge numbers of American troops to furlough in Bangkok, to the Soviet practice of minimizing the Russian presence in such states as the United Arab Republic (Egypt). For a discussion of the impact of a foreign presence upon a guerrilla struggle, and the sharp contrast in awareness of this impact between the United States on the one hand, and China, the Soviet Union, and North Vietnam on the other, see Connor, "Ethnology and the Peace of South Asia," 51–86.

53. See, for example, Karl Deutsch's comment, cited above on p. 34.

54. Particularly recommended for their incisiveness are the works of Nathan Glazer, Milton Gordon, and Daniel P. Moynihan.

55. It is not implied that most Afro-Americans are black nationalists. The percentage is not known. An incisive study would have to learn also what percentage of black nationalists are separatists. It is highly probable that a substantial percentage of those who would be apt to identify themselves as black nationalists have not speculated concerning the precise goal they have in mind beyond a concept of true equality. Attitudes concerning the desirability of various forms of assimilation (schools, business, sports, marriage, etc.) would probably represent the best index as to whether or not one envisaged a separate nation. But it does not follow that attitudinal surveys can validly determine such attitudes. For a thoughtful critique of such surveys by an experienced practitioner, see Arnold Rose, *Migrants in Europe* (Minneapolis, 1969), 100 passim.

56. Government institutions and services (particularly schools), transghetto communications media, advertising, and elections are but a few of the outside forces affecting the ghetto.

57. This aspect of size helps to account for the fact that professional people are often disproportionately represented among those desiring total separation. Belgium, Canada, and Ceylon (Sri Lanka) all offer cases in point. Since goals in a less developed society are apt to be of lesser magnitude, a smaller community may suffice in less modern situations.

58. The need to be fluent in the dominant tongue in order to obtain a decent position in the central bureaucracy is a common example.

59. This inverse relationship causes the use of the term *regionalism* to be a particularly dangerous and inappropriate substitute for *ethnic nationalism*.

60. Richard Rose is among those authorities. In 1964 he observed that "today politics in the United Kingdom is greatly simplified by the absence of major cleavages along the lines of ethnic groups, language, or religion. . . . The solidarity of the United Kingdom today may be due to fortuitous historical circumstances; it is nonetheless real and important." *Politics in England* (Boston, 1964), 10, 11. But by 1970, the situation had changed so drastically that Professor Rose entitled a work *The United Kingdom as a Multi-National State*. On page 1, Rose lists A. S. Amery, Samuel Beers, Harry Eckstein, Jean Blondel, and S. E. Finer as recent writers who have failed to detect the potential significance of ethnic

divisions within the United Kingdom. These men were hardly unique in their failure to anticipate the great change in attitudes about to manifest itself in Scotland and Wales. See, for example, chapter 1 in this volume, where this author acknowledged but underestimated the imminent power of the Scottish nationalist idea. See also J. D. Mackie, *A History of Scotland* (Baltimore, 1964), 367–70, in which a scholar also fails to appreciate the submerged but emerging power of Scottishness among his own people.

61. For a number of illustrations of this tendency to confuse the absence of ethnic warfare with the presence of nation-states throughout Western Europe, see chapter 1 in this volume. Those who have been confused include such notables as John Stuart Mill, Lord Acton, Ernest Barker, and Alfred Cobban; their errors extended inter alia to the United Kingdom, Belgium, Switzerland, and Spain. Similarly, the perspicacious Frederick Engels once wrote: "The Highland Gaels (Scottish) and the Welsh are undoubtedly of different nationalities to what the British are, although *nobody* will give to these remnants of peoples *long gone by* the title of nations, any more than to the Celtic inhabitants of Brittany in France." Cited in Roman Rosdolsky, "Worker and Fatherland: A Note on a Passage in the Communist Manifesto," *Science and Society* 29 (Summer 1965): 333; emphasis added. In his most recent work, *Nationalism and Its Alternatives*, Karl Deutsch also employs Western Europe as a regional model of successfully integrated states. And in both editions of *Nationalism and Social Communication*, Deutsch describes the Bretons, Flemish, Franco-Canadians, Franco- and German-Swiss, Scots, and Welsh as totally assimilated.

62. This statement presupposes that the government is not prepared to take such extreme measures as coercive population transfers and forced intermarriages.

63. Christian Potholm, "Political Decay in Post-Independence Africa: Some Thoughts on its Causes and Cures" (Paper presented at the 1970 Annual Meeting of the New York State Political Science Association).

64. Burundi, Cameroon, Chad, Congo (Kinshasa), Ethiopia, Ivory Coast, Kenya, Nigeria, Rwanda, Sudan, Tanzania (Zanzibar), Uganda, and Zambia. Congo (Brazzaville) also experienced open ethnic warfare on the eve of independence, and Nkrumah suppressed Ashanti and Ewe separatist movements within Ghana early in his reign. Coups that took place in Dahomey and Sierra Leone were also justified as a means of avoiding ethnic warfare. Within Liberia, Tubman's government found an official guilty of treasonably attempting to start a civil, ethnic war. Ethnicity also plays an important role within the anti-Portuguese struggle in Angola and Mozambique, and ethnic violence has occurred in the French Territory of Afars and Issas (Djibouti).

65. Edward Feit has orally referred to African political parties as "the continuation of tribal warfare by other means." See also his comment to this effect in "Military Coups and Political Development: Some Lessons from Ghana and Nigeria," *World Politics* 20 (January 1968): 184.

66. Although not involving an African state, the overthrow of Norodom Sihanouk offers an instructive case concerning a very popular figure who for many years purposefully played the role of—and was popularly viewed by the Khmer people of Cambodia as—the foremost national (read "ethnic")

leader. Following the palace coup that overthrew Sihanouk, it was essential for the coup's leadership that Khmer loyalty to Sihanouk be transferred rapidly to the new government. To this end, the new government publicized a number of charges against the character and record of Sihanouk, most of which were false or exaggerated. The most effective charge, however, was, in effect, that Sihanouk had been "soft on Vietnamese," permitting the Viet Cong and other Vietnamese to violate the Khmer homeland with impunity. This charge, together with the unleashing of a general hate campaign against all ethnic Vietnamese, posed a dilemma for Sihanouk: How to maintain the mantle of Khmer nationalism while simultaneously acknowledging an alliance with Hanoi and the Viet Cong—an alliance he needed if he were to counter the forces at the disposal of the new Cambodian government. The anti-Sihanouk strategy was, therefore, to turn Khmer ethnic nationalism against its former foremost figure by depicting him as a traitor who was aiding the cause of an ethnic enemy of long standing.

Chapter Three

MORE RECENT DEVELOPMENTS

The following paper was written in 1984 for presentation at the Harvard-MIT Joint Seminar on Political Development (JOSPOD). JOSPOD was commemorating its twentieth year of existence (under the joint directorship of Myron Weiner and Samuel Huntington) by commissioning a series of papers, each to be written from the vantage of the author's special interest, which would evaluate the political development literature of the previous twenty years and make recommendations concerning future avenues of research.

There is, therefore, some necessary overlap between the first section of this article and the previous chapter, since the writing of "Nation-Building or Nation-Destroying?" fell within the twenty-year time frame. The body of the text, however, is focused on the literature of the 1970s and early 1980s, and on proposals for honing our research techniques. Parenthetically, were I to update this manuscript in order to cover the post–1984 literature, I do not believe that any substantial alteration in my evaluation of the post–1970 literature would be necessary.

Ethnonationalism*

LOOKING BACKWARD

It risks triteness to note that during the past two decades ethnonationalism has been an extremely consequential force throughout the First, Second, and Third Worlds. Even the more occasional observers of the world scene are now cognizant that Belgium, France, Spain, and the United Kingdom are not ethnically homogeneous states and that the loyalty of Flemings, Corsicans, Basques, and Welshmen to their respective states cannot be accepted as a given. Although less publicized, ethnic unrest within China, Romania, the Soviet Union, and Vietnam (to name but a few of the afflicted Marxist-Leninist states) is a matter of record. Awareness of the significance of ethnic heterogeneity within the states of the Third World has reached the point where even newspaper accounts of coups, elections, and guerrilla struggles often contain references to the ethnic dimensions that are involved.

Few indeed are the scholars who can claim either to have anticipated this global upsurge in ethnonationalism or to have recognized its early manifestations. With respect to the First World, there was a tendency to perceive the states as nation-states, rather than as multinational states, and, in any event, to presume that World War II had convinced the peoples of Western Europe that nationalism was too dangerous and outmoded a focus for the modern age. A supranational, suprastate identity as European was described as the wave of the future. With regard to the Second World, it was broadly held that a highly effective power apparatus and the indoctrination of the masses in Marxist-Leninist ideology had made the issue of ethnonationalism either superfluous or anachronistic. In effect, scholars accepted the official position of Marxist-Leninist governments that the application of Leninist national policy had solved "the national question," leading the masses to embrace proletarian internationalism. In Third World scholarship also, ethnic heterogeneity tended to be ignored or to be cavalierly dismissed as an ephemeral phenomenon. The catchphrase of political develop-

* Published in Walker Connor, "Ethnonationalism," in *Understanding Political Development*, ed. Myron Weiner and Samuel Huntington. Copyright © 1987 Walker Connor.

ment theory at the time was "nation-building," but its devotees offered few if any suggestions as to how a single national consciousness was to be forged among disparate ethnic elements.

How could this wide discrepancy between theory and reality be explained? More than a decade ago, this writer suggested twelve overlapping and reinforcing reasons:[1]

1. *Confusing interutilization of the key terms.* Major result: a tendency to equate nationalism with loyalty to the state (patriotism) and therefore to presurmise that the state would win out in any test of loyalties.

2. *A misunderstanding of the nature of ethnic nationalism resulting in a tendency to underrate its emotional power.* Major result: a perception of ethnically inspired dissonance as predicated upon language, religion, customs, economic inequality, or some other tangible phenomenon, and, *propter hoc*, a failure to probe and appreciate the true nature and power of ethnic feelings.

3. *An unwarranted exaggeration of the influence of materialism upon human affairs.* Major result: the implicit or explicit presumption that the wellsprings of ethnic discord are economic and that an ethnic minority can be placated if its living standard is improving, both in real terms and relative to other segments of the state's population.

4. *Unquestioned acceptance of the assumption that greater contacts among groups lead to greater awareness of what groups have in common, rather than of what makes them distinct.* Major result: the optimistic belief that increased ties between groups are both symptomatic and productive of harmonious relations (as reflected, for example, in transaction-flow theory).

5. *Improper analogizing from the experience of the United States.* Major result: a presumption that the history of acculturation and assimilation within an immigrant society would be apt to be repeated in multinational states.

6. *Improper analogizing from the fact that improvements in communications and transportation help to dissolve regional identities to the conclusion that the same process will occur in situations involving two or more ethnonational peoples.* Major result: a presumption that the waning of significance of regional identities in an ethnically homogeneous state, such as Germany, has precedent for multinational states.

7. *The assumption that assimilation is a one-directional process.* Major result: any evidence of a move toward acculturation/assimilation is viewed as an irreversible gain and is a basis for optimistic forecasts.

8. *Interpretation of the absence of ethnic strife as evidence of the presence of a single nation.* Major result: a tranquil period in the relations among two or more ethnonational groups causes scholars (a) to assume that

the society is ethnically homogeneous, or (b) to perceive a multiethnic "national liberation movement" as monoethnic.

9. *Improper regard for the factor of chronological time and intervening events when analogizing from assimilationist experience prior to the "Age of Nationalism."* Major result: examples of assimilation prior to the nineteenth century are employed as evidence that ethnic identity is a thoroughly fluid phenomenon.

10. *Improper regard for durative time by failing to consider that attempts to telescope "assimilationist time," by increasing the frequency and scope of contacts, may produce a negative response.* Major result: conviction that assimilation lends itself readily to social engineering.

11. *Confusing symptoms with causes.* Major result: explanations for political decay focus upon interim steps, such as the weakening of "mass parties," rather than upon the root cause of ethnic rivalry.

12. *The predisposition of the analyst.* Major result: a tendency to perceive trends deemed desirable as actually occurring.

The list is certainly not exhaustive, and at least five additional reasons suggest themselves:

13. *The mistaken belief that the states of Western Europe were fully integrated nation-states.* A number of leading theorists of political development explicitly maintained that the experiences of the states of Western Europe would be followed by those of the Third World in the course of their development. Thus, Western Europe was held up as an exemplar of something it was not, as proof that nation-states would develop in the Third World.

14. *A tendency to apply conventional scholarly approaches to the Third World.* A great deal of early Third World scholarship reflected the First World training of the analysts. Avenues of research, long applied to First World societies, were transferred to Third World states. Thus, a number of Third World studies explored political party structures and voting patterns in state assemblies, without appreciating that political parties were often viewed at the grass-roots level as the continuation of ethnic rivalry by other means.

15. *Too-exclusive concentration upon the state.* Much of the early Third World scholarship reflected only the view from the capital, to the exclusion of the view from the ethnic homelands.

16. *Too-exclusive concentration on the dominant group in the case of societies with a Staatvolk, such as Burma or Thailand.* One indication of this tendency can be found in purportedly statewide political culture studies that make no reference to the political cultures of ethnic minorities, even when the latter account for a substantial percentage of the population.

17. *The tendency of many scholars to favor explanations based on class.*[2] Ethnic
    nationalism poses a severe paradox to such scholars since it posits that
    the vertical compartments that divide humanity into Englishmen,
    Germans, Ibos, Malays, and the like constitute more potent foci of
    identity and loyalty than do the horizontal compartments known as
    classes.

· · ·

Whatever the reason(s), the "nation-building" school failed to give
proper heed to what, in most states, was *a* if not *the* major obstacle to
political development. Today, just as two decades ago, ethnic nationalism poses the most serious threat to political stability in a host of states
as geographically dispersed as Belgium, Burma [Myanmar], Ethiopia,
Guyana, Malaysia, Nigeria, the Soviet Union, Sri Lanka, Yugoslavia,
and Zimbabwe. Given, then, the failure of the political development
theorists to reflect proper concern for the problems posed by ethnic
heterogeneity, it is disturbing to find no reference to this glaring weakness in Gabriel Almond's retrospective essay on the political development literature and its critics.[*] Indeed, although numerous authors
have drawn attention over the years to this remarkable slighting of the
ethnic factor in the "nation-building" literature, the criticism has gone
unanswered by those commonly identified with the fathering of political development theory.

More Recent Developments

Scholarly indifference to problems arising from ethnic heterogeneity
evaporated rapidly in the face of increasing numbers of ethnonational
movements. By the mid-1970s, the study of ethnic heterogeneity and its
consequences had become a growth industry. Literally thousands of
articles focused principally on ethnonationalism have appeared in En-
glish-language journals in the last decade. Scores of monographs and
collections have been dedicated to the same topic, as have an impressive number of doctoral dissertations. Conferences and round tables on
ethnicity have become commonplace, and panels on the subject have
become regular parts of the programs at annual meetings of professional organizations. A number of new journals—such as the *Canadian*

---

[*] Gabriel Almond, "The Development of Political Development," in *Understanding Political Development*, ed. Myron Weiner and Samuel Huntington (Boston, 1987), 437–90.

Review of Studies in Nationalism and *Ethnic and Racial Studies*—further attest to the intensified interest in ethnicity.

That this huge body of literature has contributed magnificently to our knowledge of specific peoples, their interethnic attitudes and behavior, their leaders, and their aspirations is beyond dispute. But it must also be acknowledged that all of this scholarly activity has not produced an approximation of a coherent statement. There is a marked lack of consensus concerning how ethnic heterogeneity can be best accommodated, or, indeed, even whether it can be accommodated non-coercively. And, in turn, these disagreements reflect a lack of consensus concerning the phenomenon that is supposedly the common focus of all these studies. In some cases, research, conducted under umbrella terms such as cultural pluralism, has in fact grouped several categories of identity (e.g., religious, linguistic, regional, and ethnonational) as though they were one or, at least, as though they exerted the same impact upon behavior. Others, influenced by the common misuse of the word ethnicity within the context of U.S. society, have used this rubric when investigating nearly any type of minority found in a state (despite the fact that ethnicity was derived from the Greek word *ethnos*, connoting a group characterized by common descent). The analytical utility of such blanket categories is open to serious question. Minimally, such broad categories sidestep raising the key question as to which of several group identities is apt to prove most potent in any test of loyalties.

Still other scholars, while focusing on ethnonationalism, have described it in terms of some other "ism." Having already misassigned nationalism to loyalty to the state, they have perforce enlisted some other term to describe loyalty to one's ethnonational group. Primordialism(s), tribalism, regionalism, communalism, parochialism, and subnationalism are among the more-often-encountered alternatives. Each of these terms already had a meaning not associated with nationalism, a fact further contributing to the terminological confusion impeding the study of ethnonationalism. (Communalism, for example, which refers within Western Europe to autonomy for local governments and within the Asian subcontinent to confessional identity, has appeared in the titles of books and articles in reference to ethnonationalism in Africa and Southeast Asia.) Moreover, individually each of these terms exerts its uniquely baneful effect upon the perceptions of both the author and the reader. And collectively, this varied vocabulary risks the impression that what is misdescribed as regionalism within one country, tribalism within another, and communalism within a third are different phenomena—when in fact it is ethnonationalism that in each case is the focus of the study. Imprecise vocabulary is both a symptom of and a contributor to a great deal of the haziness surrounding the study of ethnonationalism. As noted elsewhere:[3]

> In this Alice-in-Wonderland world in which nation usually means state, in which nation-state usually means multination state, in which nationalism usually means loyalty to the state, and in which ethnicity, primordialism, pluralism, tribalism, regionalism, communalism, parochialism and subnationalism usually mean loyalty to the nation, it should come as no surprise that the nature of nationalism remains essentially unprobed.

Indeed, very few scholars have directly addressed the matter of the nature of the ethnonational bond. A common empirical approach of those who did so during the first half of this century was to ask the question: "What makes a nation?" Among the scholarly giants who raised this question were Carlton Hayes and Hans Kohn. They addressed themselves to what was necessary or unnecessary for a nation to exist. The typical response was a common language, a common religion, a common territory, and the like. Stalin's 1913 definition of a nation, which still exerts a massive influence upon Marxist-Leninist scholarship, was very much in this tradition: "A nation is a historically evolved, stable community of people, formed on the basis of a common language, territory, economic life, and psychological make-up manifested in a common culture."[4] This approach still has its devotees, most notably Louis Snyder. Certainly it has the merit of emphasizing the wisdom of employing a broadly comparative framework when studying ethnonationalism. On the other hand, comparative analyses establish that no set of tangible characteristics is essential to the maintenance of national consciousness. Moreover, this particular approach would appear to fall into the earlier-mentioned trap of mistaking the tangible symptoms of a nation for its essence.

As noted, very few of the present generation of scholars have attempted a serious probe of the nature of the ethnonational bond forcing the curious to infer their conceptualization of it from their comments concerning the causes or the solutions to ethnonational restlessness. When employing this yardstick, it appears that many authors have scant respect for the psychological and emotional hold that ethnonational identity has upon the group. To some, ethnonational identity seems little more than an epiphenomenon that becomes active as a result of relative economic deprivation and that will dissipate with greater egalitarianism. Others reduce it to the level of a pressure group that mobilizes in order to compete for scarce resources. A variation on the pressure group concept places greater emphasis on the role of elites; rather than a somewhat spontaneous mass response to competition, the stirring of national consciousness is seen as a ploy utilized by aspiring elites in order to enhance their own status. Finally, in the hands of many adherents of the "internal colonialism" model, entire ethnonational groups are equated with a socioeconomic class, and ethnonational consciousness becomes equated with class consciousness.

All of these approaches could be criticized as a continuing tendency of scholars to harbor what we termed earlier "an unwarranted exaggeration of the influence of materialism upon human affairs." They could also be criticized as examples of a tendency to misapply theoretic approaches (such as pressure group theory, elite theory, and dependency theory). They can all be criticized empirically. (The most well-known propagator of the internal colonial thesis, Michael Hechter, recently recanted his support for that thesis, citing as cause its limited explanatory power.)[5] But they can be faulted chiefly for their failure to reflect the emotional depth of ethnonational identity and the mass sacrifices that have been made in its name. Explanations of behavior in terms of pressure groups, elite ambitions, and rational choice theory hint not at all at the passions that motivate Kurdish, Tamil, and Tigre guerrillas or Basque, Corsican, Irish, and Palestinian terrorists. Nor at the passions leading to the massacre of Bengalis by Assamese or Punjabis by Sikhs. In short, these explanations are a poor guide to ethnonationally inspired behavior.

Among those scholars who demonstrate a more profound regard for the psychological and emotional dimensions of ethnonational identity, there is a small but growing nucleus who now explicitly describe the ethnonational group as a kinship group. Among them are Joshua Fishman,[6] Donald Horowitz,[7] Charles Keyes,[8] Kian Kwan and Tomotshu Shibutani,[9] Anthony Smith,[10] and Pierre van den Berghe.[11] Interestingly, despite the fact that this formulation of the nation runs counter to classical Marxism, the Soviet Union's most influential academician in the study of national consciousness, Yu. Bromley, also acknowledges the role of kinship in nation formation.[12]

Recognizing the sense of common kinship that permeates the ethnonational bond clears a number of hurdles. First, it qualitatively distinguishes national consciousness from nonkinship identities (such as those based on religion or class) with which it has too often been grouped. Secondly, an intuitive sense of kindredness or extended family would explain why nations are endowed with a very special psychological dimension—an emotional dimension—not enjoyed by essentially functional or juridical groupings, such as socioeconomic classes or states.

Unlike scholars, political leaders have long been sensitized to this sense of common ancestry and have blatantly appealed to it as a means of mobilizing the masses.[13] Listen to Mao Tse-tung in 1938 describe the

Chinese Communists as "part of the great Chinese nation, flesh of its flesh and blood of its blood."[14] Or read the current program of the Romanian Communist party that describes the party's principal function as defending the national interest of "our people," a nation said to have been "born out of the fusion of the Dacians [an ancient people] with the Romans."[15] An article written in Hungary in 1982 criticizes a Romanian publication for promoting "an ethnocratic state" predicated upon "the unity of the 'pure-blooded race' in which there is no room for the strain, the outsider."[16] Appeals to *limpieza de sangre* (cleanliness of blood) and *pureza de sangre* (purity of blood) have a long history on the part of Castilian leaders. Within Africa, Yoruba and Fang leaders have stressed a legend of common origin, as have Malay leaders within Malaysia.

It might well be asked why scholars have been so slow to discover what the masses have felt and what political leaders have recognized. There are several possible answers, including (1) the intellectual's discomfort with the nonrational (note: *not* irrational), and (2) the search for quantifiable and therefore tangible explanations. But another factor has been the propensity to ignore the vital distinction between fact and perceptions of fact. Several of the studies of the last generation to which we alluded did raise the issue of common ancestry as one of the possible criteria of nationhood. However, the authors then denied the relevance of such a consideration by noting that most national groups could be shown to be the variegated offspring of a number of peoples. Indeed they can. But it is not *what is*, but *what people believe is* that has behavioral consequences. A nation is a group of people characterized by a myth of common descent. Moreover, regardless of its roots, a nation must remain an essentially endogamous group in order to maintain its myth.

As noted, there are grounds for optimism in that a small core of influential scholars has come to recognize the myth of common ancestry as the defining characteristic of the nation. It may well be, therefore, that effective probing of the subjective dimensions of the national bond will occur during the next decade. Fishman has certainly begun excavating in this area, and in his book, *Ethnic Groups In Conflict*, Donald Horowitz indicates one avenue of possibly fruitful research, suggesting how several studies borrowed from experimental psychology (and dealing with both individual and group behavior) may lead to a better understanding of ethnonationalism. And Pierre van den Berghe now maintains that the literature on sociobiology has much to offer the student of ethnic identity.

Two other possibly productive areas of research for the probing of the emotional/psychological dimension of ethnonationalism come to mind. The poet, as an adept expressor of deep-felt passions, is apt to be a far better guide here than the social scientist has proven to be. National poetry has hardly been touched upon on a worldwide comparative basis. Quite aside from aesthetics, it would obviously be of great value to learn what feelings and images have been most commonly invoked by recognized national poets, without regard to geography, level of their people's development, and so on.

Still another potentially fruitful source when probing the nature of ethnonationalism consists of the speeches of national leaders and the pamphlets, programs, and other documents of ethnonationalist organizations. Too often these speeches and documents have been passed off as useless propaganda in which the authors do not really believe. But nationalism is a mass phenomenon, and the degree to which the leaders are true believers does not affect its reality. The question is not the sincerity of the propagandist, but the nature of the mass instinct to which the propagandist appeals. Napoleon was unquestionably more a manipulator of than a believer in nationalism, but his armies were certainly filled with soldiers fired up by nationalism. Speeches and programs should therefore be scanned from the viewpoint of comparative content. With what frequency do certain words and images appear? What referents are used to trigger the psychological response?

In any case, it is certain that very few scholars will attempt to probe the nature of nationalism. As in the past, most authors who touch on ethnonationalism will be dealing with its manifestation in one or another society and/or policies aimed at its containment. However, their general treatment of the subject and their assessment of policies will necessarily reflect their unarticulated perception of the nature of ethnonationalism, and it is to be hoped that the literature will increasingly embody that deeper respect for the emotional and psychological depths of ethnonationalism that we have noted in the works of a small but growing number of influential writers.

A COMMENT ON COMPARABILITY

Before we turn to the issue of accommodating ethnonationalism, a few words on comparability are in order. The leading scholars on nationalism have agreed that a broad comparative approach is essential. As Hans Kohn has noted: "A study of nationalism must follow a comparative method; it cannot remain confined to one of its manifestations; only the comparison of the different nationalisms all over the earth will enable the student to see what they have in common and what is peculiar to each, and thus allow a just evaluation."[17]

While few would disagree with this advice, the comparative approach has hardly proven to be a magic key to understanding. Com-

TABLE 1
Comparability Categories

States
Nation-states
Multination states
   1. unihomeland
   2. multihomeland
   3. nonhomeland
Immigrant states
Mestizo states

Peoples
Prenations/potential nations
Nations
Offshoot nations
Diasporas (migrants and refugees)
Members of immigrant societies

parative works have often disappointed, leaving the reader more struck by the dissimilarities among societies than by their commonalities. In other cases, too-facile analogies have resulted in highly questionable conclusions. Given the absence of perfect analogies, the comparative approach to ethnonationalism will remain an imperfect analytical tool, but it could be honed by developing categories of peoples and states that analogies should respect. That is to say, it should be possible to place most peoples and states in compartments that promise a measure of suitability to intracompartmental analogies, while concurrently flashing a warning signal to those who are comparing peoples or states from two or more compartments. Table 1 represents an exploratory effort to develop categories that would help to avoid some of the more fallacious analogies that have marred the study of ethnonationalism.

Space does not permit more than a passing glance at these categories, but let us begin with the classification of states. *Nation-states* are those relatively rare situations, characterized by an extremely homogeneous population, where a nation has its own state. Iceland, Japan, Norway, and post–World War II Poland are illustrations.

Multinational states are easily the most common. However, an important consideration is whether the state consists of a single homeland, two or more homelands, or no homeland. As made evident by ethnographic atlases, most of the populated world is broken down into ethnonational homelands, regions whose name reflects a special claim upon the territory by a people—Baluchistan, Nagaland, Scotland, Ukraine, and Zululand are but a tiny sampling. The notion of the homeland is intimately associated with the myth of an ancestrally related people. The feeling that this place is indeed *home* to the extended family endows it with a reverential dimension apparent in such universal terms as the fatherland, the motherland, and, not least, the *home*land. Members of a homeland people believe that they possess a primary and exclusive title to the homeland. Outsiders may be tolerated or even encouraged as sojourners (*guest*workers, for example), but the demand that the sojourners *go home* can be raised at any time and may be aimed at compatriots as well as at foreigners. A series of quite extensive studies conducted within the [former] Soviet Union confirms patterns of behavior and attitudes observed in other parts of the world. Whether people are living within or away from their homeland greatly influences, inter alia, their willingness to adopt a statewide language (other than their own), their willingness to marry outside of the group, the choice of ethnonational identity on the part of progeny of mixed marriages, and attitudes toward other ethnonational peoples. Those living within the homeland manifest greater animosity toward other groups and greater resistance to acculturation and assimilation. But the most consequential aspect of homeland psychology has been the hostility engendered by an intrusion of "the native land" by nonnatives. Examples of this phenomenon abound in the First World (Euskadi [Basqueland] and Corsica), the second world (Lithuania, Uighuristan [China], and Slovenia), and the Third World (Assam, Baluchistan, Bangsamoro [the Philippines], and Kurdistan).

A *unihomeland, multinational state* is one in which the ethnic diversity is due to immigration. The homeland people consider the entire state to be their historic homeland, although their ancestors may themselves have migrated to the region (e.g., Malaysian Malays and Sri Lankan Sinhalese). Even if in a minority (e.g., the Fijians), a homeland people will feel that as "sons of the soil" they and their culture merit a privileged position relative to the interlopers. The current great increase in global migration may be enlarging this classification of states. Guestworkers who have become "staygrants" may be transforming former nation-states, such as the German Federal Republic and Sweden, into unihomeland, multinational states.

Multihomeland, multinational states, which represent the largest category, vary tremendously in the number of homelands they contain. While some consist of essentially two homelands (Czechoslovakia),[*] some contain more than one hundred (Nigeria). The Soviet Union[**] is one of the more complex states in this category. There, the political system extends various levels of administrative recognition to fifty-three homelands, in many of which Russians now predominate numerically.

[*] Prior to its dissolution in 1993.   [**] Prior to its dissolution in 1991.

Nonhomeland, multinational states are those whose population (1) is overwhelmingly the product of migration and (2) consists of at least two significant groups, each of which is vitally aware of its ethnic difference from the other(s) and is determined to maintain that distinctiveness. The greater Caribbean offers a number of examples, including Guyana, Suriname, and Trinidad-Tobago.

Immigrant states are also nonhomeland states, but with a highly variegated population in terms of ancestry. The officially endorsed archetype—the American in the case of the United States—is not ethnically defined, that is, it is ethnically neutral. Such states are characterized by a good deal of acculturation and assimilation. A relatively few people living in small homelands (e.g., the existence of Amerindian and Eskimo homelands within the United States) do not disqualify a state from the immigrant category.

Mestizo states are limited to Latin America and are characterized by a population in which those of joint European-Amerindian ancestry are dominant (not necessarily numerically so, as in the case of Bolivia). These states have traditionally posed severe problems of classification and analysis to students of ethnonationalism. If the ethnonational image propagated by their governments approximated the self-perceptions of the masses, these states could be treated comparatively as nation-states. This image posits a new breed or race (*La Raza Cosmica*) that has evolved from the melding of the European and the Amerindian. And from this basically undifferentiated whole there has supposedly evolved a nation that is coterminous with the state—that is, a Guatemalan, Mexican, or Peruvian nation. Reality is something else, however. Very significant numbers of Amerindian peoples have clearly not surrendered their diverse ancestral identities and are manifesting increasing hostility to mestizo domination. Antimestizo sentiment is already a key ingredient of guerrilla struggles being waged in Guatemala, Nicaragua, and Peru, and threatens to become so within Bolivia and Ecuador, among others. Amerindian peoples are currently pushing for greater autonomy within Panama. The point, then, is that while the mestizo states merit a separate category for analytical purposes, they more resemble multinational states than nation-states.

Turning now from states to peoples, the first category is *prenational or potential nations*. There still exist large numbers of people for whom national identity lies in the future. For such people, meaningful identity is still limited to locale, clan, tribe, and the like. It is quite impossible to say what percentage of a people must achieve national consciousness before the group merits treatment as a nation. But it is not enough that a substantial group of intellectuals maintains the existence of nationhood. Indeed, the Arab case reminds us of the danger of placing too great emphasis upon the views of elites in general and intellectuals in particular. The Arabs were among the very earliest non-European peoples to produce an elite that was imbued with national consciousness and dedicated to its development among the masses. And yet, after more than a half-century of such efforts, Arab nationalism remains anomalistically weak. The national literati may therefore be a poor guide to the actual level of national consciousness. But while it may therefore be difficult to say with precision at what point a group becomes transformed from prenation into nation, it is essential to keep in mind the distinction between the two. Examples of a change of identity on the part of the former should not be used to document an alleged ephemerality or situational nature on the part of the second.

We have earlier discussed the essence of *nations*. They are the largest human grouping characterized by a myth of common ancestry. The historical accuracy of the myth is irrelevant.

Offshoot nations are formed when an important segment of a nation has been geographically separated from the parent group for a period of time sufficient for it to develop a strong sense of separate consciousness. Members retain an awareness that they derive from the parent stock, but they believe that the characteristics they have in common are less significant than those that make them unique. Examples include the Afrikaaners, the Formosan Hanjen, and the Québècois.

Diasporas are people living outside of their homeland who have not assimilated to the host's identity.

Members of *immigrant societies* are those whose primary sense of loyalty is not to the ethnonation(s) of their ancestors, but to the immigrant society.

The preceding classification is at best a very rudimentary scheme for avoiding some of the more obviously fallacious analogies. It could be refined to several levels. Homeland-dwelling people, for example, could be subcategorized according to whether the homeland is essentially coterminous with the state (Sweden), comprises only part of the state (Wales), is divided among states in which the group is dominant (Arabdom), is divided into states in which the group is dominant in one and nondominant in one or more others (any number of so-called irredentist situations), or is divided into states in which the group is never dominant (Kurds). These and a myriad of other refinements would certainly mitigate the shortcomings of the analogical approach. It is also evident that some states would not neatly fit the preceding schema. Canada is both part immigrant state (outside of Québèc) and part multinational homeland state. This, however, should not pose any severe problem, so long as the two are treated as separate entities for comparative purposes. "Anglo Canada" has analogical value for immigrant states, as does Québèc for the study of homeland peoples. In any case, the point is that a greater regard for "comparability compartments" would greatly assist the comparative study of ethnic heterogeneity.

The Accommodation of Heterogeneity

Questions of accommodating ethnonational heterogeneity within a single state revolve about two loyalties—loyalty to the nation and loyalty to the state—and the relative strength of the two. The great number of bloody separatist movements that have occurred in the past two decades within the First, Second, and Third Worlds bear ample testimony that when the two loyalties are seen as being in irreconcilable conflict, loyalty to the state loses out. But the two need not be so perceived. To people with their own nation-state or to those people who are so dominant within a multinational state as to perceive the state as essentially their nation's state (e.g., the English, the Han Chinese, the Thais), the two loyalties become an indistinguishable, reinforcing blur. It is in the perceptions of national minorities that the two loyalties are most apt to vie.

Over the last decade, scholarship has made some important strides in probing the attitudes of minorities toward the state, although much more remains to be done. A number of sophisticated analyses have made good use of attitudinal data to bring us beyond the stage of simply hypothesizing about the two loyalties.[18] It should be noted, however, that the literature is based overwhelmingly, although not exclusively, on First World states and on homeland peoples.

The following findings emerge from these studies:

1. Members of ethnonational minorities manifest substantially less affection toward the state than do members of the dominant group.
2. Minorities of the same state can differ significantly in this regard.
3. For most persons, however, the matter is not perceived in either/or terms. Affective ties to the state coexist with ethnonational consciousness.
4. In most cases in which a separatist movement is active, large numbers, usually a majority of the involved group, do not favor secession.
5. In some cases, the percentage represented by pro-secessionists has remained relatively constant; in other cases it has evidenced profound trends.
6. Regardless of their attitude toward secession, a preponderant number do favor major alterations in the political system that would result in greater autonomy.

7. Where separatist parties are allowed to contest elections, their vote is not an adequate index to separatist sentiment.
8. In all cases for which there are attitudinal data, members of ethnonational groups overwhelmingly reject the use of violence carried out in the name of the national group.
9. However, a large percentage, including many who do not favor separation, empathize with those engaged in violence and place the blame for the violence upon others.
10. Separatists draw their support from all social strata and age groups.
11. Disproportionate support, however, comes from those under thirty-five years of age, with above-average education and income.
12. Professional people are disproportionately represented.
13. Lack of support is particularly pronounced among those over fifty-five years of age.

Many of the preceding points probably appear trivial or trite. Given the numerous powers of the state for politically socializing its population, it is hardly surprising that affective ties to the state exist. However, it would be particularly dangerous to take this finding—predicated principally upon First World states—and apply it wholesale to a Third World environment. For one thing, most Third World states are too young to have developed the sense of institutional and symbolic legitimacy that is a central aspect of state loyalty. And the older states (such as Afghanistan, Ethiopia, Iran, Liberia, and Thailand), given the historic absence of the principal means for inculcating this sense of legitimacy (e.g., a public school system), are not true exceptions. To take perhaps an extreme case, it would be foolhardy to presume that the Kachins, Karens, and Shans harbor any noteworthy level of goodwill toward the Burman state.

The finding that most members of national minorities are prepared to settle for something less than separation probably has more universal application. The still-revolutionary idea popularly termed national self-determination holds that any people, simply because it considers itself to be a separate people, has the right, *if it so desires*, to create its own state. However, it would appear to be the rule that a majority of members of a homeland people are prepared to settle for autonomy for the homeland. Even when demands are made for actual separation, Third World elites are usually as fragmented as those in the First World between those who maintain this stance and those who announce their willingness to settle for autonomy. (The Pakistani Baluch, the Iraqi Kurds, the Moros, and the Sikhs are major current illustrations.) Moreover, a number of groups, although having engaged in violent struggle for the stated aim of independence, have subsequently entered into a peaceful relationship with the state authorities on the basis of a grant of autonomy. In the typical pattern, these periods of peace disintegrate in a flurry of charges and countercharges over whether the government's promises of autonomy have been honored. Underlying these failures at accommodation have usually been differing views concerning the content of autonomy.

Although often treated by scholars, state authorities, and ethnonational elites as alternatives, independence and autonomy are hardly that. Autonomy is an amorphous concept, capable of covering a multitude of visions extending from very limited local options to complete control over everything other than foreign policy. It can therefore incorporate all situations between total subordination to the center and total independence. Both autonomy and independence are therefore terms that tend to obscure important shadings in the attitudes that members of a group can be expected to hold concerning goals.

It should not be surprising that ethnonational peoples should blur the distinction between independence and autonomy. Ethnonational concerns, by their very nature, are more obsessed with a vision of freedom from domination by nonmembers than with a vision of freedom to conduct foreign relations with states. They are the reaction to international, not interstate, relations. The average Basque or Fleming, just as the average Kurd or Naga, does not appear to be influenced by a prospect of a seat at the United Nations or an embassy in Moscow. Indeed, in the case of most Third World peoples, meaningful autonomy would represent a return toward either the loose system of feudatory allegiances they knew under Afghani, Chinese, Ethiopian, or Persian empires or to the indirect rule that they knew under colonialism, both of which had more effectively muted ethnonational concerns than have their successor political systems. In short, ethnocracy does not presuppose state independence. It does presuppose meaningful autonomy.

The finding concerning popular sympathy for those who carry out violence in the name of the national group also has momentous implications for the political stability of states, for it explains how guerrilla struggles have been maintained for years in the face of overwhelming odds. It undergirds the wisdom of Giuseppe Mazzini's statement of more than a century and a half ago: "Insurrection—by means of guerrilla bands—is the true method of warfare for all nations desirous of emancipating themselves from a foreign yoke." In the case of wars of (ethno) national liberation, the numbers actually engaged in guerrilla struggle may be quite small, but those who fight in the name of the nation's liberation can expect that degree of sympathy that, as Mao Tse-tung, Truong Chinh, and others have noted, is indispensable to the conduct of a successful guerrilla struggle. And this is why a number of leaders of guerrilla struggles, whose own goals have had nothing to do with minority rights, have gained the necessary local support by promising independence or autonomy to ethnonational groups. Such promises played significant roles in the assumption of power by the Chinese Communist Party, the Viet Minh, and the Pathet Lao, and it is today a key element in the propaganda of revolutionary movements in Latin America. In Africa also, the numerous guerrilla struggles cannot be understood without reference to ethnic maps and aspirations.

While the thirteen findings outlined above attest to the formidable threat that ethnic heterogeneity poses to political stability, they also contain much to encourage those in search of formulae for accommodating such diversity. The fact that most members of most ethnic minorities are prepared to settle for something less than complete independence means that such formulae are not sheer whimsy. The likelihood of arriving at a mutually agreeable formula is another matter, however. A successful formula will require a significant measure of decentralization of authority, and governments, by nature, are ill-disposed toward the relinquishing of power. However, governments may come to recognize that a measure of devolution would actually increase their authority over otherwise rebellious national groups. Few students of Spanish politics prior to 1975 imagined that the highly centralized, authoritarian system of Franco would be followed by a government prepared to grant substantial autonomy to the country's non-Castilian peoples. Belgium, Canada, and Panama are other states that have recently diluted support for separatist movements by adopting power-sharing formulae. Most governments, however, have not been prepared to grant the degree of autonomy necessary to avoid the resort to separatism. But the tendency for ethnonational groups to aspire to greater autonomy, while being prepared to settle for something short of full independence, does underline the fact that a solution to ethnic heterogeneity must ultimately be found in the political sphere and not in the economic one. Myron Weiner's advice therefore appears sound:

> In exploring the factors at work in the development of national integration and political legitimacy it is important that we pay particular attention to political variables, and resist the tendency to rely upon economic, social or psychological explanations for political facts. If we use psychological variables to explain psychological behaviors, and social facts to explain social facts, so ought we first turn to one set of political facts to explain another.[19]

By Way of Summary

The literature on ethnonational heterogeneity has undergone a quantum leap in the last decade. Our knowledge of specific peoples and

problems has grown enormously as a result. This outpouring, however, has not resulted in a broad consensus concerning either the nature of ethnonationalism or means to its accommodation, although
there are grounds for optimism that substantive progress will be made
during the next decade.

My own admonitions for ensuring this progress are five in number:

1. Greater attention must be paid to avoiding imprecise and confusing
   terminology.[20]
2. Greater appreciation for the psychological/emotional depth of ethnonational identity must be reflected in the literature.
3. Greater refinements are necessary with regard to classifying peoples
   and political systems for comparative purposes.
4. Greater appreciation that ethnonational demands are at bottom political rather than economic in nature should be reflected in proposals for
   accommodating ethnic heterogeneity.[21]
5. It should always be remembered that ethnonationalism is a mass phenomenon, and keeping this in mind should counteract the tendency to
   overemphasize the role of elites as its impresarios.[22]

NOTES

1. For a lengthier discussion and illustrations of each of these items, see
chapter 2 in this volume.

2. I am indebted to Myron Weiner for drawing attention to this omission
from my list.

3. See below, chapter 4.

4. Joseph Stalin, *Marxism and the National Question* (Moscow, 1950), 16.

5. Michael Hechter, Debra Friedman, and Malka Appelbaum, "A Theory of
Ethnic Collective Action," *International Migration Review* 16, no. 2 (Summer
1982): 412–34. The article stresses rational choice as a means of overcoming the
explanatory shortcomings of group stratification.

6. Joshua Fishman, *The Rise and Fall of the Ethnic Revival in the USA* (The
Hague, 1985).

7. Donald Horowitz, *Ethnic Groups in Conflict* (Berkeley, 1985).

8. Charles F. Keyes, "Towards a New Formulation of the Concept of Ethnic
Group," *Ethnicity* 3, no. 3 (September 1976): 202–13.

9. Kian Kwan and Tomotshu Shibutani, *Ethnic Stratification: A Comparative
Approach* (New York, 1965), 47.

10. Anthony D. Smith, *The Ethnic Revival* (Cambridge, 1981).

11. Pierre van den Berghe, "Race and Ethnicity: A Sociobiological Perspective," *Ethnic and Racial Studies* 1, no. 4 (October 1978): 401–11.

12. Yu. Bromley, "Ethnography and Ethnic Processes," *Problems on the Contemporary World* 73 (Moscow, 1978).

13. For a fuller discussion and numerous illustrations, see chapter 8 in this
volume.

14. *Selected Works of Mao Tse-Tung* (Peking, 1975) 2: 209.

15. *Programme of the Romanian Communist Party for the Building of the Multi-laterally Developed Socialist Society and Romania's Advance toward Communism* (Bucharest, 1975).

16. Gyorgy Szaraz, "On a Curious Book," *Joint Publications Research Service* 82763, 3 January 1983.

17. Hans Kohn, *The Idea of Nationalism: A Study in Its Origins and Background* (New York, 1944), ix–x.

18. Particularly noteworthy has been the work of Maurice Pinard on Canada and Robert Clark on Spain.

19. Myron Weiner, "Matching Peoples, Territories and States: Post-Ottoman Irredentism in the Balkans and in the Middle East," in *Governing Peoples and Territories*, ed. Daniel Elazar (Philadelphia, 1982), 131.

20. Note, for example, Gabriel Almond's use of "the nation-state" to describe all states, and his use of "nations" to describe the states of the Middle East, Africa, and Asia. The continuing misuse of these key terms certainly reflects and may very well help to explain Almond's failure to confront the problems that ethnic heterogeneity poses for political development. Almond, "The Development of Political Development."

21. For a more detailed discussion, see chapter 6 in this volume.

22. As set forth by a scholar more than forty years ago: "A history of national consciousness should not, like a history of philosophy, simply describe the thought of a limited number of eminent men without regard to the extent of their following. As in the histories of religions, we need to know what response the masses have given to different doctrines." Walter Sulzbach, *National Consciousness* (Washington, D.C., 1943), 14.

PART TWO

A Closer Look at Some of the Key Barriers to Understanding

Chapter Four

TERMINOLOGICAL CHAOS

We turn now from the shortcoming of the literature on political development to some of the major reasons why scholars have had trouble recognizing and appreciating the force of ethnonationalism. The reader may recall that in chapter 2 ("Nation-Building or Nation-Destroying?"), in a listing of twelve reasons why scholars have had this trouble, first place was awarded to what was termed "the confusing inter-utilization of the key terms, nation and state." The following piece was written immediately after "Nation-Building or Nation Destroying?" in order to expand on that article's discussion of the problem of slipshod terminology. It was presented at the 1971 Annual Meeting of the Northeastern Political Science Association.

A Nation Is a Nation, Is a State,
Is an Ethnic Group, Is a . . .*

EVENTS OF THE past decade have by now impressed upon even the more casual observers of world politics that ethnonationalism constitutes a major and growing threat to the political stability of most states. Rather than witnessing an evolution of stable state- or suprastate-communities, the observer of global politics has viewed a succession of situations involving competing allegiances in which people have illustrated that an intuitive bond felt toward an informal and unstructured subdivision of humankind is far more profound and potent than are the ties that bind them to the formal and legalistic state structure in which they find themselves. Present or recent large-scale violence within such Third World states as Burma [Myanmar], Burundi, Chad, Ethiopia, Guyana, India, Iraq, Kenya, Malaysia, Nigeria, Pakistan, the Philippines, the Sudan, Thailand, Turkey, and Uganda (to mention but a few of the afflicted states) amply testifies to the widespread failure of governments to induce a substantial segment of their citizenry to transfer their primary loyalty from a human grouping to the state.[1] Nor have the older, more technologically integrated states of the First World proved to be immune. Austria, Belgium, Canada, Denmark, France, Italy, the Netherlands, Switzerland, and the United Kingdom have all experienced ethnically motivated unrest.[2] And though Marxist-Leninist states of the Second World officially claim that by faithfully carrying out Lenin's prescriptions for devitalizing nationalism at home, they have successfully solved what they call their national question, the restiveness of national groups constitutes a major element in the internal and external political affairs of the Soviet Union, China, Czechoslovakia, Laos, Romania, Vietnam, and Yugoslavia.[3]

Few indeed are the scholars who can claim to have anticipated even the possibility of such a trend. The conventional wisdom of the first two post–World War II decades held (1) that the newly emerging Third World states would win the battle of loyalties over "tribal" allegiance,

* Published in Walker Connor, "A Nation is a Nation, is a State, is an Ethnic Group, is a . . . ," *Ethnic and Racial Studies* 1 (October 1978): 377–400. Copyright © 1978 Routledge Journals.

(2) that World War II had taught the peoples of Western Europe that nationalism was too parochial a focus for the modern age and that, as a result, a supranational and suprastate-consciousness of being European was rapidly becoming the primary identity of the region's inhabitants, and (3) that the highly centralized, "monolithic" Marxist-Leninist structure(s), combined with the effective indoctrination of its people in the tenets of Marxist-Leninist ideology, made consideration of forces such as ethnonationalism simply irrelevant.

There are numerous reasons why so many scholars failed to anticipate the resistance that state-integration has in fact encountered. Elsewhere, this writer has listed twelve overlapping and reinforcing contributing elements,[4] and unquestionably the list could be enlarged. But, the theme of this paper is that the most significant factor accounting for the divergence between scholarly expectations and actuality has been a basic misunderstanding concerning the nature of nationalism.

The most fundamental error involved in scholarly approaches to nationalism has been a tendency to equate nationalism with a feeling of loyalty to the state rather than with loyalty to the nation. This confusion has led scholars to assume that the relationship of nationalism to state-integration is functional and supportive rather than dysfunctional and defeatist. And since there is general agreement that nationalism remains a compelling and dominant motivational force, the linking of nationalism to the state has been viewed as all but guaranteeing the victory of the latter against all competitors for the loyalty of its inhabitants.

The error of improperly equating nationalism with loyalty to the state is the consequence of a much broader terminological disease that plagues the study of global politics. It would be difficult to name four words more essential to global politics than are state, nation, nation-state, and nationalism. But despite their centrality, all four terms are shrouded in ambiguity due to their imprecise, inconsistent, and often totally erroneous usage. In 1939 a study of nationalism undertaken by the Royal Institute of International Affairs noted that "among other difficulties which impede the study of 'nationalism,' that of language holds a leading place."[5] In the four decades that have subsequently elapsed, the linguistic jungle that encapsules the concept of nationalism has only grown more dense.

It is particularly paradoxical that the widespread misuse of the most elemental terms should be tolerated during a period in which so many authorities within the discipline are emphasizing the need for more precise and scientific vocabulary. Karl Deutsch has praised the great strides already made in this direction:

In science, including social science, a word is only a kind of noise unless we sooner or later use it to lead to a procedure that will tell us whether or not a certain event or fact belongs under the word. The meaning of a word is defined by its limits, by knowing what does not belong under it as clearly as what does. Any word that could include everything and anything has no place in science. . . . Today when someone speaks about "natives," the immediate questions are, "How do you define 'native' "? "How do you know who is a native"? The same questions arise when we speak of "workers," "patriots," or any general social classification of this sort. Such terms can no longer be taken casually.[6]

Yet despite this tribute to terminological precision, the same work by Professor Deutsch is honeycombed with illustrations of improper and contradictory usage of the four terms we have described as pivotal.[7] Professor Deutsch is *not* singled out here because he has been unusually uncircumspect in this regard, but rather in order to illustrate the breadth of the problem. That even an acknowledged scholar of nationalism and one who espouses the cause of vocabular precision should improperly and inconsistently utilize these fundamental terms indicates how acceptable such malpractice has become.

One of the most common manifestations of terminological license is the interutilization of the words state and nation. This tendency is perplexing because at one level of consciousness most scholars are clearly well aware of the vital distinctions between the two concepts. The state is the major political subdivision of the globe. As such, it is readily defined and, what is of greater moment to the present discussion, is easily conceptualized in quantitative terms. Peru, for illustration, can be defined in an easily conceptualized manner as the territorial-political unit consisting of the sixteen million inhabitants of the 514,060 square miles located on the west coast of South America between 69° and 80° West, and 2° and 18°, 21' South.

Defining and conceptualizing the nation is much more difficult because the essence of a nation is intangible. This essence is a psychological bond that joins a people and differentiates it, in the subconscious conviction of its members, from all other people in a most vital way. The nature of that bond and its well-spring remain shadowy and elusive, and the consequent difficulty of defining the nation is usually acknowledged by those who attempt this task. Thus, a popular dictionary of International Relations defines a nation as follows:

A social group which shares a common ideology, common institutions and customs, and a *sense* of homogeneity. "Nation" is difficult to define so precisely as to differentiate the term from such other groups as religious sects, which exhibit some of the same characteristics. In the nation, however, there is also present a strong group *sense* of belonging associated with a particular territory considered to be peculiarly its own.[8]

Whereas the key word in this particular definition is *sense*, other authorities may substitute *feeling* or *intuition*, but proper appreciation of the abstract essence of the nation is customary *in definitions*. But after focusing attention upon that essential psychological bond, little probing of its nature follows. Indeed, having defined the nation as an essentially psychological phenomenon, authorities, as we have noted, then regularly proceed to treat it as fully synonymous with the very different and totally tangible concept of the state.

Even when one restricts *nation* to its proper, nonpolitical meaning of a human collectivity, the ambiguity surrounding its nature is not thereby evaporated. How does one differentiate the nation from other human collectivities? The above-cited definition spoke of "a sense of homogeneity." Others speak of a feeling of sameness, of oneness, of belonging, or of consciousness of kind. But all such definitions appear a bit timid, and thereby fail to distinguish the nation from numerous other types of groups. Thus, one can conceive of the Amish, Appalachian hill people, or "down Mainers" as all fitting rather neatly within any of the preceding standards.

With but very few exceptions, authorities have shied away from describing the nation as a kinship group and have usually explicitly denied that the notion of shared blood is a factor. Such denials are supported by data illustrating that most groups claiming nationhood do in fact incorporate several genetic strains. But, as earlier noted, such an approach ignores the wisdom of the old saw that when analyzing sociopolitical situations, what ultimately matters is not *what is* but *what people believe is*. And a subconscious belief in the group's separate origin and evolution is an important ingredient of national psychology. When one avers that he is Chinese, he is identifying himself not just with the Chinese people and culture of today, but with the Chinese people and their activities throughout time. The Chinese Communist Party was appealing to just such a sense of separate origin and evolution in 1937:

> We know that in order to transform the glorious future into a new China, independent, free, and happy, all our fellow countrymen, every single, zealous descendent of Huang-ti [the legendary first emperor of China] must determinedly and relentlessly participate in the concerted struggle. . . . Our great Chinese nation, with its long history is inconquerable.[9]

Bismarck's famous exhortation to the German people, over the heads of their particular political leaders, to "think with your blood" was a similar attempt to activate a mass psychological vibration predicated upon an intuitive sense of consanguinity. An unstated presumption of a Chinese (or German) nation is that there existed in some hazy, pre-recorded era a Chinese (or German) Adam and Eve, and that the couple's progeny has evolved in essentially unadulterated form down to the present. It was recognition of this dimension of the nation that caused numerous writers of the nineteenth and early twentieth centuries to employ *race* as a synonym for *nation*, references to a German race or to the English race being quite common.

Since the nation is a self-defined rather than an other-defined grouping, the broadly held conviction concerning the group's singular origin need not and seldom will accord with factual data. Thus, the anthropologist may prove to his own satisfaction that there are several genetic strains within the Pushtun people who populate the Afghani-Pakistani border-region and conclude therefrom that the group represents the variegated offspring of several peoples who have moved through the region. The important fact, however, is that the Pushtuns themselves are convinced that all Pushtuns are evolved from a single source and have remained essentially unadulterated. This is a matter which is *known* intuitively and unquestionably, a matter of attitude and not of fact. It is a matter, the underlying conviction of which is not apt to be disturbed substantially even by the rational acceptance of anthropological or other evidence to the contrary. Depending upon the sophistication of the treatise, this type of sensory knowledge may be described as "a priori," "an emotional rather than a rational conviction," "primordial," "thinking with the heart (or with the blood) rather than with the mind," or "a 'gut' or 'kneejerk' response." Regardless of the nomenclature, it is an extremely important adjunct of the national idea.[10] It is the intuitive conviction which can give to nations a psychological dimension approximating that of the extended family, that is, a feeling of common blood lineage.

The word *nation* comes from the Latin and, when first coined, clearly conveyed the idea of common blood ties. It was derived from the past participle of the verb *nasci*, meaning to be born. And hence the Latin noun, *nationem*, connoting *breed* or *race*. Unfortunately, terms used to describe human collectivities (terms such as race and class) invite an unusual degree of literary license, and *nation* certainly proved to be no exception.[11] Thus, at some medieval universities, a student's *nationem* designated the sector of the country from whence he came. But when introduced into the English language in the late thirteenth century, it was with its primary connotation of a blood related group. One etymologist notes, however, that by the early seventeenth century, *nation* was also being used to describe the inhabitants of a country, regardless of that population's ethnonational composition, thereby becoming a substitute for less specific human categories such as *the people* or *the citizenry*.[12] This infelicitous practice continues to the present day and accounts for often encountered references to the American citizenry as the American nation. Whatever the American people are (and they may well be *sui generis*), they are not a nation in the pristine sense of the word. However, the unfortunate habit of calling them a nation and thus verbally equating American with German, Chinese, English, and the like, has seduced scholars into erroneous analogies. Indeed, while proud of being "a nation of immigrants" with a "melting pot" tradition, the absence of a common origin may well make it more difficult, and conceivably impossible, for the American to appreciate instinctively the idea of the nation in the same dimension and with the same poignant clarity as do the Japanese, the Bengali, or the Kikuyu. It is difficult for an American to appreciate what it means for a German to be German or for a Frenchman to be French, because the psychological effect of being American is not precisely equatable. Some of the associations are missing, and others may be quite different.

Far more detrimental to the study of nationalism, however, has been the propensity to employ the term nation as a substitute for that territorial juridical unit, the state. How this practice developed is unclear, though it seems to have become a relatively common practice in the late seventeenth century. Two possible explanations for this development present themselves. One involves the rapid spread of the doctrine of popular sovereignty that was precipitated about this time by the writings of men such as Locke. In identifying *the people* as the font of all political power, this revolutionary doctrine made the people and the state almost synonymous. *L'etat c'est moi* became *l'etat c'est le peuple*. And therefore the nation and the state had become near synonyms, for we have already noted the tendency to equate nation with the entire people or citizenry. Thus, the French *Declaration of Rights of Man and Citizen* would proclaim that "the source of all sovereignty resides essentially in the nation; no group, no individual may exercise authority not emanating expressly therefrom." Though the drafters of the Declaration may not have been aware, "the nation" to which they referred contained Alsatians, Basques, Bretons, Catalans, Corsicans, Flemings, and Occitanians, as well as Frenchmen.*

It is also probable that the habit of interutilizing *nation* and *state* developed as alternative abbreviations for the expression *nation-state*. The

---

* In a brilliant work (*Peasants into Frenchmen: The Modernization of Rural France, 1870–1914* [Stanford, 1976]), Eugen Weber would later establish that the vast majority of people living within France were not conscious of being French until long after the French Revolution.

very coining of this hyphenate illustrated an appreciation of the vital differences between *nation* and *state*. It was designed to describe a territorial-political unit (a state) whose borders coincided or nearly coincided with the territorial distribution of a national group. More concisely, it described a situation in which a nation had its own state. Unfortunately, however, *nation-state* has come to be applied indiscriminately to all states. Thus one authority has stated that "a prime fact about the world is that it is largely composed of nation-states."[13] The statement should read that "a prime fact about the world is that it is *not* largely composed of nation-states." A survey of the 132 entities generally considered to be states as of 1971, produced the following breakdown:

1. Only twelve states (9.1 percent) can justifiably be described as nation-states.
2. Twenty-five (18.9 percent) contain a nation or potential nation accounting for more than 90 percent of the state's total population but also contain an important minority.[14]
3. Another twenty-five (18.9 percent) contain a nation or potential nation accounting for between 75 percent and 89 percent of the population.
4. In thirty-one (23.5 percent), the largest ethnic element accounts for 50 percent to 74 percent of the population.
5. In 39 (29.5 percent), the largest nation or potential nation accounts for less than half of the population.[*]

Were all states nation-states, no great harm would result from referring to them as nations, and people who insisted that the distinction between *nation* and *state* be maintained could be dismissed as linguistic purists or semantic nitpickers. Where nation and state essentially coincide, their verbal interutilization is inconsequential because the two are indistinguishably merged in popular perception. The state is perceived as the political extension of the nation and appeals to one trigger the identical, positive psychological responses as appeals to the other. To ask a Japanese *kamikaze* pilot or a *banzai-charge* participant whether he was about to die for *Nippon* or for the Nipponese people would be an incomprehensible query since the two blurred into an inseparable whole. Hitler could variously make his appeals to the German people in the name of state (Deutsches Reich), nation (Volksdeutsch), or homeland (Deutschland) because all triggered the same emotional associations. Similar responses can be elicited from members of a nation that is clearly predominant within a state, even though significant minori-

---

[*] These statistics appear also in chapter 2 and are repeated here simply to emphasize the marked ethnic heterogeneity of states.

ties are also present. But the invoking of such symbols has quite a different impact upon minorities. Thus, "Mother Russia" evokes one type of response from a Russian and something quite different from a Ukrainian. De Gaulle's emotional evocations of *La France* met quite different audiences within the Ile de France and within Brittany or Corsica.

Whatever the original reason for the interutilization of *nation* and *state*, even the briefest reflection suffices to establish the all-pervasive effect that this careless use of terminology has had upon the intellectual-cultural milieu within which the study of nationalism is perforce conducted. The League of Nations and the United Nations are obvious misnomers. The discipline called International Relations should be designated *Interstate* Relations.[15] One listing of contemporary organizations contains sixty-six entries beginning with the word *International* (e.g., the International Court of Justice and the International Monetary Fund), none of which, either in its membership or in its function, reflects any relationship to nations. International law and international organization are still other significant illustrations of the common but improper tendency to equate state and nation. National income, national wealth, national interest, and the like, refer in fact to statal concerns. A recently coined malapropism, *transnational* (and even *transnationalism*) is used to describe interstate, extragovernmental relations. *Nationalization* is still another of the numerous misnomers that muddy understanding of the national phenomenon.

With the concepts of the nation and the state thus hopelessly confused, it is perhaps not too surprising that *nationalism* should come to mean identification with the state rather than loyalty to the nation. Even the same International Relations Dictionary whose definition of the *nation* we cited for its proper appreciation of the psychological essence of the nation, makes this error. After carefully noting that "a nation may comprise part of a state, or extend beyond the borders of a single state," it elsewhere says of *nationalism* that "it makes the state the ultimate focus of the individual's loyalty."[16] It also says of nationalism that "as a mass emotion it is the most powerful political force operative in the world."[17] Few would disagree with this assessment of the power of nationalism, *and this is precisely the problem. Impressed with the force of nationalism, and assuming it to be in the service of the state, the scholar of political development has been preprogrammed to assume that the new states of Africa and Asia would naturally become the foci of their inhabitants' loyalties.* Nationalism, here as elsewhere, would prove irresistible, and alternative foci of loyalty would therefore lose the competition to that political structure alternately called the nation, the state, or the nation-state. This syndrome of assumptions and terminological confusion which has generally characterized the political development school is reflected in the early self-description of its endeavors as "nation-building." Contrary to its nomenclature, the "nation-building" school has in fact been dedicated to building viable states. And with a very few exceptions, the greatest barrier to state unity has been the fact that the states each contain more than one nation, and sometimes hundreds. Yet, a review of the literature will uncover little reflection on how the psychological bonds that presently tie segments of the state's population are to be destroyed. One searches the literature in vain for techniques by which group-ties predicated upon such things as a sense of separate origin, development, and destiny are to be supplanted by loyalty to a state-structure, whose population has never shared such common feelings. The nature and power of those abstract ties that identify the true nation remain almost unmentioned, to say nothing of unprobed. The assumption that the powerful force called nationalism is in the service of the state makes the difficult investigation of such abstractions unnecessary.

As in the case of substituting the word *nation* for *state*, it is difficult to pinpoint the origin of the tendency to equate nationalism with loyalty to the state. It is unquestionably a very recent development, for the word *nationalism* is itself of very recent creation. G. de Bertier de Sauvigny believes it first appeared in literature in 1798 and did not reappear until 1830. Moreover, its absence from lexicographies until the late nineteenth and early twentieth centuries suggests that its use was not extensive until much more recently. Furthermore, all of the examples of its early use convey the idea of identification *not* with the state, but with the nation as properly understood.[18] While unable to pinpoint nationalism's subsequent association with the state, it indubitably followed and flowed from the tendency to equate state and nation. It also unquestionably received a strong impetus from the great body of literature occasioned by the growth of militant nationalism in Germany and Japan during the 1930s and early 1940s.

As outstanding illustrations of the fanatical responses that nationalism can engender, German and Japanese nationalism of this period have come to occupy an important place in subsequent scholarship on nationalism. And, unfortunately, these manifestations of extreme nationalism have been firmly identified with loyalty to state. The most common word applied to them has been *fascism*, a doctrine postulating unswerving obedience to an organic, corporate state. The most popular alternative descriptive phrase, *totalitarianism*, perhaps even more strongly conveys the idea of the complete (total) identification of the individual with the state.

The linking of the state to these examples *par excellence* of extreme nationalism suggests the likelihood that other states will also become the object of mass devotion. If some states could elicit such fanatical devotion, why not others? Granted, few would wish to see such extreme and perverted dedication to the state arise elsewhere. But if the concept of a Japanese state could, during World War II, motivate "banzai charges," kamikaze missions, and numerous decisions of suicide rather than surrender (as well as the many postwar illustrations of people enduring for years an animal-like existence in caves on Pacific islands) because of a loyalty to the Japanese state that was so unassailable as to place that state's defeat beyond comprehension, then surely the states of the Third World should at least be able to evoke a sufficiently strong loyalty from their inhabitants so as to prevail against any competing group allegiances. If a loyalty to a German state could motivate Germans to carry on a war long after it became evident that the cause was hopeless and that perseverance could only entail more deprivation, destruction, and death, then surely other states could at least elicit a sense of common cause and identity from their populations that would prove more powerful than any counter-tendencies to draw distinctions among segments of the populace. If the German and Japanese experiences were pertinent elsewhere, then optimism concerning the stability of present state structures would be justified.

But what has been too readily ignored is the fact that Germany and Japan were among the handful of states that clearly qualify as nation-states. As earlier noted, in such cases the state and the nation are indistinguishably linked in popular perception. Japan to the Japanese, just as Germany to the Germans, was something far more personal and profound than a territorial political structure termed a state; it was an embodiment of the nation-idea and therefore an extension of self. As postulated by fascist doctrine, these states were indeed popularly conceived as corporate organisms, for they were equated with the Japanese and German nations. As Hitler wrote in *Mein Kampf*: "We as Aryans, are therefore able to imagine a State only to be the living organism of a nationality which not only safeguards the preservation of that nationality, but which, by further training of its spiritual and ideal abilities, leads it to its highest freedom."[19]

But could such an emotion-laden conception of the state take root where the nation and the state were not popularly equated? The single rubric of fascism was applied to Hitler's Germany, Tojo's Japan, Mussolini's Italy, Franco's Spain, and Perón's Argentina. It is evident, however, that appeals in the name of Spain did not elicit any great emotion from the Basques, Catalans, and Galicians. In polygenetic

Argentina, Perón's message was not a unifying appeal to all Argentinians, but was in fact a divisive call in the name of socioeconomic class. Within Italy, a sense of loyalty to the state proved woefully and surprisingly inadequate in the face of its first major test, the invasion by Allied forces. The reason appears to be that the concept of a single people (national awareness) has not yet permeated the subconsciousness of the Italians to the same measure as a similar concept had permeated the German and Japanese people.[20] In equating nationalism with loyalty to the state, scholars had failed to inquire how many cases there have been where fanatical devotion to a state has arisen in the absence of a popular conception of the state as the state of one's particular nation. Rather than suggesting certain victory on the part of new states in the competition for loyalty, the experiences of Germany and Japan exemplify the potential strength of those emotional ties to one's nation with which the multiethnic state must contend. German and Japanese nationalism were more prophetic auguries of the growth of concepts such as, inter alia, Ibo, Bengali, Kikuyu, Naga, Karen, Lao, Bahutu, Kurd, and Baganda, than they were auguries of the growth of concepts such as Nigeria, Pakistan, Kenya, India, Burma [Myanmar], Thailand, Rwanda, Iraq, and Uganda.

Mistakenly equating nationalism with loyalty to the state has further contributed to terminological confusion by leading to the introduction of still other confusing terms. With nationalism preempted, authorities have had difficulty agreeing on a term to describe the loyalty of segments of a state's population to their particular nation. Ethnicity, primordialism, pluralism, tribalism, regionalism, communalism, and parochialism are among the most commonly encountered. This varied vocabulary further impedes an understanding of nationalism by creating the impression that each is describing a separate phenomenon. Moreover, reserving nationalism to convey loyalty to the state (or, more commonly, to the word *nation* when the latter is improperly substituted for state), while using words with different roots and fundamentally different connotations to refer to loyalty to the nation, adds immeasurably to the confusion. Each of the above terms has exercised its own particular negative impact upon the study of nationalism.

ETHNICITY

Ethnicity (identity with one's ethnic group) is, if anything, more definitionally chameleonic than *nation*. It is derived from *Ethnos*, the Greek word for *nation* in the latter's pristine sense of a group characterized by common descent. Consonant with this derivation, there developed a general agreement that an ethnic group referred to a basic human category (i.e., not a subgroup). Unfortunately, however, American sociologists came to employ *ethnic group* to refer to "a group with a common cultural tradition and a sense of identity which exists as a subgroup of a larger society."[21] This definition makes ethnic group synonymous with minority, and, indeed, with regard to group relations within the United States, it has been used in reference to nearly any discernible minority, religious, linguistic, or otherwise.

The definition of ethnic group by American sociologists violates its original meaning with regard to at least two important particulars. In the traditional sense of an ancestrally related unit, it is evident that an ethnic group need not be a subordinate part of a larger political society but may be the dominant element within a state (the Chinese, English, or French, for example) or may extend across several states, as do the Arabs. Secondly, the indiscriminate application of ethnic group to numerous types of groups obscures vital distinctions between various forms of identity. In a stimulating and often cited introduction to a volume entitled *Ethnicity*, Nathan Glazer and Daniel Patrick Moynihan, while rejecting the notion that ethnicity refers only to minorities, defended the incorporation of several forms of identity under this single rubric: "Thus, there is some legitimacy to finding that forms of identification based on social realities as different as religion, language, and national origin all have something in common, such that a new term is coined to refer to all of them—ethnicity. What they have in common is that they have all become effective foci for group mobilization for concrete political ends."[22] However, despite the usefulness that such a categorization possesses for the study of the politics of special interest groups, there is little question but that it has exerted a damaging influence upon the study of nationalism. One result is that the researcher, when struggling through thousands of entries in union catalogs, indices to periodicals, and the like cannot be sure whether a so-called ethnic study will prove germane to the study of nationalism. Sometimes the unit under examination does constitute a national or potential national group. Other times it is a transnational (inter- or intrastate) group such as the Amerindians. And, in most instances, it is a group related only marginally, if at all, to the nation, as properly understood (e.g., the Catholic community within the Netherlands). Moreover, a review of the indices and bibliographies found in those ethnic studies that do deal with a national or potential national group, illustrates all too often that the author is unaware of the relationship of his work to nationalism. The student of nationalism and the student of ethnicity seldom cross-fertilize. The American journal, *Ethnicity*,* and the *Canadian Re-*

* Ceased publishing in 1982.

view of Studies in Nationalism, for example, are remarkably free of over-lap with regard to (1) the academic background of their contributors and (2) footnoted materials.

Even if the author uses the term *ethnicity* solely in relation to national groups, his equating of nationalism with loyalty to the state will predispose him to underestimate the comparative magnetism of the former.[23] But the much more common practice of employing ethnicity as a cloak for several different types of identity exerts a more baneful effect. Such a single grouping presumes that all of the identities are of the same order. We shall reserve further comment on the adverse consequences of this presumption to a later discussion of *primordialism* and *pluralism,* noting here only that this presumption circumvents raising the key question as to which of a person's several identities is apt to win out in a test of loyalties.

Anthropologists, ethnologists, and scholars concerned with global comparisons have been more prone to use *ethnicity* and *ethnic group* in their pristine sense of involving a sense of common ancestry.[24] Max Weber, for example, noted: "We shall call ethnic groups those human groups that entertain a subjective belief in their common descent . . . , this belief must be important for the propagation of group formation; conversely, it does not matter whether or not an objective blood relationship exists. Ethnic membership (*Gemeinsamkeit*) differs from the kinship group precisely by being a presumed identity."[25] This definition would appear to equate *ethnic group* and *nation,* and, as earlier noted, Weber did indeed link the two notions.[26] However, elsewhere Weber made an important and useful distinction between the two:

> The idea of the nation is apt to include the notions of common descent and of an essential though frequently indefinite homogeneity. The "nation" has these notions in common with the sentiment of solidarity of ethnic communities, which is also nourished from various sources, as we have seen before [ch. V:4]. *But the sentiment of ethnic solidarity does not by itself make a "nation."* Undoubtedly, even the White Russians in the face of the Great Russians have always had a sentiment of ethnic solidarity, yet even at the present time they would hardly claim to qualify as a separate "nation." The Poles of Upper Selesia, until recently, had hardly any feeling of solidarity with the "Polish nation." They felt themselves to be a separate ethnic group in the face of the Germans, but for the rest they were Prussian subjects and nothing else.[27]

Weber is here clearly speaking of prenational peoples or, what we termed earlier, potential nations.[28] His illustrations are of peoples not yet cognizant of belonging to a larger ethnic element. The group consciousness to which he refers—that rather low level of ethnic solidarity which a segment of the ethnic element feels when confronted with a foreign element need not be very important politically and comes closer to xenophobia than to nationalism. To the degree that it represents a step in the process of nation-formation, it testifies that a group of people must know ethnically what they *are not* before they know what they *are*. Thus, to Weber's illustrations, we can add the Slovaks, Croats, and Slovenes who, under the Habsburg Empire, were aware that they were neither German nor Magyar, long before they possessed positive opinions concerning their ethnic or national identity. In such cases, meaningful identity of a positive nature remains limited to locale, region, clan, or tribe. Thus, members need not be conscious of belonging to the ethnic group. An ethnic group may be readily discerned by an anthropologist or other outside observer, but until the members are themselves aware of the group's uniqueness, it is merely an ethnic group and not a nation. While an ethnic group *may*, therefore, be other-defined, the nation *must* be self-defined.[29] Employing ethnic group or ethnicity in relationship to several types of identities therefore beclouds the relationship between the *ethnic group* and the *nation* and also deprives scholarship of an excellent term for referring to both nations and potential nations.

PRIMORDIALISM

Primordialism, another common substitute for nationalism, is usually associated with Clifford Geertz, although Geertz has acknowledged his debt in this matter to Edward Shils.[30] Moreover, Geertz did not in fact write of primordialism but of primordial sentiments. The use of the plural was not accidental, for Geertz does not conceive the matter of competing loyalty dichotomously as loyalty to the state versus loyalty to the nation. Rather, he perceives "primordial sentiments" or "primordial attachments" as a number of distinct and only sometimes overlapping phenomena. Psychological ties stemming from a common linguistic, racial, tribal, regional, or religious background are treated by Geertz as totally separable, though often reinforcing, fundamental identities.

As noted in our comments concerning ethnicity, Geertz is certainly not alone in treating fundamental ties as multinatured. Thus the conflict between Walloon and Fleming is described by a number of writers as essentially linguistic, since there is no religious or other easily discerned division present; the problem in Northern Ireland is, by contrast, regularly identified as religious since there is no language or racial problem present; the problem in Singapore is often described as racial because there are visible distinctions that can be made between the typical Malay and Chinese; Indonesia's problems of identity are often described as regional because the islandic character of its geography is readily perceived; Taiwanese self-identity is apt to be referred to as ethnic only because there is no tangible difference between the Taiwanese and the Mainland Han. The question, however, is whether each of these examples does in fact constitute a separate species, or whether their description as essentially religious, linguistic, and so on, is the result of mistaking the tangible manifestations of the nation for its psychological essence.

Any nation, of course, has tangible characteristics and, once recognized, can therefore be described in tangible terms. The German nation can be described in terms of its numbers, its religious composition, its language, its location, and a number of other concrete factors. But none of these elements is, of necessity, essential to the German nation. The essence of the nation, as earlier noted, is a matter of *self*-awareness or *self*-consciousness. Many of the problems associated with defining a nation are attributable precisely to the fact that it is a self-defining group. That is why scholars such as Ernest Barker, Rupert Emerson, Carleton Hayes, and Hans Kohn have consistently used terms such as self-awareness and self-consciousness when analyzing and describing the nation. It is this group-notion of kinship and uniqueness that is the essence of the nation, and tangible characteristics such as religion and language are significant to the nation only to the degree to which they contribute to this notion or sense of the group's self-identity and uniqueness. And it is worth noting that a nation can lose or alter any or all of its outward characteristics without losing its sense of vital uniqueness which makes it a nation. Thus, the Irish and the Highland Scots could lose their language without losing their conviction of a separate national identity. Similarly, Jews can sever their affiliation with Judaism, while remaining very consciously tied to the Jewish nation. Indeed, in a period in which the traditional costumes, ceremonies, and other customs that formerly helped the outsider to identify distinctive nations are giving way to increasing global conformity, nationalism, in its proper sense, is obviously on the rise. Tangible characteristics, therefore, do not constitute the essential factor, and all of the above situations, although identified as essentially linguistic, religious, racial, and so on, are in fact all of the same genus, ultimately being predicated upon divergent national identities.

There are several reasons accounting for the propensity to mistake the tangible manifestations of the nation for its psychological essence. One factor is that tangible elements are the most readily seen and easily conceptualized. Moreover, for the television commentator, the news reporter, and even the scholar, tangible considerations are not only more easily perceived, but they are also more easily transmitted in understandable terms to one's audience. The new scholarly emphasis on quantification is also involved, as researchers have overly concentrated their efforts on the search for quantifiable determinants of nationalism.[31]

The problem, however, cannot be totally blamed upon the outsider. Those most involved in a conflict of national identity can also contribute to this emphasis on the more visible elements in at least three ways. A specific characteristic of a nation often becomes the rallying point in a national struggle and, in such event, is described as indivisible from the nation itself. The Ukrainians, the Franco-Canadians, and several national groups within India and Pakistan thus insist that their particular language must be preserved or their national identity will disappear. The "primordial" imperative in these cases is thus described as linguistic. We have noted, however, that several nations have lost their language without losing their national consciousness. It is particularly pertinent to note that Irish nationalists of the nineteenth and early twentieth centuries made the same assertion concerning the linkage of language and national uniqueness, but postindependence attempts to resurrect Gaelic have been spurned by the majority of the Irish people who have nonetheless clearly retained their national identity.[32] A second contributing element is that people of one nation, as a short-hand method of describing a more complex set of standards by which they distinguish another group, have a tendency to grasp upon a single attribute. Thus to the people of Scottish and English extraction in Northern Ireland, the Irish are "Catholics." The reverse of the process produces "the Prods." The observer is therefore easily lulled into believing that the issue can be reduced to a religious struggle, although the real issue involves differences in fundamental national identity.[33] A third and more difficult consideration to document is essentially psychological. People involved in a conflict of national identities appear to experience a need to express or explain their emotional responses to the other group in more "logical" and concrete form. The *sense* or *feeling* of uniqueness that creates the gulf between them must be translated into more tangible form, such as into differences of religion, customs, or dialect. A clearly related phenomenon is the apparently widely felt compulsion to "justify" one's prejudices (i.e., the emotional responses to foreign stimuli) by ascribing readily perceived (or readily misperceived) distinguishing attributes to the other group.

Quite apart from obscuring the root cause and psychological depth of the particular issue, the practice of describing such situations as, for example, essentially linguistic, racial, or religious, involves the same danger that we noted with regard to the use of multiple-meaning terms such as ethnicity: there is the risk of concluding that each term is describing a separate phenomenon. Analyses that emphasize a tangible element are often interspersed with expressions such as "cultural nationalism," "religious nationalism" or "linguistic nationalism." Though such terms have the merit of noting that nationalism is present, they give the impression that it is but one of several different species and that it could not survive the disappearance of tangible factors. The use of *primordialism* is therefore at least preferable to "primordial sentiments" in that it does not further fractionalize the national concept. The major criticism of primordialism is that its suggestion of primitiveness, as in the case of *tribalism*, implies that it will wither away as modernization progresses. There is a strong hint that it does not affect "modern" societies. But a listing of the European states that have recently experienced national friction illustrates that national consciousness is not limited to the Third World. The Soviet Union, Romania, Cyprus, Czechoslovakia, Yugoslavia, Italy, France, Spain, Switzerland, Belgium, and the United Kingdom have all recently known problems stemming from growing national consciousness on the part of segments of their populations. "Black Nationalism" in the United States and Franco-Canadian unrest in Canada offer further testimony that industrialization, intensive communication systems, high ratings on a global educational index, and impressive Gross National Products do not constitute safeguards against frictions arising from growing national consciousness.

PLURALISM

The origin of *pluralism* is customarily linked to the anthropologist, J. S. Furnivall. Furnivall was particularly interested in colonial milieux in which indigenes, colonials, and nonindigenous peoples who had been imported by the colonials, lived side-by-side. Such a unit he called a *plural society*: "It is in the strictest sense a medley, for they mix but do not combine. Each group holds by its own religion, its own culture and language, its own ideas and ways. As individuals they meet, but only in the market-place, in buying and selling. There is a plural society, with different sections of the community living side-by-side, but separately, within the same political unit."[34] Though Furnivall was describing a very particular form of society, and one now largely passé, his terminology was soon applied by others to describe any society containing heterogeneous characteristics. Thus, the third edition of *Webster's New International Dictionary* (1971) contains the following definition of *pluralism*, no counterpart of which had appeared in the previous edition: "a state or condition of society in which members of diverse ethnic, racial, religious, or social groups maintain an autonomous participation in and development of their traditional culture or special interest within the confines of a common civilization."

The inclusion of social groups makes *pluralism* an even more inclusive term than *ethnicity*, for the latter excluded socioeconomic class. Pluralism therefore encompasses seemingly all forms of group-identity that are less than statewide, and the adjective, *cultural*, which customarily precedes it, does little to mitigate its catch-all nature.[35] This lack of discrimination implies that all group identities are of the same order. And when linked to pluralism's a priori acceptance of the society as an enduring given, it lends itself to the Madisonian concept of the balancing of cross-cutting interests. Since the regional, economic, social, religious, ethnonational, racial, and other identities of the individual do not perfectly coincide with one another, this theory postulates that the competing interests arising from all identities will tend to check the fissiparous tendency of any particular one, thus guaranteeing the continued viability of the state. But such a prognostication ignores the evidence, offered by several ethnonational separatist movements, that the well-springs of national identity are more profound than are those associated with religion, class, and the like, and the presence of other shared characteristics may, therefore, *not* be sufficient to preserve the state. That the individual partakes of several group identities simultaneously is beyond dispute. But that these identities are not of the same order was the basis for Rupert Emerson's sage description of the nation as "the largest community which, when the chips are down, effectively commands men's loyalty, overriding the claims both of lesser communities within it and those which cut across it or potentially enfold it within a still greater society."[36]

TRIBALISM

As currently applied, the words *tribe* and *tribalism* are usually associated with non-Arab Africa where they have added a special dimension to the obscurity surrounding the study of nationalism. Though the term tribe is far from precise and its meaning a matter of contention among anthropologists, it has traditionally been employed to describe an ethnically homogeneous sociopolitical unit, but one which forms *only part* of a larger interrelated grouping. This concept of the tribe as an ethnically subordinate unit is usually honored outside of Africa; thus, the key sociopolitical units that comprise such Asian peoples as the Azerbaijani, Kurds, and Pushtuns are called tribes, thereby conveying that in each case there exists a single ethnic group which embraces all of the tribal units. In non-Arab Africa, on the other hand, the preponderant number of human categories to which the term *tribe* is most commonly affixed, constitute separate nations or potential nations in and by themselves. Well known examples include the Ashanti, Kongo,

Hausa, Ibo, Xhosa, and Zulu. There is liable to be as much difference—psychologically as well as tangibly—between two African "tribes" as there is between Frenchman and German. In referring to them as tribes rather than as nations or potential nations, scholars have been lulled into badly underestimating the emotional magnetism that these collectives exert upon individuals. Calling this magnetism *tribalism*, while reserving *nationalism* to describe attachment to the new states, both reflects and strengthens a presumption that the loyalty of the individual will assuredly over time be transferred from the part (which is actually the nation but called the tribe) to the whole (actually the state but called the nation).

This presumption is reinforced because "tribe," in addition to conveying the idea of subethnic status, also popularly connotes a primitive, evolutionary stage in human organization. Thus, the Celtic and Germanic tribes were ultimately absorbed in a transtribal, national unit. By analogy, it can be assumed that the "tribes" of Africa will be absorbed in, for example, "the Nigerian nation." Time is thus perceived as clearly on the side of the states, and they and not the tribes are viewed as the wave of the future.

There is a final problem concerning the meaning of the tribe as applied to non-Arab Africa. Most of the distinctive ethnic groups, though called tribes, are themselves organized on a multitribal basis. As a result, parent and subordinate groups are often identically described. This dual use of the term makes it very dangerous to generalize concerning the probability of *all so-called tribes* becoming absorbed in a larger identity. Increased contacts should cause ethnically subordinate units to become increasingly aware of what they have in common, thus giving rise to the nation-concept. But increased contacts between different ethnic groups cannot be presumed to have any such effect.

REGIONALISM

Much that has been said concerning tribalism pertains also to the use of the word *regionalism* as a substitute for nationalism. Part of the confusion is due to the fact that regionalism in today's parlance has two quite incompatible meanings, one involving a transstate identity and the other an intrastate identity. Thus, the transstate integration of a segment of the globe is called, for example, European *regionalism*; and structures such as NATO, SEATO, the EEC, and the Arab League are called *regional* organizations. On the other hand, regionalism is used to describe intrastate divisions based upon sentimental ties to the locale. It is in the second sense, that of sectionalism, that nationalism is often improperly referred to as regionalism.

To an even greater degree than primordialism and tribalism, regionalism simply does not convey the same sense of emotional commitment as does nationalism, so the mere use of the former reflects and reinforces a conviction that it will not prove a worthy competitor for a person's most fundamental allegiance.[37] Moreover, the equating of regionalism with nationalism is confusing because regionalism, as properly used, often coexists with true nationalism. German nationalism, for example, has not precluded differences in regional attitudes among Prussians, Rhinelanders, Bavarians, and so on. The important fact, however, is that in any test of loyalties, those factors which all members of the German nation feel they have in common are deemed more important than are regional distinctions.

There are, to be sure, a number of cases in which the national "idea" (national consciousness) has not yet fully coalesced, and in which regional identity therefore remains a true competitor with nationalism for people's loyalty. Thus, the concept of the Arab West (al-magrib al Arabi) still exerts a substantial impact upon the identity of Arabs to the west of Libya. While Arab nationalism is penetrating the area, some of the inhabitants still sense that there are vital differences between Arabs of western and eastern Arabdom, which outweigh in importance their common Arabness.[38] However, it is generally conceded that sectionalism wanes with increased contacts among the various parts of an ethnically homogeneous population. Developments in a series of situations support the proposition that more intensive contacts among parts of a population that has some foundation for a sense of common origin will increase that consciousness. Today's nations were once composed of segmented peoples whose fundamental sense of identity did not extend beyond the family, village, clan, or tribe. Moreover, once a sense of national consciousness is established, further increases in interregional contacts clearly tend to homogenize the populations's customs, tastes, and attitudes. But where one is dealing not with a single potential nation, but with groups whose customs and beliefs bespeak, on balance, not a common history but distinctive origins and development, increased contacts tend to have the opposite effect. Rather than strengthening the appeal of those traits held in common, there is a tendency to emphasize the traits which divide. The great increase in tensions which a multitude of multiethnic states have been experiencing underlines this dichotomy. Expanded contacts have made the Kurds, Laotians, Flemings, Welsh, and Franco-Canadians more nationally conscious, but it has also made them more opposed to, respectively, the Arabs and Turks, Thais, Kikuyus, Walloons, English, and Anglophones.

Increased communications and transportation within a state thus have one impact among members of the same nation or potential nation, but have quite another among members of separate nations. The error of referring to nationalism as regionalism has thus led authorities to assume that the variations in identity with which they are dealing will disappear with modernization. But the body of actual evidence points in the opposite direction.

COMMUNALISM

As still another substitute for true nationalism, *communalism* also raises a number of problems. Communalism entered recent literature involving nationalism with respect to political developments in South Asia. Communalism became a popular way of describing the tendency of South Asian people to divide along an Islamic-Hindu breakdown. In the period prior to the British withdrawal from India, communalism there came to mean the growing tendency of people to stress the importance of an identity linked to religion rather than to stress what was commonly but erroneously called an "Indian nationalism." In this region, then, communalism came to be viewed as a competitor with what was termed "nationalism" (i.e., what, in fact, was what we have termed state loyalty), but it was not used (as primordialism, tribalism, and regionalism have been used elsewhere) as synonymous with what we have identified as "true nationalism." Rather, communalism, by postulating a fundamental identity along religious lines that would both incorporate several nations and sever others, repudiated the importance that we have ascribed to the nation-concept.

Support for this contention was offered by the pre-independence ferment for dividing India into two states, one of which openly aspired to be identified as an Islamic republic; by a number of plebiscites in which nations were divided along religious lines in their affinity toward Pakistan; and by the bloodletting perpetrated by religious groups upon one another both at the time of British withdrawal and at periodic intervals since then. It is clear, however, that growing national consciousness has characterized the peoples of the area. The fact that the multinational union of India is still territorially intact is not without significance, but the price of continued union has been a series of concessions to various nations concerning India's internal boundaries, acceptable levels of group autonomy, and so on. In some cases, for example among the Kashmiri, Mizos, and Nagas, such concessions have not even sufficed to gain passivity. And in Pakistan, separatist agitation among the Sindi and Pushtuns seriously questions the power of religious over national sentiment. But clearly the most serious rebuttal to the claim that communalism is more powerful than the nation-idea has been occasioned by the Bengali. It is not just their secession from Pakistan that is noteworthy, but also the many illustrations, particularly poignant during the secession struggle, that the common Bengali bond straddles both the Hindu-Islamic division and the Pakistani-Indian division of the Bengali people.[39]

While communalism has been treated as a competitor with the nation-concept in literature on South Asia, there is a growing tendency to equate the two elsewhere.[40] The term, therefore, has the remarkable versatility to connote a number of concepts that are in no way related to nationalism; or to signify a religious identity that contests the validity of nationalism; or to be synonymous with nationalism while never being identified as such. As a sower of confusion, it has few equals.

PAROCHIALISM

If *primordialism* and *tribalism* suggest something of a patronizing view of nationalism in the Third World as a quaint echo of something Europeans had shed before the end of "the Dark Ages," the connotation that the word *parochialism* has acquired within American intellectual circles causes its equation with nationalism to result in an accusing finger being pointed at anyone who recognizes a bond of loyalty to his nation. The third edition of *Webster's New International Dictionary* defines parochialism as "the quality or state of being parochial; esp: selfish pettiness or narrowness (as of interests, opinions, or views)." The use of such judgmental terms tells us more about the author's emotional biases concerning, among other things, the state-nation competition than it does about the national phenomenon.[41] It also suggests that dispassionate analysis and evaluation of the national bond are not apt to follow.

SUBNATIONALISM

It is fitting that we should conclude this list of improper substitutes for nationalism with that of *subnationalism*.[42] Granted, the users of this term at least indicate an awareness that they are confronting some approximation of nationalism. However, in its clear presumption that nationalism is in the employ of the state and in its relegation of loyalty to the ethnonational group to a subordinate order of phenomena, *subnationalism* has no peer. In and of itself, it is an affirmation of the ultimate victory of state loyalty over ethnic loyalty.

. . .

Where today is the study of nationalism? In this Alice-in-Wonderland world in which nation usually means state, in which nation-state usually means multination state, in which nationalism usually means loyalty to the state, and in which ethnicity, primordialism, pluralism, tribalism, regionalism, communalism, parochialism, and subnational-ism usually mean loyalty to the nation, it should come as no surprise that the nature of nationalism remains essentially unprobed. Indeed, careless vocabulary has even precluded a realistic assessment of the magnitude of nationalism's revolutionary potentiality. Unidentified as such, nationalism has tended to be either ignored or misunderstood in the literature on political development. When identified under an im-proper appellation, it has been dismissed as something that will wither away as modernization progresses or as something too distasteful to be countenanced. So long as nationalism remains unrecognized and mul-tititled, its implications are apt to remain unappreciated. And if both it and its implications are unrecognized, then greater understanding of the nature of nationalism is not apt to follow.

But while it is a major contributing element to the ambiguity sur-rounding nationalism, careless terminology is also a reflection of nationalism's intangible nature. As philosophers are well aware, termi-nological carelessness finds fertile soil in the area of abstraction. The abstract, illusive quality of the national bond in itself impedes scholarly investigation. It may well be, therefore, that knowledge of the quintes-sence of nationalism will continue to evade us. In a most thought-pro-voking article, Ladis Kristof has suggested that the scientific form of inquiry may be inappropriate for phenomena of this type.[43] Dissection and logic, even in concert, may prove not only inadequate but mislead-ing when applied to the study of sensory loyalties. Rupert Emerson, whose scholarly dedication and sensitive insight into nationalism has benefited all who have pondered his works, has expressed essentially the same sentiment in a few prefacing words to an impressive investi-gation of the elements that most commonly accompany nationalism:

> The simplest statement that can be made about a nation is that it is a body of people who feel that they are a nation; and it may be that when all the fine-spun analysis is concluded this will be the ultimate statement as well. To advance beyond it, it is necessary to attempt to take the nation apart and to isolate for separate examination the forces and elements which appear to have been the most influential in bringing about the sense of common identity which lies at its roots, the sense of the existence of a singularly important national "we" which is distinguished from all others who make up an alien "they." This is necessarily an overly mechanical process, for nationalism, like other profound emotions such as love and hate, is more than the sum of the parts which are susceptible of cold and rational analysis.[44]

Emerson's comments suggest that the basic prerequisite for greater understanding of nationalism may be a measure of humility. Some doubt concerning one's ability to penetrate its innermost core may prove more appropriate than confidence for gaining insight into the national phenomenon. An acknowledgment that total understanding might continue to evade best insures that one will maintain a proper appreciation for the complexity of the subject and will not, as so often has been the case, confuse the most apparent manifestations with essence. Acknowledging that one cannot explain the quintessence of nationalism need not preclude advances in understanding. Even in a totally physical area, people of medicine have made great strides in learning about the symptoms and responses to stimuli of melanomic cancer, while remaining ignorant of its basic cause and nature. But it was first necessary that melanoma be identified and distinguished from other phenomena. Similarly, the prerequisites to greater understanding of nationalism are (1) that it be recognized and (2) that it and only it be identified as such.

NOTES

1. For a more complete listing and additional details concerning the states of Asia, see this writer's "An Overview of the Ethnic Composition and Problems of Non Arab Asia," *Journal of Asian Affairs* 1 (Spring 1976): 9–25, and, for the states of Africa, chapter 2 in this volume.

2. For details, see this writer's "The Political Significance of Ethnonationalism within Western Europe," in *Ethnicity in an International Context*, ed. Abdul Said and Luiz Simmons (Edison, N.J., 1976), 110–33, and chapter 7 in this volume.

3. For details, see this writer's *The National Question in Marxist Theory and Strategy* (Princeton, 1984).

4. See chapter 2 in this volume.

5. *Nationalism: A Report by a Study Group of Members of the Royal Institute of International Affairs* (London, 1939), xvi.

6. Karl Deutsch, *Nationalism and Its Alternatives*, (New York, 1969), 138.

7. Ibid. *Nation*, for example, is used to denote (a) the total population of a country, regardless of its ethnonational composition (pp. 23, 33); (b) only the assimilated part of the country's population (pp. 40, 43); the state (pp. 32, 33, 79); and specific multinational states such as Belgium and Switzerland (p. 70). *Nation-state* is first correctly defined as "a state that has become largely identical with one people" (p. 19) and then is employed indiscriminately to describe all states (pp. 32, 33, 35, 49, 60, 61, 63, 112, 113, 114, 120, 125, 171, 172, 176), specifically including such multinational states as Czechoslovakia, Romania, and Yugoslavia (p. 62); it is also used to connote a unitary in contradistinction to a federal state (p. 120). *Nationality* refers to an ethnonational identity (pp. 54, 68)

or to citizenship (p. 125). *Nationalism* refers to "concern for fellow nationals, for countrymen" (p. 25), regardless of ethnonational differences, and yet the author can speak of the nationalism of minorities (p. 53).

8. Jack C. Plano and Roy Olton, *The International Relations Dictionary* (New York, 1969), 119; emphasis added. [The fourth edition, published in 1988, made no substantive changes in the definition of *nation* and *nationalism*.]

9. Conrad Brandt, Benjamin Schwartz and John Fairbank, *A Documentary History of Chinese Communism* (London, 1952), 245; parenthetical material added.

10. Max Weber notes that "the concept of 'nationality' [or 'nation'] shares with that of the 'people' (Volk)—in the 'ethnic' sense—the vague connotation that whatever is felt to be distinctively common must derive from common descent." Weber, *Economy and Society*, ed. Guenther Roth and Claus Wittich (New York, 1968), 1: 395. An old European definition of a nation, though intended to be humorous and derisive and which Karl Deutsch cites as such, hit almost the same mark: "A nation is a group of people united by a common error about their ancestry and a common dislike of their neighbors." Deutsch, *Nationalism and Its Alternatives*, 3.

11. A recent example of the loose manner in which nation may be used is: Jill Johnston, *Lesbian Nation: The Feminist Solution* (New York: Simon and Schuster).

12. Raymond Williams, *Keywords: A Vocabulary of Culture and Society* (New York, 1976), 178.

13. Louis J. Halle, *Civilization and Foreign Policy* (New York, 1952), 10. For another example of this practice of referring to states as nation-states, see Dankwart Rustow, *A World of Nations* (Washington, D.C., 1967), 30, for a reference to the United Kingdom and the Soviet Union as nation-states. Note also Rustow's concluding remarks (p. 282): "More than 130 nations, real or so-called, will each make its contribution to the history of the late twentieth century." For other illustrations, see chapter 7 in this volume.

14. By a potential nation is meant a group of people who appear to have all of the necessary prerequisites for nationhood, but who have not as yet developed a consciousness of their sameness and commonality, nor a conviction that their destinies are interwound. They are usually referred to by anthropologists as ethnolinguistic groups. Such peoples' sense of fundamental identity is still restricted to the locale, extended family, clan, or tribe. The Andean states and southwestern Asia offer several illustrations of such prenational people.

15. A random survey of books, published within the United States and designed for college courses in global politics provides ample documentation of the impact this misuse of terminology has exerted upon the discipline. In addition to the host of titles consisting of or containing the expressions *International Relations* or *International Politics* are such well-known examples as *Politics Among Nations*, *The Might of Nations*, *Nations and Men*, *The Insecurity of Nations*, *How Nations Behave*, and *Games Nations Play*. Another illustration is offered by the American professional organization called the International Studies Association. Its official raison d'être, as set forth in the early issues of its Quarterly, notes that the organization "is devoted to the orderly growth of knowledge concerning the impact of nation upon nation."

16. Plano and Olton, *The International Relations Dictionary*, 119, 120.

17. Ibid. 120. [As noted above, later editions contained no substantive changes in the definitions of *nations* and *nationalism*.]

18. See G. de Bertier de Sauvigny, "Liberalism, Nationalism, and Socialism: The Birth of Three Words," *The Review of Politics* 32 (April 1970): 155–61 particularly.

19. Adolph Hitler, *Mein Kampf* (New York, 1940), 595.

20. For details, see this writer's "The Political Significance of Ethnonationalism within Western Europe," particularly 126–30.

21. George Theodorson and Achilles Theodorson, *A Modern Dictionary of Sociology* (New York, 1969), 135. For a similar definition, see H. S. Morris's selection on "Ethnic Groups" in *The International Encyclopedia of the Social Sciences* (New York, 1968).

22. Nathan Glazer and Daniel P. Moynihan, *Ethnicity: Theory and Experience* (Cambridge, Mass., 1975), 18.

23. See, for example, Peter Busch, *Legitimacy and Ethnicity* (Lexington, Mass., 1974), in which ethnicity refers to the breakdown of the population of Singapore into Chinese, Malay, and other such components, and in which nationalism refers to identity with the Singaporean state.

24. See, for example, Tomotshu Shibutani and Kian Kwan, *Ethnic Stratification: A Comparative Approach* (New York, 1965), 47, where an ethnic group is defined as composed of "those who conceive of themselves as being alike by virtue of their common ancestry, real or fictitious, and who are so regarded by others."

25. Max Weber, *Economy and Society*, 389.

26. See above, note 10.

27. Weber, *Economy and Society*, 923.

28. See chapter 3 in this volume.

29. As Charles Winick has observed with regard to an *ethnos*: "A group of people linked by both nationality and race. These bonds are usually unconsciously accepted by members of the group, but outsiders observe the homogeneity." Winick, *Dictionary of Anthropology* (New York, 1956), 193.

30. Clifford Geertz, "The Integrative Revolution: Primordial Sentiments and Civil Politics in the New States," in *Old Societies and New States*, ed. Clifford Geertz (New York, 1963), particularly 109.

31. For a rather unusual claim concerning the degree to which nationalism has already succumbed to modern analysis, see the *New York Times*, 16 March 1971, for a prepublication review of a study by Karl Deutsch, John Platt, and Diter Senghaas, which lists what the authors consider to be "the 62 major accomplishments in the behavioral and social sciences since 1900." Among them is listed "quantitative models of nationalism and integration (mathematical study of nationalistic response)." The contributors are listed as K. Deutsch, B. Russett, and R. L. Merritt, and the time of the accomplishment is placed between 1942 and 1967.

32. Still another interesting example is that of the Basques. Though their level of nationalism is obviously very high, they are the least interested of all non-Castilian speaking groups within Spain in requiring education in their lan-

guage. This attitude is reflected in a poll cited in Milton da Silva, *The Basque Nationalist Movement: A Case Study in Ethnic Nationalism* (Ph.D. diss., University of Massachusetts, 1972).

33. Contrary to most analyses, both sides in the conflict do not consider themselves Irish. A poll indicates that less than 50 percent do. For more details, see chapters 2 and 7 in this volume.

34. J. S. Furnivall, *Colonial Policy and Practice* (Cambridge, 1948), 305.

35. For example, the multivolume *Case Studies on Human Rights and Fundamental Freedoms*, produced by the Foundation for the Study of Plural Societies, the Hague, as well as the Foundation's journal, *Plural Societies*, contain articles dealing with such diverse groups and topics as, inter alia, national minorities, religious groups, sex discrimination, castes, and races.

36. Rupert Emerson, *From Empire to Nation* (Boston, 1960), 95–96.

37. For an article grouping ethnonational movements (such as those in Brittany, Corsica, Scotland, and Wales) with localism (such as that evidenced within a number of German Länder) under the single rubric of "subnational regionalism," see Werner Feld, "Subnational Regionalism and the European Community," *Orbis* 18 (Winter 1975): 1176–92. The result is a confusing comparison of different phenomena. For a description of Scottish nationalism as regionalism (and a corresponding underevaluation of its potency), see John Schwartz, "The Scottish National Party," *World Politics* 22 (July 1970): 496–517, and particularly 515, where the author speaks of a "regional identity." See also Jack Haywood, *The One and Indivisible French Republic* (New York, 1973), 38, 56, where the movement within Brittany is referred to as regionalism. No reference to ethnonationalism is made, nor are there any references to France's other ethnic minorities. Since the term region implies a larger whole, the indivisibility of France (as indicated by the title) is assured. The propensity to refer to ethnonational movements within France and Italy as regionalism has probably been heightened in recent years by "regionalization" plans to decentralize authority. In both cases, the borders of the new regions often closely correspond with the distribution of ethnic groups.

38. One manifestation of a separate regional identity is found in a comparison of constitutions. While the constitutions of most Arab states contain statements that their populations are part of an "Arab nation," the constitutions of Morocco and Tunisia each omit this expression and emphasize that their state is part of "the Greater Maghrib." Still another manifestation of regionalism is the progressive lessening of emotionalism sparked by the Arab's "arch enemy," Israel, as one moves toward the Arab West. President Bourguiba of Tunisia was able many years ago to recommend that Arab states recognize Israel, without raising much domestic furor. A similar position would be foolhardy for a leader in the Levant.

39. For details, see Connor, "An Overview of the Ethnic Composition and Problems of Non-Arab Asia."

40. See, for example, Robert Melson and Howard Wolpe, "Modernization and the Politics of Communalism: A Theoretical Perspective," *American Political Science Review* 64 (December 1970): 1112–30. See too, F.H.H. King, *The New Malayan Nation: A Study of Communalism and Nationalism* (New York, 1957).

41. While less innately prejudicial, other often encountered terms, such as particularism, suggest this same pro-state bias on the part of the author.

42. See for example, Victor Olorunsola, ed., *The Politics of Cultural Sub-Nationalism in Africa* (Garden City, N.Y., 1972). See also Feld, "Subnational Regionalism and the European Community."

43. Ladis Kristof, "The State-Idea, the National Idea and the Image of the Fatherland," *Orbis* 11 (Spring 1967): 255.

44. Emerson, *Empire to Nation*, 102.

Chapter Five

ILLUSIONS OF HOMOGENEITY

We have earlier recounted the tendency of many scholars to perceive or to assume homogeneity within states where heterogeneity is the fact. In turn, this tendency is part of a much broader tendency to perceptually divide the world into huge segments on the basis of assumed uniformity of cultural, historical, and behavioral patterns. A current example can be found in ubiquitous references to "the Islamic World." Implicitly and often explicitly in works using this expression is the notion that valid generalities concerning thought and behavior patterns can be applied to the predominantly Muslim peoples stretching from Morocco to western China and Indonesia. Reality, of course, is quite different, for everywhere Islam reflects the influence of pre-Islamic culture. Thus, although Islamic tradition is militantly monotheistic ("There is no god, but Allah . . ."), as practiced by the majority of Muslims in Indonesia (the Abangans) Islam is outrightly polytheistic. Similarly, although Islamic precepts are stringently egalitarian, pre-Islamic caste structures remain powerful among many Muslim communities of South Asia.

Although an "Islamic World" is not considered in the following article, the tendency to perceive Muslims as an undifferentiated group has certainly influenced the literature on national identity. The Islamic tradition holds that it is religious identity (membership in the *ummah* or community of believers) that is the key group-identity, and many scholars have accepted this ordering of identities. Thus, prior to the demise of the Soviet Union, numerous authorities on Soviet Central Asia maintained that Kazakhs, Turkmen, Uzbeks, and others, viewed themselves first and foremost as a single Muslim people. But as the Soviet Union began to disintegrate, the Central Asia nations showed at least as much hostility to other predominantly Muslim nations as they did to non-Muslim nations. What follows is a description of the manner in which still other misperceptions of homogeneity have influenced scholars and public policy.

Myths of Hemispheric, Continental, Regional, and State Unity[*]

ONE OF THE MORE enduring and consequential myths of human relations is the assumption that groups who dwell on a single land mass
share certain common interests and traits because of that territorial
contiguity, even though the groups in question may be separated by
great distances.[1] An illustration of this phenomenon is offered by the
phrase popularly ascribed to United States relations with Latin America in the post-1933 period, "the Good Neighbor Policy." By the term
neighbor, U.S. leaders were obviously implying the existence of a special relationship based upon a concept of relative proximity. Among
the neighbors were the so-called "ABC" states of Argentina, Brazil, and
Chile. Beyond the pale of the neighborhood were such states as the
United Kingdom, France, Germany, Italy, Liberia, and the USSR. Yet, in
navigable distances, each of these states was closer to the United States
than was any of the "ABC" group.[2] Contrariwise, Argentina and Brazil
were closer to Europe than they were to the "colossus of the north."

In terms of its basic assumption that a special relationship exists
among all of the states of the Western Hemisphere due to geography,
the Good Neighbor Policy did not represent a departure from earlier
attitudes, but rather furnished testimony to the tenacity of a myth
which had been prevalent at least since the first stirrings of independence movements in Latin America. Thomas Jefferson, for example,
noted in private correspondence in 1811:

> The European nations constitute a separate division of the globe; their
> localities make them a part of a distinct system; they have a set of interests
> of their own in which it is our business never to engage ourselves. Amer-
> ica has a hemisphere to itself. It must have its separate system of interests;
> which must not be subordinated to those of Europe. The insulated state in
> which nature has placed the American continent, should so far avail that

[*] Published in Walker Connor, "Myths of Hemispheric, Continental, Regional
and State Unity," *Political Science Quarterly* 84 (Winter 1969): 555–82. Copyright
© 1969 *Political Science Quarterly*. Reprinted with permission from *Political Science Quarterly* 84 (Winter 1969): 555–82.

no spark of war kindled in other quarters of the globe should be wafted across the wide oceans which separate us from them and it will be so.[3]

In a similar vein, Henry Clay declared on the floor of the House of Representatives a few years later:

> There cannot be a doubt that Spanish America, once independent, whatever may be the form of governments established in its parts, these governments will be animated by an American feeling, and guided by an American policy. They will obey the laws of the system of the New World, of which they will compose a part, in contradistinction to that of Europe.[4]

Both statements predicate a mystical bond arising from an equally mystical proximity. From their sharp differentiation between Europe and all that is European on the one hand, and the New World and all that is "New Worldly" on the other, it is evident that both men had assumed a direct relationship between physical geography and contemporary human affairs. The oceans were viewed as constituting barriers to human relations, and the landed interconnection between the United States and the states to the south was viewed, at least by contrast with the oceans, as constituting a cultural and political bridge.

This same a priori assumption underlay the clarion of "Manifest Destiny," which called upon Americans to conform to Nature's law by making their political-cultural domain coterminous with the land mass. While president, John Q. Adams found "it a settled geographic element that the United States and North America are identical." He was followed by others who pursued the logic of the concept of "natural frontiers" (ocean borders) to its conclusion. In 1845, for example, a congressman from Illinois prophesied on the floor of the House that the Speaker would soon recognize not just the gentleman from Oregon, but the one from Canada, from Cuba, from Mexico, "aye, even the gentleman from Patagonia." And he was supported in his prophecy by Stephen A. Douglas, who made clear, however, that he "did not wish to go beyond the great ocean—beyond the boundaries which the God of nature had marked out."[5]

Although the United States was later to settle for something far less territorially ambitious than the Arctic and the Straits of Magellan, the idea of the hemispheric bond was to remain the ideological nucleus of United States–Latin American policy. From the espousal of the Monroe Doctrine in 1823 to the Alliance for Progress, the United States has steadfastly assumed the existence of special ties between itself and all of Latin America (1) because of their common separation from Eurasia by oceans and (2) because of their landed interconnection. Considering again that the United States and some of the South American states are closer to Europe than they are to each other, how else is to be explained the words of the Monroe Doctrine: "With the movements in this hemisphere we are of necessity more immediately connected, and by causes which must be obvious to all enlightened and impartial observers"? Or Secretary of State Olney's 1895 contention that "the States of America, South as well as North, *by geographic proximity,* . . . are friends and allies"?[6] Or Theodore Roosevelt's 1904 denial that the United States wanted anything in the Western Hemisphere other than "to see the neighboring countries stable, orderly, and prosperous"?[7] Or Franklin Roosevelt's reference to "good neighbors"? Or the official wording of the congressional rationale for the Alliance for Progress: "It is the sense of the Congress that the historic, economic, political, and *geographic* relationships among the American peoples and Republics are unique and of special significance . . ."?[8]

It is evident that this "unique" and "special" relationship is based upon the sharing of a single land mass, for the United States shares little else with all of the states of Central and South America. Surely not culture, for the United States is a predominantly Anglo-Saxon, English-speaking, Protestant culture while its neighbors to the south are predominantly Latin, Spanish/Portuguese-speaking, and Catholic. Economically, some of the states of Central and South America have been important providers of raw materials to the United States, others have been essentially unimportant to the United States economy, and still others, such as Argentina, have been competitive with the United States.

But how important has the fact of sharing a common land mass actually been? The reality, of course, is that relations with all states south of Mexico have been conducted as though they and the United States were distinct islands. And this is true of the most important relations between Mexico and the United States as well. The "land-bridge" represented by the Isthmus of Panama is, in fact, a barrier (containing mountains and tropical jungle, and not completely crossed by a single north-south highway), which has been bypassed rather than utilized by man in his north-south travels. The major importance of the Isthmus in the relations among the states of the Western Hemisphere has been due to its manmade, east-west severance at Panama, rather than to its north-south continuity. Intercourse between the United States and other American states to the south has been conducted primarily by sea or, so far as passenger service in recent years is concerned, by air, but practically not at all by land. Yet, would the United States have been apt to postulate a "unique" and "special" relationship between itself and, say, Argentina, if the two states had been "separated by ocean," rather than "connected by land"?

I

The prevalence of the myth of landed relationships is not limited to the Western Hemisphere. There exists a common tendency, when looking at a world map, to conceive of the blue-painted oceans and large seas as chasms and voids, effectively separating the land masses—particularly Eurasia, Africa, and the Americas—into inward-looking, intrarelated wholes. Meaningful relations, it follows, end at the water's edge. As a formula this conception would read: *Two points, connected by land, are closer than two points, equally distant, but separated by water.*

The formula admittedly possessed validity prior to the late fifteenth century, if two points separated by water meant two points separated by a wide expanse of open ocean. But even in prehistoric times man had discovered and put into practice what his successors have continued to practice while often failing to perceive, that water poses less of a barrier to movement and to transcommunication than does land.

The sociopolitical consequences of the comparative advantage of water travel are manifest in the arterial role which navigable rivers have played throughout history. Thus, the first political integration of a large territory and population occurred in Egypt, where even today almost 99 percent of the inhabitants dwell in that 4 percent of the territory which stretches along the Nile. Other early societies developed along the Tigris-Euphrates, the Indus, and the Yellow rivers.[9]

This integrating influence of rivers possesses great significance for contemporary South Asian politics. In the case of Burma [Myanmar], for example, an examination of the linguistic and relief maps illustrates that the Burmese-speaking people are limited essentially to the Irrawady and Sittang river valleys, their deltas, and a stretch of coastal plain. In Thailand the Siamese-speaking element is essentially restricted to coastal areas and the Chao Praya Valley. In Vietnam the Vietnamese speakers are restricted to the Red and Mekong river valleys, their deltas, a thin coastal strip, and the river and canal infested Cochin-China plain. It is therefore evident that the rivers and off-coast waters have been the main passageways for cultural and economic intercourse throughout South Asian history. People separated by great distances along a navigable river or sea coast are very often culturally interrelated and, what is of key political importance, are conscious of that interrelationship because it has been nourished by continuing contacts. By contrast, people only short distances away (for example, the Karens, Kachins, Mons, and others in Burma [Myanmar]; the mountain tribesmen of the north, and the Lao-speaking people of the northeast in the case of Thailand; the "montagnards" in the case of Vietnam) have been comparatively isolated from the dominant people within the political state in which they now find themselves. Many of the major problems of contemporary South Asia are the *in tandem* consequence of the attempt to combine within single territorial-political units what have hitherto been effectively separated highland and riverine-coastal culture groups.

Coastal waters have also served as intercontinental avenues since early times. The key role that was played by the Mediterranean in a number of ancient civilizations is impressed upon all "Western" schoolchildren. What is seldom emphasized in childrens' history books, however, is that "the cradle of Western civilization" actually consisted of the intertwined civilizations of Asia and Africa, as well as Europe. Moreover, even prior to the Christian era, goods from monsoon Asia regularly reached the Mediterranean by way of the Indian Ocean, the Red Sea, and the shortest possible overland route across the Isthmus of Suez. Similarly, a thriving ocean trade between east-coast Africa and the Indian subcontinent existed long before Vasco de Gama rounded southern Africa. The advances in navigational devices and shipbuilding which made possible "the Age of Discovery" represented, therefore, only an evolutionary, albeit a giant step in the pattern of human relations. Transocean voyages did not herald a radical departure from earlier patterns.

Significant overland movements have also occurred, of course. Overland migrations of people, covering great distances, are quite common facts of history; caravan routes for the carriage of goods long existed between the Orient and the Mediterranean and between the north and south Sahara; there have been empires such as the Khanate of the Golden Horde, which were based primarily upon overland relationships. But three points are evident: (1) Where navigable waters are available man, throughout history, has utilized them in preference to overland routes. In the conduct of relations beyond the immediate proximity, navigable waters have been a more important avenue than has land. (2) Both quantitatively and qualitatively, overwater relations have proved more pervasive than have overland relations. Thus, the historic overland migrations tended to be single-shot in nature; their routes did not form the channel for continuing cross-fertilization of the cultures located at the originating and terminal points of the migration. Similarly, the overland empires, such as that of the Golden Horde, proved to have little enduring impact upon the peoples of their further reaches.[10] The Chinese cultural impact remained confined to the river valleys and coastal plains, but had little impact upon the peoples of southern China, Tibet, Sinkiang, and Mongolia. Portuguese and Spanish culture had an enduring impact upon the variegated coastal-oriented people of South America, but much less a one upon those of the interior. Indeed, the influence of Castilian culture upon the coastal and riverine people of those territories in South America once controlled by Spain has been greater than it has been upon the Basques and Catalonians of territorial Spain. It is apparent, therefore, that the interrelationship which was noted between water transport and acculturation in South Asia is not unique to that region. (3) Important overwater contacts have been conducted, often without distance having any discernible impact, while territorially adjacent areas frequently have experienced little intercommunication.

II

The impact of technology upon "meaningful distance" has been a great and an accelerating one in quantitative measure. But has it altered or merely magnified the comparative disadvantage of land travel? An answer requires that one differentiate distance in terms of transportation, communications, and military strategy.

The continuous erection of road, rail, and pipeline networks is certainly evidence of man's progress in overcoming barriers to overland transportation. Nonetheless it remains the case that the water transport of bulk items is by far the most efficient method. As but one illustration, consider the cost ratio of various forms of bulk-oil transport within the United States as compared with ship transport: movement by pipeline is four times as expensive; by railroad, twenty-two times; and by truck, seventy-five times more costly.[11*]

Despite the proliferation of networks of other forms of surface transport, such figures make evident that water transport, wherever available, would be the preferred method for the movement of bulk goods.[12] Illustrative of this preference is the fact that 70 percent of all tonnage

---

* These comparative costs altered significantly in the course of the next quarter-century. In 1987, James Morris wrote ("America's Stepchild: The Maritime World," *Wilson Quarterly* 11 [Summer 1987]: 118) that tramp ships (ships usually hired for a single carriage) moved goods for "one percent the cost of aircraft, five percent that of trucks, and ten percent that of trains." Ship transport therefore retained a substantial comparative advantage, although the gap between it and both trucks and trains had been very substanially altered. The alteration was due to new technology, including so-called RO/RO (Roll-on/Roll-off) ships, and worldwide adoption of standard size containers for the carriage of bulk goods (which permitted the rapid interchange of cargo among ship, truck, and train).

shipped in and out of United States ports represents intra-United States trade.* Similarly, in functional though not in political terms, there is justification for considering the Panama Canal an internal waterway; one-sixth of all shipping through the canal is merely en route from one United States coast to the other.** San Francisco is closely tied to New York by water transport, despite the fact that the navigable water distance between the two is more than twice the overland distance, is greater than the distance from New York to Rio or Istanbul, and is greater than the distance from San Francisco to the ports of Japan and Korea. The same comparative advantage explains why the transport of goods between Alaska and the group of forty-eight states south of Canada is conducted essentially as though each were an island. And it lends a measure of truth to the occasional slip of writers and speakers when they refer to the forty-eight states as "the continental United States," in contradistinction to the Hawaiian and, inferentially, the Alaskan Islands. It also explains why the Alaska Highway, constructed during World War II for strategic reasons, has been of negligible economic importance. Where alternate sea lanes are available, lengthy roads such as the Alaska and the still uncompleted Pan American Highways are principally of touristic, psychological, and highly localized economic value.

Air freight is also at a disadvantage. Its importance is still limited to those classes of goods which enjoy a high value-to-volume ratio, to situations in which rapid delivery is important, and to situations in which alternate methods of transport are unavailable.

---

* Owing in large part to the change in comparative costs, the figure of 70 percent had dropped to 51 percent by 1989. [Extrapolated from table 1060 in U.S. Bureau of the Census, *Statistical Abstract of the United States: 1992* (Washington, D.C., 1992).]

** The marked increase in the size of vessels (both containerships and supertankers) has subsequently decreased the significance of the Canal to U.S. trade, as the percentage of vessels too large for the Canal's lock system has accelerated. However, so far as oil shipments from Alaska to the East Coast are concerned, the narrowness of the Isthmus retains its importance; the building of a petroleum pipeline system paralleling the Canal means that the overwater transport of this commodity is only interrupted by the narrow width of the Panamian Isthmus. By contrast, as a result of (1) the container revolution, and (2) the long delays suffered by even the smaller vessels waiting to use the Canal, the latter has lost important West Coast to East Coast cargo (particularly Japanese motor vehicles) to U.S. railroads. Whether an often proposed sea-level canal would reroute this trade through the Isthmus is a subject of some debate both in Japan and the United States.

The role of water travel relative to passenger transport is, of course, vastly different; and it loses primacy to air travel and to land travel where adequate roads and railways are available. The pattern is not a simple one, however. While air travel is quite obviously the most important means of traversing long distances between important urban areas, it remains an inadequate means of reaching destinations of lesser import. Tales concerning the need to expend more time in reaching a relatively nearby airport than in traveling between two distant cities are now common ingredients of travelers' lore. Since commercial intercontinental flights have long been a reality, such tales emphasize once more the inherent danger of assuming "land connects, water divides." They also raise the far broader question of the degree to which personal travel possesses significance for intercultural relations.

Capitals of Third World states may be hours from Paris or Washington, and days, or even weeks, from points within their own states. As a result, the impact of air travel upon the great majority of the world's people has been negligible. Indeed, even in the case of states which possess a good intrastate transportation system, the direct impact of personal travel upon the society is minute. The average American, Frenchman, or Russian is not significantly affected by the coming and going of interstate travelers at New York, Paris, or Moscow airports; nor is his culture. On the other hand, if one is talking about the simultaneous visits of a foreign element in sufficiently large numbers to have a cultural impact,[13] then one could contend that the presence of the foreigner in such numbers is at least as apt to give rise to cultural isolation characterized by ethnocentrism and xenophobia. Intercultural person-to-person contacts, unless the necessary concomitant of some mutually desired function (trade or the prosecution of a military alliance in the face of a mutually recognized threat, for example), are apt to prove either unimportant or pernicious.

To contend that the impact of transcultural person-to-person contacts is probably not very great is not to be blind to the evidence that most societies today are culturally less isolated than formerly, and, therefore, more closely reflect one another in current tastes in music, dress, movies, architectural and structural design, student riots, and so forth. But two points should be noted. The first is that this transstate acculturation has not been due to personal contacts but to (1) the greatly increased interchange of goods, including such particularly pertinent items as machine tools, films, and technological and popular journals, (2) more efficient transcultural communications, and (3) the proliferation of multistate corporations such as General Motors, Uniroyal (formerly U.S. Rubber), and the International Business Machines Corporation, which facilitate the unencumbered intracorporate, interstate exchange of research results, style design, production methodology, and patents.[14] The second point is that the degree of this transcultural impact varies tremendously among states. Its most highly developed manifestation is most commonly held to be the recent impact of the United States upon the states of Western Europe—a transocean, not a transland relationship!

Technology appears to be reinforcing the primacy of water as an intercultural connector. Super-tankers, container-cargoes, proportionately smaller crews, nuclear propulsion advances, artificial deep-draft harbors, increasing mechanization of unloading and loading processes, and more powerful ice-breakers are all increasing the relative efficiency of sea transport. Investments in such developments by industry and the continued emphasis by governments upon improving water travel indicate their expectation of the indefinite paramountcy of sea transport. The current plan of the government of the Soviet Union, for example, calls for increased outlays for inland waterways, and its efforts to make the "northeast passage" along the Arctic coast utilizable during longer periods of the year continue to have a high priority. Farther west plans are now underway to connect the Baltic and Black seas via the Rhine and Danube rivers.* United States interest in improving the Saint Lawrence Seaway and in creating a larger canal across the Isthmus of Panama offer still additional evidence of the optimistic future anticipated for water transport.[15] The advent of the "Air Age" and, more recently, the "Space Age," have not signified the deathknell of the "Sea Age."

The concept of communications distance offers a number of parallels with what has been said concerning air transport. Principal urban areas of the world are interconnected by communication channels without regard to distance or intervening oceans, while it is often much more difficult to make contact between those urban areas and nearby hinterlands. Despite some past technical problems in developing underseas telephone cables, the tendency for interstate channels of communication to be determined by demand rather than by distance or the intervening physical medium is evidenced by the often publicized fact that telephonic communication between South American capitals travels through New York, and two African points are in many instances telephonically joined only by a European detour.[16] The significance of such routes is in the lie they give to concepts of continental insularity and solidarity.

Recent technological developments and projected advances in the use of telecommunication satellites will bring all states, without regard

* By late 1992, the canal had been completed and was in service.

to location, closer together in communicative distance. Intelsat satellites are even now available for the commercial use of telephone, telegraph, radio, and television transmission, and a vast extension of services is contemplated.

By itself, however, such a globe-girdling system will not affect areas otherwise poorly serviced by communications facilities. Continents will be more closely joined, capitals will be more closely joined, but sections of many states may remain essentially incommunicado.

Much publicity has been given in recent years to the integrating impact which the spread of the inexpensive transistor radio is having upon the less accessible areas of the states of Africa and Asia. Two warnings are appropriate, however. The first is that very little is known concerning either the degree or the nature of the impact of one-way communications. The phrase "meaningful monologue" is yet to be coined. Second, if the basic language, dialect, and colloquialisms common to the transmitting area are indistinguishable from those in the receiving area, then the two areas have long enjoyed an intensive, intracultural relationship. In such case, radio is merely augmenting an existing interrelationship, not creating a new one. If, on the other hand, language or dialect differs, then the announcer, even assuming that he can be understood, risks drawing attention to divisive rather than to common traits. If the programmers decide that it is best to make announcements in the local dialect or language, the question arises whether communications are strengthening intercultural contacts or cultural self-awareness. The transistors scattered among the tribes of northern and northeastern Thailand have been the means by which Peking and Hanoi draw attention, in the local dialect, to the distinctions and divisions between the listeners and the ruling Thais. Bangkok counters by broadcasts in the local tongues. In such a situation can one safely speak of transistorized assimilation? Or is it safer to note that cultural distance is being increased by the shortening of communications distance?[17]

III

The concept of strategic distance may appear anachronistic. In programming targets for ICBMs, distance is immaterial, and it is also inconsequential whether the target be overland or overseas. Submarine-launched, intermediate-range missiles, however, continue to play an important role in the strategic planning of nuclear powers, so it might be noted that ocean relationships between potential enemies do affect vulnerability. Here again water connects and land separates, for the only meaningful measurement in this context is the distance of a target from the nearest major body of ocean-connected water. Again, it is within this context that Omaha is one of the least vulnerable spots within the United States.

In any event, assuming that one *must* rule out the occurrence of nuclear warfare, distinctions between sea and land distances do retain strategic significance. Judging by their actions it appears most likely that those states in possession of modern weapons are not apt to confront each other directly, but that their interests are apt to be contested by proxy in relatively minor struggles. Soviet post–World War II practice, recent British and French retrenchment on international commitments, articles on people's wars by Chinese leaders, and the panoply of responses by Americans to involvement in Vietnam make it most improbable that nationals of the major states will participate directly in these struggles in large numbers. If present practices continue, however, the major states can be expected to provide essential logistics. And here one returns to the clear advantage of ship transport, for one of the strange rules of the new "proxy wars" of the major states is total respect for freedom of the seas. During the Vietnam War, Haiphong and Cam Ranh Bay were doorways between a peace zone and a war zone; the United States and the Soviet Union were able to transport supplies to Vietnam as readily as they could, in the event of similar struggles, to Germany, Tanzania, or Venezuela. If a state possesses a reserve capability with regard to its merchant marine, the discrepancy of a few days in sea journey does not strategically affect the situation once goods have begun to arrive. For example, the difference in shipping time from the Persian Gulf to Britain via the Cape of Good Hope, as compared with the Suez Canal route, is approximately seventeen days. But the longer distance necessitated by the closing of the canal during 1967 affected the scale of deliveries to Britain for only a short time. Once the time gap between the arrival of the last tanker to pass through the canal, and the arrival of the first vessel via the Cape had been closed, a compensatory increase in cargo capacity on the new run could and did neutralize the adverse effect of the canal's closing. There is, of course, an economic advantage in shortening distance. But the relative insignificance of this consideration is illustrated by the fact that much of the oil shipping will continue to use the Cape route after the canal is reopened. Costs associated with the seventeen-day delay are more than offset by the use of supertankers too large for the canal and by the avoidance of canal fees.

Similarly, the overseas distance involved in the supplying of a war has little strategic significance, if the freedom-of-the-seas principle is observed. The important logistical problems of the Vietnam War did not involve the movement of goods to Cam Ranh Bay, but rather their unloading and their movement once ashore. The logistical distance from the closest port to a point in Laos, Sikkim, Niger, or Bolivia would unquestionably prove greater than the distance from that port to the United States. Guerrilla interdiction, inadequate road and rail networks, and the natural disadvantage of land transport are all involved.

There is, to be sure, one phenomenon in relation to which water could be said to separate and land to connect. This phenomenon involves a second strange rule of contemporary warfare, as manifested in the practice of states. The rule holds (1) that in a "revolutionary warfare" situation supporters of each side will pay lip-service to the traditional view of the sanctity of borders (that is, that the government of one state should not become involved in affairs occurring on the other side of a state border without the permission of that state, nor should it permit activities on its side of the border which affect the internal affairs of the other state); (2) that the antirevolutionary government and its supporters are in practice to observe the traditional sanctity of borders; and (3) that the revolutionary movement and its supporters will then use the sacrosanct side of the border for sanctuaries and for logistical avenues. As a result of this new practice, the significance of a common border between two states, in which the leaders of one desire the revolutionary overthrow of the government of the other, has been enormous in terms of the revolution's success or failure. When Yugoslavia, following its break with the Soviet Union, closed its borders to Greek revolutionaries, the movement within Greece rapidly dissipated. Similarly, the insurrectionist movement within what was then British Malaya was never very effective, in part because the Thai government was not kindly disposed toward permitting its territory to be used by the guerrillas. On the other hand, the Algerian National Liberation Front was able to use Moroccan and Tunisian territory both for sanctuary and as a means of obtaining supplies. The post-1949 use of Chinese territory for the same two purposes by the Viet Minh is well known. So, too, is the use by Hanoi of Laotian territory for supply lines (the Ho Chi Minh Trail) and Cambodian territory for both sanctuary and supply lines. Similar use of Tanzania and the Democratic Republic of Congo has been made by groups desiring to "liberate" Mozambique and Angola.

A government is therefore more immune to revolutionary movements if it does not adjoin another state. This certainly does not mean that island states are impervious to revolutions, as evidenced by the case of Cuba. But an ocean border does preclude the establishment of sanctuarial headquarters and supply depots immediately across the border. Moreover, it is much more difficult to supply war materiel from outside the state *without detection*. Policing a coast may pose problems, particularly if the coastal waters are customarily cluttered with large numbers of fishing boats, junks, sampans, dhows, and the like; but it is vastly easier than policing a land border of equivalent length. The Huk movement within the Philippines had serious problems obtaining supplies, as did the Communist movement in Java once it became a truly revolutionary movement (once it lost the support of the government following the abortive coup). Castro's frustrated desires to export his revolution throughout Latin America are well documented. How different would be the situation had he come to power in Venezuela or some other "mainland" state. But it is the interposition of the water and not the actual overseas distance that is the key to Castro's frustration; Jamaica is as remote as Brazil.

Overwater location, then, offers a measure of insularity from the effects of the contemporary propensity of revolution-oriented states to disregard the sanctity of borders when it suits their cause to do so. At the same time another—and more significant—practice of contemporary warfare, the recognition of the freedom-of-the-seas principle, results in the potential linkage of all coastal states without much regard being owed to distance.

The impact which the air transport of military contingents is apt to have upon military strategy as yet defies measurement. France has, in a state of readiness, the capability to establish a limited presence in former French Africa on very short notice. Britain claims it will maintain a similar capacity with regard to Malaysia and Singapore. In 1968 the United States conducted trans-Atlantic air maneuvers in order to illustrate its capacity for rapidly increasing its forces in Europe; a similar airborne operation was conducted in Korea in March 1969. Even if one acknowledges severe limitations on the part of air transport as a means of supplying sustained, large-scale operations, such a capability, regardless of importance, only augments what has been said concerning sea transport and clearly points up the inaccuracy of equating strategic distance with actual mileage.

An examination of economic, communicative, and strategic distance, therefore, leads to the conclusion that distance is either meaningless— ICBM distance or intercapital communicative distance, for example— or that overwater distance is less segregative than overland distance. The forementioned formula should therefore be amended to read: *If distance is a meaningful consideration, then two points connected by water are closer than two points equally distant but separated by land.* Inexactitude, however, has not prevented the broad-scale acceptance of the uncorrected formula, as manifested in popularly held myths of hemispheric, continental, regional, and state unity. All such myths contain two potential fallacies: (1) that the particular unit, whether a hemisphere, continent, region, or state, is somehow integrated, and (2) that significant interests are not shared with those beyond the land borders of the unit.

IV

Hemispheric Myths. Enough has been said concerning the so-called "Western Hemisphere" to indicate that geographic misconceptions concerning hemispheric relations underlie many important political decisions. There is a fallacy built into the division of the world into two parts and in assigning to each half a title such as "Western" and "Eastern" or "Northern" and "Southern." It lends a sense of naturalness to a dissection that is in fact totally arbitrary, and it posits the existence of intrahemispheric relations, which may be absent, to the exclusion of interhemispheric relations, which *are* present. Even if cultural distances could be measured in actual mileage—which they cannot—it should be evident that two points immediately on either side of a mythical hemisphere dividing line are closer than either is to the geographic center of its respective hemisphere. Perhaps televised views of earth from space flights will ultimately rid man of one of his favorite myths, for even while he watches the earth is offering to his vision an uninterrupted series of hemispheres. When man at the subconscious level comes to realize that the number of hemispheres is infinite he will perhaps also realize that the number of possible interhemispheric relations of a cultural and political nature are likewise infinite. The patterns of intercultural relations have little to do with hemispheres. British and United States cultural ties are, at least in this period of history, more pervasive than those between the United States and Mexico. Similarly, Australia and New Zealand are closely tied to Britain and the United States despite an intervening equatorial line which demarcates northern and southern hemispheres.

Continental Myths. It is in continental myths that the "land connects, water divides" fallacy most commonly manifests itself. African continentalism, perhaps because it is the most youthful, has recently been the most vehemently articulated. African cohesion has been an a priori assumption of a number of statesmen such as Touré, Nkrumah, and Nyerere, and the assumption has been institutionalized in the Organization of African Unity. One of its more colorful articulations was made by Gamal Abdal Nasser [of Egypt] in 1953:

If we consider next . . . the continent of Africa—I may say without exaggeration that we cannot, under any circumstances, however much we might desire it, remain aloof from the terrible and sanguinary conflict going on there today between five million whites and 200 million Africans. We cannot do so for an important and obvious reason: we are *in* Africa. The peoples of Africa will continue to look to us, who guard their northern gate, and who constitute their link with the outside world. We will never in any circumstances be able to relinquish our responsibility to support, with all our might, the spread of enlightenment and civilization to the remotest depths of the jungle.[18]

The quotation is interesting as an example of how one who, according to the most common anthropological taxonomy, is a caucasoid may nevertheless identify himself with nonwhites by stressing a georacial relationship; it is also a declaration of what might be termed "the Arab man's burden," which has been thrust upon him because some of the Arabs live in Africa. But for present purposes it is most interesting because it raises the question: In what way does Egypt or the entire northern littoral of Africa represent "the link with the outside world" for Dakar, Lagos, Cape Town, Cape Elizabeth, Dar es Salaam, and others?

Even a cursory glance at the transportation map of Africa will dramatize the absence of interconnecting facilities among the widely separated, important pockets of population. There is no African hub from which roads and railways emanate outward. Rather, the pattern of the transportation system, including navigable rivers, caravan routes, roads, and railways, consists of a number of seldom interconnected inward thrusts, usually short, from various points on the coast. South Africa is the only state whose interior could be said to be adequately serviced by a transportation system. There is no transcontinental railroad from north to south and, north of Rhodesia [Zimbabwe], none from east to west. The transportation map makes clear that economic and cultural ties among nonadjoining sub-Saharan African states have been practically nonexistent. Most societies of interior Africa have been essentially culturally isolated, while those riverine, coastal, and railroad-neighboring peoples who have been affected by other societies have been most affected by ones outside Africa.

The case of South America is similar. The area has indeed merited the epithet "the hollow continent," for climate and topography have combined to orient the important enclaves outward—that is, the key societies have had their backs to the continent. The dominance of a common Latin culture in most of the states is not denied, but this same culture is shared by the peoples of many of the islands of the Caribbean and the

Iberian Peninsula. By itself, then, the common culture does not prove continental solidarity. More instructive is the persistence of the more indigenous Indian cultures which dominate most of the interior and separate the Latin enclaves. Only in recent years has there been a real attempt by many of the capitals to make highway and cultural contact with the interior. That interstate relations have occurred among Buenos Aires, Bogota, and Lima is fully acknowledged, but their landed relationship has quite evidently been relatively insignificant.

The Asian pattern is also characterized by a number of major cultural pockets, each oriented to the periphery rather than to the interior. Contacts between the steppe- and highland-dwelling peoples on the one hand, and the riverine- and coastal-dwelling peoples on the other have been insignificant, as shown, for example, by the rather meager impact that Han-Chinese culture has had upon the peoples of noncoastal, peripheral China. Moreover, transcontinental relations often have been more significant than intracontinental, as signified by the impact of British culture upon the language and political institutions of the subcontinent. Finally, it might be noted that while the phrase is geographically incorrect, the relative absence of overland contacts does cause references to the Chinese of South Asia as "overseas Chinese" to acquire a measure of cultural accuracy.

Of all the expressions conveying continental unity, one would anticipate "European" to be the most meaningful. For generations "the Continent" has meant mainland Europe, and to be "continental" has been to display cultural mannerisms common to Europe. A large measure of cultural integration would certainly appear consonant with the often publicized common Greco-Roman heritage. But how is one to reconcile this concept of "Europeanness" with the history of that area for the past two hundred years? No area of similar size has offered so drastic an illustration of divisiveness, reflecting strong national jealousies and rivalries. There is no reconciliation because a single European culture is a fiction, and a multiplicity of languages, dialects, religious denominations, and other cultural manifestations is the fact. The smallest of the multistate continents is incredibly diverse; a land connection has not made the German more French or vice versa. Emphasis has been on the particular cultural unit, and "Europeanness" has been only a myth. Historically, attempts to unify Europe (1) have not been the result of a "natural" growth of contacts but of coercive superimposition, (2) have been undertaken not in the name of Europe, but in the name of a particular national group, and (3) have been defeated by the stout resistance of groups desirous of cultural and political autonomy.

With the notable exception of Charles de Gaulle, few have spoken of European unity in the post–World War II period, because of the Communist/non-Communist division. On each side of that line, however, there has been a subsequent attempt at regional integration. By increasing economic contacts, both the EEC and CEMA hopefully envisage the unification of six states. Though the total area of each represents only a small segment of all of Europe, the problems with which each has been confronted due to competing nationalisms are instructive. At the minimum they can be said to illustrate the fallacy of automatically assuming historic common interests and characteristics among even adjoining states.

The illusory nature of continental concepts is perhaps best illustrated by a question with which scholars and orators have grappled for centuries: Where does Asia end and Europe begin? The fictitious bifurcation of the land mass is an acknowledgment that overland contacts between its Pacific and Atlantic shores have been unimportant, but the attempt at geographic division is, in essence, the attempt to determine a line on one side of which all the immediately local people look westward while, on the other side, they look eastward. Such an inanity would hardly warrant consideration were it not for the impact that it continues to exert on human convictions. De Gaulle, for example, often spoke of a Europe for the Europeans, stretching from the Atlantic to the Urals, as though the Soviet Union [Russia] were prepared either to divest itself of its holdings east of that mountain range or were able to differentiate between the interests of its European and Asian components. A physical watershed need not be a human one.

The problem of differentiating Europe and Asia does not end with the Soviet Union. Is Turkey, with territory on either side of the straits, to be considered Asian? The matter is further complicated by the fact that the Ottoman Turks came originally from central Asia, but at least since the time of Attaturk have considered themselves European. Does Europe stop even at the eastern border of Turkey? Turkic peoples stretch almost uninterruptedly from Turkey to western China. Moreover, how is one to explain the exclusion from Europe of the Indo-European language area of Iran, West Pakistan, and northern India? Cultural contacts and political borders have shown a remarkable disregard for continental divisions.

The term *continent* derives from *continere*, meaning to hold together, to repress, to contain. The expression, therefore, least applies to Europe, because culture groups of that region can claim a greater global impact for ideas and customs than can be claimed for the cultures of any other region. "The Sea Age," "The Age of Discovery," "The Age of Imperialism," "Colonialism," "Neo-colonialism," and the prevalence of French, Spanish, Portuguese, and English in the most widely scattered regions of the world are all testaments to the fact that Europe was certainly not a contained unit. Myths need not accord with reality, but it is particularly ironic that former French leader de Gaulle should have opposed an Atlantic community, denying a role to the United States with regard to the states of Europe, simply because the United States is not European. Conveniently ignored were such matters as early French interest in the exploration of North America, France's alliance with the United States in the Revolutionary War, the United States–French transaction involving the Louisiana Territory, the United States–French alliances of World Wars I and II, de Gaulle's own interest in Quebec, and France's continued control of the trans-Atlantic islands of Saint Pierre and Miquelon, Guadeloupe, and Martinique, and of the trans-Atlantic mainland territory of French Guiana.

V

Regional Myths.   As in the case of hemispheres one can postulate as many regions as imagination permits. "Latin America," for example, is larger than a single continent, although regional terms are usually employed in reference to an area smaller than a continent but containing a number of states. The minimal implication is that the peoples of the region possess a number of important characteristics in common, which justifies its treatment as a distinct and separate entity. Seldom, however, do regional terms warrant such an unqualified ascription. Although it always possessed the danger of obscuring essential distinctions, the phrase "Latin America" was, until recently, a convenient shorthand expression for all of the independent states of North and South America plus the neighboring islands, minus Canada and the United States. The acquisition of statehood by Guyana, Jamaica, Trinidad-Tobago, and Barbados, as well as the anticipated statehood of British Honduras [Belize], however, antiquates the expression and again emphasizes the dangers of indiscriminately relating culture and location.

Other regional expressions are seldom more satisfying. Their arbitrariness is evident by the great variations in their geographic definitions over different periods and among authors in any given period. Changes in political borders and the relative knowledge of the complexities of the societies within the region help account for the geographic disparities in their descriptions. The region of the Near East, for example, is defined in the third edition of *Webster's New International Dictionary* as follows: "used originally of the Balkan States, later of the region included in the Ottoman Empire, and now often of all the countries of southeastern Europe, entire area extending from Libya or Morocco, Ethiopia, and Somalia to Greece, Turkey, Iran, Afghanistan, and sometimes India." One is tempted to ask: Inclusive or exclusive? The task of giving definition to the multiple definitions of such terms merits only sympathy, not criticism, and one can readily excuse, therefore, the oversight concerning Turkish territory in southeastern Europe; Greece's exclusion from southeastern Europe is more perplexing.

The incredible lack of precision in such terms would be humorous were it not for their tendency to evoke stereotyped images predicated upon the myth of cultural homogeneity. The images, in turn, hamper proper analysis.

The phrase "Southeast Asia" in most texts refers to Burma [Myanmar], Thailand, Malaysia, Singapore, Laos, Cambodia, the Vietnams, Indonesia, and the Philippines. The usual pattern of restricting regional groupings to landed relationships is broken here by the inclusion of Indonesia and the Philippines. Indonesia, which stretches some three thousand miles from west to east, reaches farther east than the farthest of the Far East states, Japan. Australia, which is excluded, is only a few miles across the Torres Strait from Indonesian territory. The Philippines, although also close to Indonesia, are markedly farther from the southeast Asian mainland than they are from China and Taiwan. The inclusion of the archipelagoes is due, of course, to the common ethnic heritage of the dominant group of mainland Malaysia with that of the Philippines and Indonesia. In the case of the Philippines this approach stresses early history, and, by contrast, ignores the fact that since 1500 Spain and the United States have had a greater cultural impact on the Philippines than have intraregional contacts, as evidenced by the prevalence of Catholicism and the widespread use of English. Moreover, it overlooks the fact that the dominant culture of Java is not the dominant culture of all of the Indonesian islands, including the two largest in terms of territory. But what is more important, if dominant culture is to be the criterion of membership, the off-African island of Madagascar (the Malagasy Republic) should have been included because of its Malay heritage. And Singapore, because of its dominant Chinese culture, should be considered part of the Far East not Southeast Asia. So, too, should that area populated by the Vietnamese. The puzzled responses evoked by the political activism of Buddhist monks in Vietnam would have been less common if there were broader awareness that Vietnamese culture is much more a reflection of the cultures to its north than it is of those to its west, and that the northern, Mahayana Buddhism, common to China, Korea, Japan, and Vietnam, differs from the more pacifist Theravada (Hinayana) Buddhism of Burma, Thailand, and Cambodia.

Two points are clear. Southeast Asia, just as the Far East, the Middle East, the Near East, Western Europe, sub-Sahara Africa, and other such geographic regions, is a highly diversified area, and it is the distinctions rather than common characteristics which are usually of key political importance. Second, regional categorization is dangerous not only because it tends to obscure important distinctions, but also because it tends to ignore important interregional relationships.

State Myths.   Of all the territorial concepts—hemisphere, continent, region, and state—it is the last which most resists generalization in terms of the degree of cultural, economic, and political integration. Some states, such as Japan, are quite thoroughly fused; others, such as Nigeria, are characterized by marked heterogeneity and centrifugal tendencies. Perhaps such discrepancies should be expected in confronting a unit which is found in such disparate territorial sizes. Canada, for example, is larger than Europe, and the Soviet Union [was] two to three times as large as either; at the other extreme, the Maldive Islands are approximately one-tenth the size of Rhode Island. Yet, from earlier statements, it should be evident that more important than the area is the distribution of population in relation to ease of intercommunication.

It is likely, however, that one must further differentiate between "natural" avenues of easy access, such as rivers and coasts, and artificial, manmade avenues, such as railroads and highways. There is little question that a highly intensive, modern transportation and communications network indicates extensive economic interrelationships, but its intercultural impact is less certain. Granted, it is a truism that centralized communications and increased economic contacts help to dissolve sectional cultural distinctions within what is fundamentally a one-culture state such as the United States. On the other hand, if one is dealing with two distinct cultures, is it possible that increased contacts are apt to perpetuate and perhaps exacerbate nationalistic proclivities and particularism? Problems between the Walloons and Flemish of Belgium, the French-speaking and English-speaking Canadians, the Serbs and Croats of Yugoslavia, and the Czechs and Slovaks of Czechoslovakia have increased with increased contacts.

The fact is that very little is known concerning the assimilation process. Because its essence is psychological, involving self-acceptance, it is very conceivable that programs designed for its accomplishment are doomed to failure; or, to put it more positively, that successful assimilation may best be achieved by contacts which are not made for that purpose. The Arab trader who in the midst of the busy bazaar of a sub-Saharan city quite unselfconsciously prostrates himself on his prayer rug may exert greater cultural magnetism than the dedicated proselytizer. The Soviet Union, despite a half-century of ethnic plans and programs, is still plagued by "the national question." The failure of India and Pakistan to achieve their formal, constitutional commitment to have their varied peoples accept Hindi and Urdu respectively is also pertinent. So, too, is Franco's failure to Castilianize the Catalans and Basques. Such examples of resistance to governmental programs of assimilation could be multiplied. Programmed assimilation appears to produce an opposite effect. Assimilation is apparently most apt to be achieved as an accidental by-product, not by design.

A related factor is that assimilation probably requires a period of great duration, extending well beyond a generation. More intensive contacts, whether by design or accident, may not only fail to telescope the process, but may well arouse a psychological barrier. Variations in tempo of intercultural contacts may not be merely a matter of degree, but may represent a qualitative consideration which determines whether a people move toward assimilation or ethnocentrism. The assimilation of all of the riverine people of China into the Han culture was accomplished only over many centuries. The post-1949 Chinese attempt to bring its remaining minorities into the state's cultural mainstream through greatly expanded contacts has resulted in substantial intergroup antagonisms.[19] Many contemporary states, indeed most of the states of Africa, Asia, and Latin America, contain large areas which have hitherto not been connected by arteries of transportation and communication. Such isolation is expected to alter rapidly, but the nature of the cultural result may be very different from that which is usually envisaged. Cultural integration cannot be assumed.

It is also probable that assimilation involves not only the question of duration but of chronological time as well. At least in "assimilationist time" the telephone, radio, train, and motor vehicle are very recent introductions and, what is of greatest importance, postdate the advent of the age of nationalism. The people who succumbed to foreign cultural inroads prior to the eighteenth century were not aware of belonging to a developed, competing civilization, in which they had hitherto taken great pride. By contrast, peoples everywhere today are much more apt to be aware of their membership in a group possessed of a history, customs, beliefs, and perhaps a language which distinguish it from other ethnic groups.[20] There are many reasons for this increase in ethnic consciousness, a major one of which has been the great increase in the frequency, the scope, and the type of intra- and intercultural contacts. But regardless of its cause, such cultural awareness is apt to hamper seriously any movement toward assimilation, and intercultural contacts are apt to strengthen the ethnic bond. It has been broadly assumed that an excellent communications and transportation network throughout a state has been a contributor to the cultural integration of all affected parts. While granting that such a network has tended to neutralize minor regional distinctions, it is more likely that the growth of an arterial system has occurred within what was already a fundamentally homogeneous cultural unit. Communications and transportation connections often strengthen common ties. But does this not portend an Iboland rather than a Nigeria, a Kurdistan rather than an Iraq, a Tibet instead of present China, a true Ukraine State rather than the USSR, a Flanders instead of a Belgium? *The "Age of Nationalism" may have heralded the end of assimilation.* And the end of assimilation portends increasing demands for the radical redrawing of most of today's political borders.

The matter is of the greatest importance, for the majority of states are multi-ethnic. Growing ethnic consciousness translated into self-determination movements is already challenging existing political structures without regard to hemisphere, continent, or region. Myths of unity to the contrary, even most states are culturally divided. The growing demand today, for good or evil, is to make reality approximate the myth of state unity by redrawing borders to reflect ethnic unity.

VI

Myths vary greatly in the degree to which they accord with fact. Regardless of their factual basis, however, myths engender a reality of their own, for it is seldom *what is* that is of political significance, but what people *think is*. If United States leaders have believed that a special relationship has existed between the United States and the states of South America because of their landed connection, then special ties do in fact exist, regardless of the questionability of their underlying assumption. Why, then, refute myths of unity? Surely a misconception which gives rise to a conviction of a trans-state mutuality of interests, thereby promoting harmony, deserves cultivation not criticism.

The response must be that while myths of unity have a capacity for engendering harmony they also have a capacity for accentuating division. And the myths are invoked more often for the latter. The notion of "Africa for the Africans" is the result of a fallacious belief in intracontinental relations which never existed. It has also been the justification for expelling people of Asian heritage from East Africa, despite (1) the fact that the expellees were in most instances born in East Africa, and (2) that East Africa has had interrelations with Asia going back thousands of years, while its relations with the African interior have been virtually nonexistent. Any geographic myth of unity, short of global scope, presupposes exclusivity.

Basing one's assumptions on myths also hampers logical analysis and can lead to questionable judgments. For example, it has long been accepted that colonialism per se is bad. But implicit in the popular definition of colonialism is the myth "water separates, land connects." Thus only if salt water flows between the mother country and the territory is it colonialism. The Soviet Union and China are seldom castigated for perpetuating colonialism, despite the fact that each contains huge areas, residues of an imperial age, which are populated by distinct minorities.

Another illustration of a questionable conclusion predicated upon the "water separates" myth is the concept of "spheres of influence." A recent manifestation is the position which holds that United States involvement in South Asia [i.e., during the Vietnam War] violates geographic logic. It is "natural," according to this school, for the Chinese "colossus of the north" to exert predominance throughout the region. As has been noted, however, the premise is not historically correct. Moreover, as long as freedom of the seas is observed, the United States advantage in sea transport places the coast of South Asia, including that of South Vietnam, closer to the United States than to China.

Myths of geographic unity not only obscure important interunit relations but also tend to obscure important intraunit distinctions. It is what divides men and not what they have in common which is the catalyst of political history. Surely tribal nationalism is a more momentous fact of the politics within Africa than is African harmony. Ethnic nationalism may well be the most explosive challenge to the survival of the Soviet Union. Proper analysis, therefore, requires that one differentiate myth from fact.

It is not one world but a highly variegated world. The same is true of hemispheres, continents, regions, and most states. The patterns of distinctions and similarities, of shared and competing interests, are incredibly complex and kaleidoscopic in their dynamism. Although no set of relations is truly global, attempts to restrict a description of human relations to any subdivision of the globe are intrinsically unsatisfactory. A knowledge of the geographic backdrop is essential to an understanding of contemporary world politics, but it is seldom a sufficient explanation and often a deluding one.

NOTES

1. For an earlier article concerned with this myth, see Eugene Staley, "The Myth of the Continents," *Foreign Affairs* 19 (1941): 481–94. Staley's analysis was essentially limited to the Western Hemisphere, and his primary aim was to counter the tendency, prevalent in the period prior to the attack on Pearl Har-

bor, to stress a hemispheric concept of defense at the expense of European ties. For a still earlier reference to the myth as applied to the Western Hemisphere, see William Stevens and Allan Wescott, *A History of Sea Power*, (New York, 1920), 2.

2. The statement is based upon the distance between New York City and the major port of each of the other states. It holds true for both sea and air travel. To anticipate a possible objection it might be noted that the ports of Chile are closer to New York than they are to U.S. west coast ports. Argentina is the farthest from New York, comparing unfavorably in this regard even with Turkey and the UAR [Egypt].

3. From a letter to his friend, Alexander von Humboldt. Quoted in Dexter Perkins, *A History of the Monroe Doctrine* (Boston, 1963), 22; emphasis added. It is assumed that the statement can be considered an accurate reflection of Jefferson's convictions, since it was not intended for publication.

4. Speech of 24 March 1818, cited in Perkins, *A History of the Monroe Doctrine*, 3–4; emphasis added.

5. Frederick Merk, *Manifest Destiny* (New York, 1963), 16, 28.

6. Perkins, *A History of the Monroe Doctrine*, 149; emphasis added.

7. Annual Message from President Roosevelt to the United States Congress, 6 December 1904, in William Williams, ed., *The Shaping of American Diplomacy* (Chicago, 1956), 530.

8. *Foreign Assistance Act of 1962, Title VI—Alliance for Progress*, sec. 251, par. (a); emphasis added.

9. There is some evidence that the Tigris-Euphrates civilization may antedate that of the Nile.

10. If, as it has long been assumed, the early Incas were not seafarers, the Inca empire would be an exception. But recent discoveries of pottery raise serious doubts about this assumption. See Walter Sullivan's article in the *New York Times*, 1 June 1969, and a description of a voyage by reed boat from Peru to Panama in the *New York Times*, 22 June 1969.

11. John Alexander, *Economic Geography* (Englewood Cliffs), N.J., 1963), 347.

12. The distance, of course, must be sufficiently great to offset the cost and inconvenience of transloading goods from truck or train to ship and vice versa. If the trip is relatively short, the advantage of direct rail or road transport from source to final destination will counter the lesser ton-mileage expense of ship transport. This fact accounts for the great loss in the *relative* importance of intrastate shipping within many states in recent years.

13. Recent illustrations might include Allied occupation forces following World War II, population transfers of Russians and Ukrainians into Kazakstan and other Asian areas of the Soviet Union, similar Chinese settlement in Sinkiang and Tibet, and the United States presence in South Vietnam and Thailand.

14. For a report of an interesting speech on multistate companies by the chairman of a large British concern, see the *Christian Science Monitor*, 25 April 1969. The speaker referred to such companies as "the decisive business institution of our time" and cited a prediction that "by 1988, the free world's economy

will be dominated by some 300 large companies responsible for most of the world's industrial output."

15. Perhaps the most publicized recent example of faith in the future of sea transport was offered by a private corporation, the Humble Oil and Refining Company, when in 1969 it supported a $30,000,000 venture in order to prove the feasibility of a year-round sea route along the northern coast of the North American continent. The venture was justified on the grounds of the immense savings that could be obtained by complete ship transport of the oil on the Alaskan North Slope to United States east coast ports. It was estimated that the alternative of moving oil to ships by a north-south trans-Alaskan pipeline would jump the total delivery price from $0.96 to $1.81 per barrel. See the *New York Times*, 18 August 1969.

16. See, for example, Albert Wohlstetter, "Illusions of Distance," Foreign Affairs 46 (1968): 248.

17. This subject is treated in greater detail below.

18. Gamal Abdal Nasser, *Egypt's Liberation: The Philosophy of the Revolution* (Washington, D.C., 1955), 109–10.

19. For some remarkably frank admissions concerning this matter by the Chinese Deputy Chairman of the Commission of Nationalities, see Liu Chun, *The National Question and Class Struggle* (Peking, 1966), particularly 18–22.

20. See chapter 1 in this volume.

Chapter Six

THE SEDUCTIVE LURE OF ECONOMIC
EXPLANATIONS

In chapter 2, we noted that a prevalent tendency among the "nation-building" school was "an unwarranted exaggeration of the influence of materialism upon human affairs." In chapter 3, we noted this same tendency on the part of scholars who have become aware of the growing power of ethnonationalism but who explain it in terms such as "relative economic deprivation," "internal colonialism," "competition for scarce resources," and the like. The following piece attempts to counter this very common tendency among scholars to explain ethnonationalism in economic terms. It was first presented at a conference at the University of Washington (Seattle) in 1976 and later, in expanded form, at Saint Antony's College, Oxford University, in 1979.

Eco- or Ethno-Nationalism?[*]

WHEN COMMENTING on a case of ethnonational conflict, spokesmen for at least one of the groups, newsmen, and scholars have all tended to emphasize the economic dimension of the struggle. Data concerned with intergroup differences in income, occupation, and general living standards are customarily given great prominence in such case studies, and the implicit or explicit message is that the conflict would tend to evaporate if these economic discrepancies were reduced or eradicated. The frequency of such analyses both reflects and reinforces a more generalized theory of group relations (usually called "the theory of relative economic deprivation") that maintains that ethnonationalism is at bottom economic in impulse.[1]

The tendency to stress economic forces can be viewed as one manifestation of a broader tendency to mistake the overt characteristics of a nation for its essence. The essence of the nation is psychological, a vivid sense of sameness or oneness of kind, which, from the perspective of the group, sets it off from all other groups in a most vital way. Following Max Weber's lead, we shall here employ the further refinement that this sense or consciousness of kind is derived from a *myth* of common descent.[2] Members of the nation feel or intuitively sense that they are related to one another.

Although the defining characteristic of the nation is psychological, a matter of group self-perception, any nation necessarily has its tangible characteristics. Any human grouping can be described in terms of a certain set of overt traits: vital statistics, population distribution, religious and linguistic composition, and so forth. But such characteristics are relevant to the notion of the nation only to the degree to which they contribute to the intuitive sense of kinship as well as to the sense of vital uniqueness from nonmembers. Nevertheless, in those cases in which a difference in some tangible characteristic tends to coincide rather closely with the division between two national groups, conflict between the two groups is apt to be explained in terms of the tangible discrepancy. Overt distinctions between the protagonists are found to be at the root of the struggle. Thus, the conflict between Walloon and

[*] Published in Walker Connor, "Eco- or Ethno-Nationalism?" *Ethnic and Racial Studies* 7 (October 1984): 342–59. Copyright © 1984 Routledge Journals.

Fleming has been quite regularly described as essentially linguistic, there being present no evident racial or religious differences. The turmoil in Northern Ireland between those who think of themselves as Irish and those who do not is facilely explained as a religious struggle, no other readily identifiable distinction, such as language or race, being in evidence. Guyana's major problem is seen as racial (between "Asians" and "Africans").

One of the more obvious ways in which the analyst can establish that such tangible considerations are not essential prerequisites for ethnonational conflict is through a broad comparative study of such conflicts. Such an approach confirms that ethnonational struggles have often arisen in the absence of language, race, and/or religious differences. However, the comparative approach does not so readily repudiate explanations for ethnonational conflict which are tied to economic causation because of the near universality with which economic factors *appear* to be involved in ethnonational problems. Analysts have been beguiled by the fact that observable economic discrepancies are near universal concomitants of ethnic strife. A comparison of the per capita income figures and occupational status of groups involved in such an issue will quite consistently show that a substantial variation exists between the groups.

Chi square assumptions to the contrary, however, this near-perfect frequency correlation may not tell us much about causation. With but very rare exceptions, ethnonational groups populate distinct territories, as is evidenced by the fact that it has been possible to produce ethnic maps covering all sectors of the globe. Granted, such cartographic projects have not been without problems. Zones particularly resistant to ethnic mapping have included (1) the shatter zones where two or more ethnic homelands converge and (2) immigrant societies composed of peoples who (or, more likely, whose ancestors) have left a variety of ethnic homelands. Additional complexities are caused by the fact that territories in which one group predominates often contain polygenetic cities and/or more broadly dispersed minorities. Nevertheless, as indicated by such terms as Bengal, Brittany, Croatia, Iboland, Ukraine, etc., ethnonational groups tend to populate distinctive territories.

The geographic distribution of ethnonational groups into distinctive homelands is sufficient in itself to assure the existence of economic discrepancies among groups. There is what might be termed a "law" of uneven, regional economic development. Though the unevenness is apparent when we contrast huge areas such as continents, most, if not all states also reflect economic differentials between regions. This is true of ethnically homogeneous and heterogeneous states alike; Germany, as well as France, illustrates notable sectional differences. Among the contributing factors are regional variations in such categories as (1) topography (ease of transportation), (2) climate, (3) soils, (4) availability of natural resources and raw materials, (5) population density, (6) the current technological capabilities of the local populace, (7) distance from potential markets, (8) the comparative advantage of local industry with regard to (a) age of plant and equipment and (b) margin of profit, and (9) the enduring effect of earlier decisions regarding investments and the locating of support industries and facilities (the infrastructure).[3]

As a result of (1) the geographic distribution of ethnonations and (2) the uneven economic development of regions, defining ethnonational conflicts in terms of economic inequality is a bit like defining them in terms of oxygen: where you find the one, you can be reasonably certain of finding the other. One of the great dangers of economic statistics when applied to ethnonational groups, therefore, is that the figures are apt to convey far more than they warrant. As noted, any categorization of humans can be expected to reflect statistical divergencies. Groups, whether ethnically heterogeneous or homogeneous, will customarily reflect variations not just with regard to socioeconomic matters, but also with regard to such diverse matters as median height and weight, age and sex distribution, and the per capita consumption of alcohol.[4] When, as in the case of economic statistics, the factor of uneven regional development is added, *statistically* significant variations between geographically distinguishable groups can be anticipated.

Spokesmen for ethnonational movements can nevertheless be expected to point to economic disparities as primia facie evidence of discrimination. "The figures speak for themselves!" is a well-worn saw. Armed with firm statistical evidence of economic disparities and supported by the protestations of disadvantaged groups, observers of ethnonational problems have been partial to socioeconomic explanations and to solutions aimed at a closing of economic gaps between groups, including, if necessary, recourse to quotas as a means of ensuring adequate group representation at all levels of professional attainment.

An interesting aspect of the charge of discrimination being practiced toward an ethnonational group is that it is essentially restricted to the state within which the purportedly aggrieved group resides. So far as economic statistics are concerned, it is well to remember that substantial variations among ethnic groups are not limited to *intra*state situations but exist as well relative to the dominant nationalities of other states (e.g., Scotsmen as contrasted with Great Russians, Germans, Han Chinese, or Swedes). Nevertheless, transstate accusations concerning the exploitation of one ethnonation by another have largely taken the form of very broad, abstract assertions concerning the world's "haves" and "have nots" (more recently, "the rich north" of the world versus "the poor south"), and have been limited in their appeal to a relatively few political elites and intellectuals. Charges that have struck a popular chord have been *intra-* rather than *inter*state in scope.[5] No popular charge has been made, for example, that the citizens of Kuwait, who enjoy one of the world's highest per capita incomes, do so as a result of the exploitation of peoples outside that country's borders. And Englishmen seldom blame Americans for the fact that their per capita income is substantially less than that of the latter. On the other hand, Scottish and Welsh national leaders are much more apt to charge discrimination for the much smaller discrepancy between their per capita income and that of the English.

The quite evident reason for the greater propensity to charge discrimination in an *intra*state than in an *inter*state situation is that economies are generally construed to be primarily statewide enterprises. Thus, we speak of the American, British, or Soviet economy. Whether such a compartmentalized view of economics is valid, particularly in an age of growing trading blocs and so-called "multinational corporations," is beside the point. Today people perceive the government as the chief regulator of the economy and take umbrage if they feel that their group is not getting its fair share of their country's total pie. But even if one accepts this view of the government as the essentially unfettered judge of how resources are to be distributed within a state's borders, why does it follow that disparities among ethnonations are due to purposeful discrimination? If true, why do even greater disparities characterize the much less controlled global economy?

The possibility that ethnonational discrimination is at work within a given state is, of course, quite strong. Discrimination within Northern Ireland, for example, is a major element in the poorer economic and occupational status of the Irish as contrasted with the non-Irish.[6] But as a last bit of evidence that discrimination need not be present to produce economic discrepancies between ethnonations, consider the relative economic positions of the Castilians, Malays, and Serbs. As just noted, government is usually considered the not-too-invisible hand behind the allocation of economic resources. Yet, although each of these groups is the politically dominant nation within its respective state (Spain, Malaysia, and Yugoslavia), Basques and Catalans enjoy higher living standards than Castilians, Chinese (within Malaysia) higher than Malays, and Croats and Slovenes higher than Serbs.

Although many of the supporters of the theory of relative economic deprivation have presumed the omnipresence of discrimination, the theory does not require it. The fact of intergroup discrepancies, regardless of the reason therefor, could still support the thesis that ethnonational conflicts are, at bottom, the result of economic inequalities. Casting doubt on discrimination as a satisfactory explanation for inequalities between nations does not automatically weaken the theory of relative deprivation. However, if the theory is valid, the following two propositions should be empirically verifiable:

PROPOSITION I

If economic differentials are primary, responses to similar economic discrepancies between groups should approximate one another within both homogeneous and heterogeneous societies. The absence or presence of national diversity should not be determinative.

PROPOSITION II

If ethnonational competition is fundamentally economic in causation, then *substantial* changes over time in the economic relationship should come to be reflected in the ethnonational relationship.[7] A corollary relating to a comparison of ethnonational relations between different sets of ethnonational groups, would hold that when the sets are characterized by marked differences in the degree of economic discrepancies, then the sociopolitical relationships should also vary substantially from set to set.

Neither of these propositions withstands empirical validation. Consider first, Proposition I. Contrary to its postulate, in situations where no ethnonational division is present, regionally defined groups will accept unfavorable economic disparities between themselves and others in the state which, had they coincided with ethnonational groups, would bring charges of discrimination and rumblings of political separatism. Consider the case of two adjoining regions of Canada and the United States, Québèc and Maine. As table 2 indicates, median family income in real terms for the two regions is quite comparable. And, so far as their relative situation within their respective state is concerned, Québècers occupy a more favorable position in the economic structure than do Mainers. Nevertheless, the Parti Québècois, which mustered more than half of the Franco-Canadian vote in the last provincial election, makes much of the economic discrepancies between Québèc and Ontario as evidence of discrimination and of the fact that Québèc would be better off to go it alone. Mainers are also quite well aware that the economic plight of their state is unfavorable when contrasted with the rest of the Union as a whole, and politicians are regularly elected there on the promise to bring more industry and higher living standards to Maine. But Mainers see no conspiratorial discrimination in

TABLE 2
Comparison of Median Family Incomes

Unit	Median family income	Standing relative to all comparable units	As percentage of countrywide median figure	As percentage of wealthiest comparable unit[b]	As percentage of poorest comparable unit[c]
Québèc	$18,592[a]	4/10	94.3	87.1	136.9
Maine	$16,208[a]	48/50	81.4	57.3	112.9

Sources: U.S. Bureau of the Census *Statistical Abstract of the United States, 1982–1983* (Washington, D.C., 1982); and *Canada Yearbook, 1980–1981* (Ottawa, 1981).

[a] Figures are for 1978 in the case of Canada and for 1979 in the case of the United States. Taking into account the 9 percent U.S. inflation rate in 1978/1979, as well as the offsetting exchange-rate for 1978 (1 Canadian dollar = 0.85 U.S. dollar), the median income for Québèc families remained higher than that for Maine families, $15,803 to $14,749.

[b] British Columbia and Alaska.

[c] Prince Edward Island and Arkansas.

their situation, and acknowledge that geography (location at the end of the railhead) is much more to blame. Demands for autonomy or separatism have not been heard.

The Québèc-Maine illustration is not unusual. Most states, as noted, reflect sharp regional variations in income. But autonomist and separatist movements, which have truly deserved being described as regionalist rather than as nationalist, have been scarce indeed. On the other hand, approximately 50 percent of all states have been confronted by ethnonational movements in recent years, and many of the afflicted states have been simultaneously facing several such movements.[8]

Another interesting sidelight on this issue of the homogeneous versus the heterogeneous situation is that regional economic variations within a single state are very unlikely to have precipitous edges. In the absence of state borders, economic regions are set off one from another by twilight zones rather than by sharp demarcations.[9] So far as ethnic homelands are concerned, this means that any economic discrepancy between peoples immediately on either side of an ethnonational border is apt to be infinitesimal. Thus, the general economic plight of the peoples living on either side of, and in proximity to, the English-Scottish border is comparable, and, if economics determined social consciousness, both these adjacent peoples should respond as one. But Englishmen and Scotsmen view the same facts quite differently. It is the sharp separation between membership and nonmembership in an ethnonational group and not the far more subtle economic shading between regions that takes precedence in determining viewpoint.

As to the second proposition (which holds that substantial alterations in the economic gap should bring about a corresponding alteration in ethnonational attitudes), comparative data strongly suggest that
this is also not the case. At a macrocosmic level of analysis, it can be
noted that while the spread of socialism and welfare statism are evidence of an age characterized by an important role being ascribed to
governments as "levelers" (at least to the degree of curbing extreme
wealth and poverty), it has also been an age characterized by rapidly
growing ethnonationalism. Without in any way suggesting an alternative causal relationship between these two developments, the pattern
clearly does not support the thesis that closing the economic gap between groups will result in a lessening of ethnonational dissension.

The experiences of Belgium and Czechoslovakia are therefore not
atypical. Flanders and Slovakia each received a disproportionately
large share of their country's statewide investments during the 1950s
and 1960s.[10] Yet, in each case, the resulting rapid closing of the economic gap between the two principal ethnonational groups was accompanied by increased demands for autonomy.

To avoid the possibility that two or three decades might be too abbreviated a period in which to discern trends, we can turn to the nearly
seventy-year history of the Soviet Union. Consonant with the Marxist
interpretation of history and the specific precepts of Lenin, the Soviet
leadership has, since 1917, consistently maintained that the prevalence
of antagonisms among nations can be explained as the product of economic forces. Do away with the exploitation of one nation by another,
Lenin and his legatees have contended, and national antagonisms will
also disappear. The "equality of nations" has therefore been a corner-
stone of Soviet nationality policy from the beginning. In the words of
one Soviet writer:

> The establishment of the Union of Soviet Republics brought to the fore the
> task of promoting the progress of the people of the former Russian em-
> pire. The removal of socio-economic barriers, of everything that had con-
> tributed toward kindling strife among nations, provided the basis for ac-
> celerating and levelling up the economic development of the backward
> regions and for the final eradication of all forms of national inequality.[11]

Still another Soviet author succinctly answers his own question, "What
is the main point in tackling the nationalities question in a multinational country? It is to ensure the real equality of the nations."[12] And
though the Soviet policy of national equality has a cultural, as well as
an economic aspect, its attainments have been largely publicized in
economic terms. Thus, in the just cited article, the strides toward equality are documented as follows:

Throughout the Soviet period, the Party has ensured higher economic growth rates in the non-Russian republics than the average for the country as a whole. In 1968, growth of industrial output for the Union was 79 times the 1913 level, but in Kazakhstan it was 125 times, in Kirghizie 152 times, in Armenia 146 times, and even higher in some autonomous republics (Komi Republic 223 times, Bashkira 477 times, etc.). The Party and the state set aside a relatively larger share of capital investments for the national areas so as to raise them to the level of the advanced nations.[13]

But after more than a half-century of experimentation with national policy, Soviet leaders publicly acknowledge that problems persist.

Some scholars, while aware of this failure of ethnonationalism to dissolve in the face of economic betterment, still perceive a relationship between ethnonationalism and economics. They contend that the former depends not upon economic inequality but upon economic change. Here is how one author described the relationship in the case of the Slovaks:

In fact economic and social conditions had improved in Slovakia. . . . This may indeed have been one of the reasons why Slovak national consciousness had increased. Economic dissatisfaction is not always the main source of nationalism; very often nationalism becomes overt with the improvement of economic conditions. Slovak nationalism would have existed and grown even if the country had had no reason to complain of unjust economic treatment from Prague.[14]

This thesis that ethnonationalism is tied to the process of change is, in turn, questioned by ethnonational stirrings among a multitude of Third World peoples, such as the Baluchis, Ewes, Hutus, Karens, Kongo, Nagas, Shans, and Somalis, whose economic situation would be better described as stagnant rather than fluid. Moreover, the fact that a change in economic status is *not* a prerequisite for the stimulation of ethnonationalism is illustrated by the Basques and Catalans of Spain and the Croatians and Slovenes of Yugoslavia. As earlier noted, these people enjoy a decided economic advantage over their state's politically dominant group. The gap, in fact, has continued to widen.[15] Yet all four peoples have manifested mounting ethnonationalism. Indeed, if two Yugoslav opinion polls are at all accurate, then the Slovenes, who are easily the wealthiest of Yugoslavia's eight major ethnonational groups (and who have enlarged that advantage over all competitors since World War II) are also quite easily the most dissatisfied people within Yugoslavia.[16]

The conclusion would appear to be that the theory of relative economic deprivation offers an unsatisfactory explanation for ethnonational dissension. The growing tendency of peoples to resent and resist being ruled by those deemed aliens appears to operate quite independently of the economic variable. Rich and poor states, and rich and poor nations, have been rather indiscriminately susceptible to the ethnonational virus. Economically static and economically fluid environments have both witnessed increased ethnonational dissension.

Is this, then, to deny any role to economic considerations? Not at all. As evidenced by the great emphasis that is placed upon economic deprivation (real or imaginary) in ethnonational propaganda, economic arguments can act as a catalyst or exacerbator of national tensions. But this is something quite different than acknowledging economic deprivation as a necessary precondition of ethnonational conflict. Deprivation is but one of several possible catalysts. As noted at the outset, language, religion, and race are among other possibilities. In situations where language is a principal issue, for example, the "aggrieved" group will typically perceive the preservation of the native language as indispensable to the survival of the national "soul"; liquidate the language and you liquidate the nation, it is charged. Campaigns to have the native language made (or continued as) the language of the communications media, of literature, of instruction in the schools, and even of shop and street signs, become emotional crusades, often leading to bloodshed. The Ukrainians, for example, have waged their national struggle largely in terms of language, maintaining that their continued existence as a separate nation is at stake. That they are sincere in the conviction of their contention can be assumed. But that the loss of the language would mean the loss of Ukrainian identity cannot. Irish nationalists of the late nineteenth century shouted similar linguistic slogans while marching under the banner of language preservation. But with independence achieved, the same tongue, which was a chief focus of contention during the liberation struggle, suddenly lost its emotional content and significance, and the new state became on balance more English speaking than it had been when ruled from London. Similarly, we have seen that economic discrepancies which become invested with an emotional dimension when the discrepancy coincides with an ethnonational division are not so invested when an ethnonational division is absent (Maine versus Québec). But though the struggle may therefore be conducted in economic (or linguistic) terms, the issue at bottom is predicated upon two distinct group-identities and the question of the right of one of these people to rule the other. Remove economic inequality or reverse it (Basques, Catalans, Chinese of Malaysia, Croats, Flemings, and Slovenes), and the conflict remains. Remove the ethnonational issue while maintaining economic inequality between regions, and the conflict dissolves (Maine).

Beyond acting as a catalyst, exacerbator, and/or choice of verbal battleground, economic discrepancies between two peoples can exert a
major but *indirect* influence, if the discrepancy results in significant levels of in- or outmigration from an ethnic homeland. Ethnonationalist
propaganda often makes much of emigration data, noting that the failure of the economy to offer sufficiently attractive employment at home
has led to the partial breakup of the ethnonational "family." Here is
how one author put it in the case of the Slovaks:

> The Slovak economists were certainly bitter about the migration of Slovak
> labour to the Czech lands. Tens of thousands of Slovaks were forced to
> settle there permanently because they could not find employment at
> home. It was felt that those Slovaks, or at least their children, would be lost
> to the nation. The Czech local authorities did not bother to provide Slovak
> schools for them. This "de-Slovakization" probably worried the national-
> ists more than the purely economic aspects of the matter. No nation, and
> for that matter, no region, welcomes a situation in which a large part of its
> population finds it necessary to emigrate, even if it is a case of inner-state
> migration.[17]

On the other hand, an invasion of the homeland because of an economic boom, is even more incendiary than an outmigration. The name
of the movement designed to oust foreign workers from Switzerland
was well-designed to elicit just such an emotional response: *Nationale
Aktion gegen die Uberfremdung von Volk und Heimat* (National Movement
against Foreign Domination of People and Homeland). The willingness
of people to accept a lower living standard rather than to permit such
immigration is perhaps the most remarkable testament to the primacy
of ethnonational sentiment over economic considerations. For example, in 1974 more than one-third of all Swiss voters opted to deport
huge numbers of immigrant workers, despite the fact that all of the
customary formulators of public opinion were opposed to the ouster,
more specifically, both Houses of Parliament (157 to 3 and 42 to 0),
political parties from left to right, religious leaders, and both labor and
management organizations. Moreover, all parties agreed that the expulsion would cause serious economic dislocation and a drop in living
standards. In a similar development, the Baltic peoples have *resisted*
new investment capital from the Soviet government because of the conviction that greater industrialization brings with it more Russians into
the Estonian, Latvian, or Lithuanian homeland, a *price* deemed too high
to pay for increased living standards.[18] A corollary of this negative psychological response is the unwillingness of people to leave their ethnonational hearth in order to seek employment in a different home-

land, a problem of psychology which seriously retards the mobility of labor within multinational states. Thus, one authority on Yugoslavia has noted that positions in the north of Yugoslavia go begging because of the reluctance of ethnically dissimilar people from the south to migrate from their homelands. Moreover, what movement does occur is heavily influenced by ethnonational considerations: Serbs from Bosnia go to Serbia, while Croats go to Croatia. The richest area, Slovenia, attracts relatively few immigrants, and the poorest, Kossovo (the homeland of the Albanians), has actually experienced a net inflow of migrants over a forty-year period.[19] The magnetic tug of an ethnic homeland and the desire to preserve its ethnonational integrity can thus counter economic incentives.

Economic considerations could logically be expected to have a maximal impact in situations (1) where the principal economic unit ("the economy") coincided with the ethnonation or (2) where socioeconomic classes within a given economy coincided with ethnonations. The first situation would be comparable to a case in which a linguistic or religious cleavage coincided with an ethnonational cleavage. (Possible illustrations would be the Fleming-Walloon cleavage and the Jewish-Arab cleavage, respectively.) In such case, the linguistic or religious factor will reinforce the ethnonational factor. But since, as earlier noted, it is the state which constitutes the primal unit of modern economics, nation and economy could only coincide in the case of true nation-states, that is, those units where political and ethnonational borders coincide. If we exclude both the multinational states and those states which, although themselves homogeneous, are characterized by that so-called irredentist situation in which the dominant group extends beyond the state's borders, our only illustrations would be Denmark, Iceland, Japan, Luxembourg, the Netherlands, Norway, and Portugal. These states would account for less than 4 percent of the world population and, if we exclude Japan, for less than 1 percent. With so few nation-states, analyzing ethnonationalism in terms of total economies (G.N.P.s, labor forces, etc.) is not apt to prove very edifying.

One could perhaps make a case for the proposition that it is the fact that the state forms the principal economic crucible that causes ethnonational groups to demand their own states. Being "masters of our own house," "architects of our own destiny," subsumes, inter alia, the notion of control over the economy. But the fact that any number of colonies and ethnonational groups have agitated for independence while aware that independence would probably bring on a worsened economic situation again militates against assigning primacy to economic motivation. Separatists, as we are reminded by the plethora of so-called microstates and a still larger number of small, secessionist movements, are not apt to be dissuaded by the argument that their state will simply be too small to support a viable economy.

Analyses based upon the second eventuality—the coincidence of nations with socioeconomic classes—have a long history. Both Marx and Engels, particularly after 1848, were given to expositions in which nations had replaced classes as the major vehicles of history. There were nations (such as the Germans, Magyars, and Poles) who had come to denote the forces of enlightenment and progress, that is to say, a role reserved in their classical treatises to the proletariat. Other nations, particularly the non-Russian, non-Polish, Slavic peoples, were substituted for the feudal aristocracy and the bourgeoisie in the role of darkness and reaction, whose "chief mission [was] to perish in the revolutionary holocaust."[20]

It is, of course, possible that a society might be stratified according to ethnonational group. The traditional class system throughout Rwanda-Burundi, that coincided with the division between the ruling Tutsis and the subservient Hutu, approximated such a situation. As in the case of language, religion, and race, the coincidence of class with nation would reinforce the ethnonational cleavage (see figure 1). But within developed societies, class lines customarily cut across ethnonational units. In these cases, the two types of divisions (the vertical one which separates the ethnonation as a unit from all others and the horizontal one which divides the nation into classes) are potential competitors for the loyalty of people (see figure 2). As writers on nationalism conventionally point out, ethnonational consciousness is predicated upon a division of humankind into "us" and "them." But this sense of an ethnonational "us" does not preclude the existence of lesser "us"-"them" relationships within the ethnonation, nor larger ones which transcend it. Class, religious, and sectional sentiments commonly crosscut a single nation. The significant question, however, is which one of the many "us's" to which a person belongs will win out in a test of loyalties. Which loyalty is primary? Herein lies the profundity underlying Rupert Emerson's disarmingly simple definition of the nation as "the largest community, which when the chips are down, effectively commands men's loyalty, overriding the claims both of lesser communities within it and those which cut across it or potentially enfold it within a still greater society."[21]

As Lenin discovered during World War I, Emerson's definition indeed holds true when the chips are down. Forced to choose between their proletarian consciousness and ethnonationalism, the working class of France and Germany elected to fight as Frenchmen and Germans. Indeed, nationalism even pervaded the proletariat's vanguard,

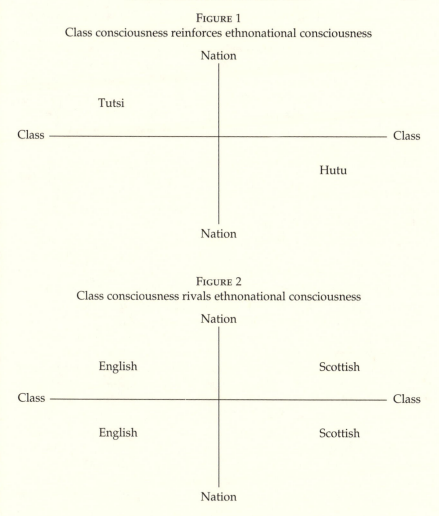

FIGURE 1
Class consciousness reinforces ethnonational consciousness

FIGURE 2
Class consciousness rivals ethnonational consciousness

an apostasy which Lenin would describe following the war as "the despicable betrayal of Socialism by the majority of the leaders of the proletariat of the oppressing nations in 1914–19."[22] With this harshly learned lesson concerning the relative strength of class-loyalty versus ethnonational loyalty behind them, Lenin et al. decided that it was strategically advisable to give the appearance of allying themselves with national causes, and the most blatant appeals to ethnonational aspirations thereafter became a staple in Marxist-Leninist propaganda. Thus, all communist parties were informed in 1924 of the absolute need to take a public stand on "one of the basic principles of Leninism, requiring the resolute and constant advocacy by communists of the right of national self-determination (secession and the formation of an independent State)."[23] The parties were further informed that this appeal to ethnonationalism "forms one of the most important constituents in the policy of winning the masses and preparing a victorious revolution."[24] And yet again, the parties were warned against "the mistake of underestimating the national question, a mistake which deprives them of the opportunity of winning over substantial, at times decisive strata of the population."[25] This emphasis upon appealing to ethnonational aspirations reaped rich dividends, for the strategy played a *vital* role in the assumption of power by the communist parties of the Soviet Union, the People's Republic of China, Vietnam, and Yugoslavia, that is to say, the four parties which can lay claim to having come to power largely by their own devices, without the aid of foreign troops.[26] Marxist-Leninists, therefore, owe their major success more to the power of ethnonationalism than to either the popular appeal or the predicted inevitability of historical dialectical materialism. It is indeed a powerful testament to the primacy of ethnonational over economic motivation, that a school predicated upon economic determinism should turn to ethnonationalism to propel them into power.

Since nations tend to be conglomerates of socioeconomic classes, a broad-based ethnonational movement will also likely demonstrate a multiclass base. The leadership of a movement may for a period reflect upper class or "rightist" leanings, a situation more characteristic of pre– rather than post–World War II movements. In another period, the leadership may reflect "radical leftist" leanings, as when the *Front for the Liberation of Québèc* held center stage in the Québèc drama during the late 1960s and early 1970s. By and large, one could say that the intelligentsia (whether of right or left) have been the most consistently prominent among the leadership of ethnonational movements. But none of these class elements is essential for the development of such a movement. Indeed, a leadership that permits itself to be identified too closely with a specific interest or class, thereby reduces the likelihood of being able to project itself as the legitimate representative of the entire nation. Communist parties, the self-styled vanguard of the proletariat, have often exemplified a keen awareness of this danger by cloaking themselves in a broader "united front of all national and patriotic forces."

To note that an ethnonational movement must appear to transcend class and other special interests is not to contend that an ethnonational goal, such as separatism, will be uniformly acceptable to all classes. Nor is it to contend that the leadership will not face factionalization along lines of socioeconomic philosophy, just as it may face factionalization predicated upon personalities and/or tactics.[27] However, ethnonationalism, by definition, posits the primacy of the ethnonational unit over its class divisions.[28] Indeed, in addition to positing the primacy of the ethnonational bond over all internal cleavages, ethnonationalism also maintains that the ethnonational bond is stronger than any ties that transcend the national group. The case of Northern Ireland is instructive on this point. Table 3 shows the results of an opinion poll indicating the self-ascription of people there by class and religion, but we can safely presume that Catholicism is a relatively safe index to Irish identity and Protestantism an index to non-Irishness. Two points are notable: (1) the lack of coincidence between class and national group, each national group being divided into several classes; (2) the rather remarkable parallel between the two groups in terms of their self-perceived class spectrum. But despite the striking similarities in class composition between the two peoples, political events within Northern Ireland make evident that "when the chips are down," nation-transcending class consciousness is either absent or inconse-

TABLE 3
Self-perceived Class

	Protestant (%)	Catholic (%)	Total (%)
Upper class	1	0	—
Middle class	52	41	47
Working class	29	34	31
Lower, poor class	2	4	3
Average, ordinary class	2	5	3
Don't believe in classes	2	2	2
Don't know, miscellaneous	12	14	12

Source: Richard Rose, *Governing Without Consensus* (Boston, 1971), 286.

quential. National consciousness has proven stronger than both *intra*national class divisions and *inter*national class solidarity.

In retrospect, it is likely that the tendency to perceive economic causation behind ethnonational developments is due in large part to a fortuitous accident of chronology. Both the Industrial Revolution and the age of ethnic nationalism were inaugurated at approximately the same time. The temptation to assign a causal interrelationship to their concurrent birth and growth is understandable. But as Carleton Hayes so perspicaciously pointed out nearly a half-century ago:

It is important to bear in mind that the Industrial Revolution is not necessarily an intellectual revolution. Of itself it is neither nationalist nor internationalist. It is essentially mechanical and material. It has merely provided improved means and greater opportunities for the dissemination of
any ideas. . . . Now it so happened that when the Industrial Revolution
began, nationalism was becoming a significant intellectual movement,
even more significant than internationalism. Consequently, while the
newer industrial machinery has been utilized for international ends, it has
also been utilized, even more, for nationalist purposes. The obvious international fruits of the Industrial Revolution must not blind our eyes to its
intensely nationalist contribution and implications.[29]

Causal connection between economic forces and ethnonationalism
should not be inferred simply from the fact of coexistence.

.   .   .

To recapitulate, many authorities have tended to perceive ethnonational struggles in terms of economic discrimination. Two reasons help
to account for this tendency:

1. The propensity to mistake the tangible characteristics of a nation for its
   essence.
2. The fact that observable economic discrepancies are near universal concomitants of ethnic strife.

The practice of inferring discrimination directly from statistical documentation of economic differentials overlooks three elements:

1. The geographic distribution of ethnic groups into distinct homelands
   guarantees discrepancies because of the "law" of uneven regional economic development.
2. Although the *possibility* of exercising centralized, effective, manipulat-
   ive control over the regional allocation of new industrial plants, wage
   differentials, governmental subsidies, and the like is far greater at the
   intrastate than at the interstate level, the greatest economic discrepancies are those between states.
3. There are several states in which the national group that controls the
   ruling apparatus is economically disadvantaged relative to national
   minorities, thus confirming that the fact of economic discrepancies cannot be accepted as prima facie evidence of discrimination.

If the theory of relative economic deprivation were valid, two propositions would follow:

1. Group responses to similar economic discrepancies should be essentially the same, whether in an ethnically homogeneous or heterogeneous situation.
2. A closing of an economic gap between ethnonational groups should result in the dissipation of national particularism. *Corollary*: Variations in economic differential between sets of groups should be accompanied by corresponding differences in group relations from one set to another.

Both propositions are challenged by comparative data.

The conclusion that ethnonationalism appears to operate remarkably independent from the economic variable is not tantamount to denying a role to economic factors. The latter are very apt to serve as catalytic agent, exacerbator, or choice of battleground. They can also exert a significant effect upon immigration to or emigration from the ethnic homeland, migrations which in turn can become highly volatile issues. But catalysts and indirect forces should not be confused with cause.

Economic considerations can be expected to exert maximal impact where socioeconomic class and nationhood coincide. However, the vertical category of nationhood is normally divided by the horizontal category of class, which is why Marxism and nationalism are fundamentally incompatible. Marxist-Leninists have discovered that, when forced to choose between national and class loyalty, people are most apt to opt for the former.

Although nations are apt to be conglomerates of socioeconomic classes, the leaders of national movements may be motivated primarily by hoped-for material gains or by class-oriented philosophy. The essence of nationalism is not to be sought in the motives of elites who may manipulate nationalism for some ulterior end, but rather in the mass sentiment to which elites appeal. Those who would manipulate the national sentiments of the masses must hide their motive or risk losing support. Thus, Marxist-Leninist movements have learned to cloak their prerevolutionary appeals in ethnonational garb.

A final reason advanced for the tendency to perceive a close linkage between ethnonationalism and economic forces was the parallel histories of the growth of nationalism and industrialization. But chronological coincidence does not establish a causal relationship.

NOTES

1. A variation on the thesis of relative economic deprivation is that of "the competition for scarce resources," in relation to which ethnonationalism is per-

ceived as the product of a decision to mobilize an ethnic group or, what in the context of U.S. politics, is termed a "pressure group."

A slightly broader variation of the deprivation thesis is offered by those who introduce the notion of *status* within the society. Because *status* is a rather nebulous or amorphous concept, not perfectly equatable with economic standing, its introduction into an analysis offers a measure of protection against a charge of positing an overly simplistic theory of economic causation. In reality, however, describing a nation in terms of a lower status group and maintaining that their nationalism is the result of frustration at being denied higher status does not vary significantly from analyses that describe (1) a nation as an economically deprived class and (2) nationalism as the product of deprivation.

The internal colonial model and the rational choice model, as applied to the behavior of ethnonational groups, are also currently popular analytical frameworks that reflect a high regard for the explanatory power of economic motivation. Moreover, those who associate the rise or fall of ethnic nationalism with a specific economic stage ("industrial" or "postindustrial") or with "modernization" also thereby make ethnic nationalism subservient to material considerations.

Given all this, it is evident that most social scientists writing on ethnic nationalism could be included on a list of those who ascribe great significance to the explanatory power of economic forces. For those who would like specific names, see Jeffrey Ross, "A Test of Ethnicity and Economics as Contrasting Explanations of Collective Political Behavior," *Plural Societies* 9 (Winter 1978): 69–71 particularly, and Joshua Fishman, "The Rise and Fall of the Ethnic Revival in the USA," in *Mexican Americans in Comparative Perspective*, ed. Walker Connor (Washington, D.C., 1985).The former's list includes such luminaries as J. S. Furnivall and M. G. Smith. The latter's list is extremely extensive; he traces the tendency to seek economic explanations to the work of Karl Deutsch.

2. For an expanded discussion of the meaning of such key terms as nation, ethnic group, and nationalism, see chapter 4 in this volume.

3. There are also more abstract elements involving the cultural traditions of the local people, including their work habits, predispositions toward urban versus rural life, their yardstick for "the good life," the general aptitude for business, and so on.

4. Such discrepancies are often surprisingly substantial. For example, in 1970 the number of males per one hundred women varied from 91.5 in New York to 101.8 in North Dakota. U.S. Bureau of the Census, *Statistical Abstract of the United States: 1974*, 95th ed. (Washington, D.C., 1974).

5. During the age of overseas territories, the charge of colonial exploitation was very popular. However, in its allegation of discrimination within a single economic and political crucible, it differed little from a purely intrastate situation. "Neocolonialism" also involves the charge of exploitation within one's own state, even though engineered from abroad.

6. The Irish and non-Irish of Northern Ireland are also less territorially segregated from one another than are most ethnonational groups.

7. The word *substantial* is used to allow for what Marxists term "the law of the transformation of quantity into quality," that is to say, incremental altera-

tions in the economic substructure need not be *immediately* reflected in the superstructure.

8. For a list of the afflicted states, see Walker Connor, "The Politics of Ethnonationalism," *Journal of International Affairs* 27, no. 1 (1973): 2 particularly.

9. State borders can correspond with sharp economic differentials because of very uneven overall wealth between the bordering states (for example, Mexico and the United States) combined with strict restraints upon transborder intercourse (tariffs, strict antimigration laws, etc.). Even in free-trade areas (such as within the EEC), borders may correspond with sharp differentials in living standards because of differences in the levels of welfare statism conducted by the two state governments.

10. See, for example, Eugen Steiner, *The Slovak Dilemma* (Cambridge, 1973), 129–38, and Joseph Rudolph, *The Belgian Front Democratique des Bruxellois Francophones—Rassemblement Wallon (F.D.F.-R.W.) and the Politics of Sub-National Institution Building* (Paper presented at the 1973 Annual Meeting of the Northeastern Political Science Association), 3.

11. L. Lebedinskaya, "The Nationality Question and the Formation of the Soviet State," *International Affairs* (Moscow) (December 1972): 11.

12. S. Gililov, "The Worldwide Significance of the Soviet Experience in Solving the Nationalities Question," *International Affairs* (Moscow) (July 1972): 61.

13. Ibid.

14. Steiner, *Slovak Dilemma*, 132.

15. See Milton da Silva, "Modernization and Ethnic Conflict: The Case of the Basques," *Comparative Politics* 7 (January 1975): 238–42 particularly; and Richard Burks, *The National Problem and the Future of Yugoslavia* (Santa Monica, 1971), particularly 50–54.

16. Compare the tables on pp. 43 and 55 in Burks, *The National Problem and Future*.

17. Steiner, *Slovak Dilemma*, 134.

18. See, for example, the *New York Times*, 21 March 1971 and 19 July 1971 and the *Christian Science Monitor* of 1 April 1972.

19. Burks, *The National Problem and Future*, 57. Interregional migration has increased since Burks's study was undertaken.

20. *Democratic Panslavism* in Paul Blackstock and Bert Hoselitz, eds., *The Russian Menace to Europe: A Collection of Articles, Speeches, Letters and News Despatches by Karl Marx and Friedrich Engels* (Glencoe, Ill., 1952); the citation is from p. 59. See also, in the same volume, *Hungary and Panslavism*.

21. Rupert Emerson, *From Empire to Nation* (Boston, 1960), 95–96.

22. *Preliminary Draft of Theses on the National and Colonial Question, June 1920*, in *Lenin on the National and Colonial Questions: Three Articles* (Peking, 1967), 28.

23. *Extracts from the Resolution of the Fifth Comintern Congress of the Executive Committee of the Communist Internatioal, June 26, 1924* in Jane Degras, ed., *The Communist International 1919–1943: Documents* (London, 1960) 2: 106.

24. *Extracts from the Theses on Tactics Adopted by the Fifth Comintern Congress (July 1924)* in Degras, *Documents*, 142–56.

25. *Extracts from the Theses on the Bolshevization of Communist Parties Adopted at the Fifth Executive Plenum (April 1925)* in Degras, *Documents*, 188–200.

26. Though Castro also came into power without foreign troops, his Marxist-Leninism was a well-guarded secret until well after his assumption of power. For details on the experiences of the Soviet, Chinese, Vietnamese, and Yugoslavian parties, see this writer's *The National Question in Marxist-Leninist Theory and Strategy* (Princeton, 1984), chapters 3 through 6.

27. For further comment and illustrations, see Connor, "The Politics of Ethno-

nationalism," 17.

28. A remarkable illustration of a willingness to submerge class interests in the name of the ethnonational interest over a long period of time is offered by the Swedish community within Finland, wherein an overwhelming percentage of all identifiable groups—intelligentsia, industrial workers, management, small businessmen, and farmers—have supported the Swedish People's Party, in preference to all countrywide parties, since early in the century. The overall percentage of the Swedish electorate voting for the party reaches 85 percent. See Theodore Stoddard et al., *Area Handbook for Finland*, Department of the Army Pamphlet 550–167 (Washington, D.C., 1974), 50–51, 145–46.

29. Carlton Hayes, *The Historical Evolution of Modern Nationalism* (New York, 1931), 234–37.

Chapter Seven

AHISTORICALNESS: THE CASE OF
WESTERN EUROPE

In 1975, a Conference on Ethnic Pluralism and Conflict in Contemporary Western Europe and Canada was held at Cornell University. Scholars from Western Europe and Canada, as well as United States scholars specializing in Western Europe, were present. The conference had been occasioned by a spate of ethnonationally inspired unrest throughout a number of Western European countries. The clearly predominant view was one of surprise. Time and again, participants raised the question, "But why now?" (Actually, as recorded in chapter 1, the movements in question were visible at least a decade earlier.) Underlying that "But why now?" query was a view of these ethnonational movements as both historically rootless (and therefore unpredictable) and as inconsonant with their perceptions of contemporary Western Europe. As suggested by the following article, which was prepared for the conference, greater familiarity with the history of nationalism in Europe might have caused a change in query from "Why now?" to "Why not now?"

Ethnonationalism in the First World:
The Present in Historical Perspective[*]

UNTIL QUITE RECENTLY, the conventional view of scholars concerning the vitality of ethnonationalism within the region known as Western Europe rested upon two pillars. The first was a conviction that World War II had impressed upon the peoples of the region the realization that modern technology had made nationalism an unaffordable luxury. For an amalgam of both positive and negative reasons, the prewar tendency to ascribe primary significance to being "British," French, or German was alleged to have been succeeded by an emphasis upon a supranational consciousness of being European, with an attendant willingness to accept radical alterations in traditional political structures so as to bring the latter into line with the new European identity. In the words of Stanley Hoffmann: "If there was one part of the world in which men of good will thought that the nation-state could be superseded, it was Western Europe. The conditions seemed ideal. On the one hand, nationalism seemed at its lowest ebb; on the other, an adequate formula and method for building a substitute had apparently been devised."[1]

In identifying this first pillar, Hoffmann here quite unintentionally also bears testimony to the prevalence of the second, namely, the assumption that Western Europe was devoid of significant national minorities. States of the region were (and, all too often, still are) described indiscriminately as nation-states, that relatively rare phenomenon, characterizing less than 10 percent of all states, in which the political borders of the state contain a single ethnic group. This commonly propagated image of Western Europe held that the individual states had either successfully assimilated their disparate peoples (for example, in Belgium, France, Spain, Switzerland, or the United Kingdom) or were themselves the product of the political consolidation of a nationally conscious people (as in Germany or Italy).[2]

[*] Reprinted from Walker Connor, "Ethnonationalism in the First World: The Present in Historical Perspective," in *Ethnic Conflict in the Western World*, ed. Milton J. Esman, 19–45. Copyright © 1979 by Cornell University. Used by permission of the publisher, Cornell University Press.

The assumption that those Western European states that contained more than one ethnic group had successfully solved their national problems through assimilation was particularly consequential for the collective academic endeavor known as "nation building." Surveying with one eye the problems of sociopolitical integration faced by the ethnically complex states in Africa and Asia, while perceiving with the other an uninterrupted pattern of successfully assimilated states within the industrially advanced region of Western Europe, the "nation builders" concluded that the experience of the latter had precedential value for predicting the political future of Africa and Asia.[3] If Cornishmen, Scots, and Welsh had become thoroughly British; if Basques, Catalans, and Galicians had become Spanish; if Flemings and Walloons had become Belgian; if Alsatians, Bretons, and Corsicans had become French, then why should not Ibo, Hausa, and Yoruba become Nigerian; or Baluchi, Bengali, Pashtun, and Sindhi become Pakistani?

This thesis that the process of building nation-states, presumably undergone by Western Europe, was destined to be repeated within the Third World was not predicated upon simple chronological determinism, that is, the notion that newer states must necessarily follow the sequential evolution undergone by older counterparts. Afghanistan, Ethiopia, Iran, and Thailand, for example, could boast of being created prior to all or most of the Western European states; yet they were not held up as likely models for the future. Indeed, they were grouped with other Third World states that were thought to be about to embark on the Western European route. The key element was held to be not chronology but modernization, the term applied to that amalgam of subprocesses including industrialization, urbanization, increasing literacy, intensified communication and transportation networks, and the like. These processes and the "social mobilization" of the more isolated and inert masses that the processes heralded were considered to be at the root of successful assimilation within the First World.[4] Since modernization must also infect the Third World, a series of nation-states was the predictable outcome. But what would be left of this linkage theory and the prognostications based thereon, should the states of Europe prove not to be successfully assimilated?

As is now generally recognized, both of the scholarly pillars that I have described (a postnational Europe and a Europe of nation-states) rest upon shaky foundations. The notion of an intuitive sense of "Europeanness" that transcends national consciousness was challenged by, among other things, (1) the defeat of the European Defense Community as a result of French distrust of German militarism, (2) the broad-scale toleration with which President Charles de Gaulle's insistence on a *Europe des patries* was greeted both within and without

France, a toleration suggesting substantial though unarticulated support, (3) the rejection of European Economic Community (EEC) membership by the Norwegian electorate and a general lack of interest in membership displayed by the people within a number of other states, (4) the sporadically demonstrated proclivity for each state to look out for itself, as occurred when Arab oil-producing states elected to pursue a policy of selective embargoes, and (5) the negative responses, often bordering on xenophobia, which were accorded to migrant workers throughout Western Europe.[5] Meanwhile, the increasing manifestations of ethnic unrest throughout the area drew attention to the mirage nature of that second pillar, a Europe composed of uninational states. Among the more well-publicized cases were the revitalization of the Scottish and Welsh nationalist movements, and the frictions generated between Flemings and Walloons, between the South Tyrolean Germans and Rome, between the Basques and Madrid, between the Irish and non-Irish of Northern Ireland, and between the French- and German-speaking elements of the canton Berne in Switzerland. Less advertised, but no less pertinent, was the growing ethnonational assertiveness among the Catalans and Galicians of Spain; the Alsatians, Basques, Bretons, Corsicans, and Occitanians of France; the Slovenes and the Val D'Aostans of Italy; the Croats and Slovenes of Austria; the Norse-descendent inhabitants of the Danish-controlled Faroe Islands; and the Eskimo population of Danish-controlled Greenland.[6] Even this listing does not exhaust all of the region's groups who retain a sense of ethnic distinctiveness from their state's dominant element.[7]

The first few manifestations of ethnonationalism within postwar Europe (among the South Tyroleans, for example) could be explained away as vestigial or unique. But as ethnonationalism has become unmistakably evident on the part of several peoples whose ethnic consciousness had hitherto been considered nonexistent or, at the least, politically inconsequential, scholars have proffered a variety of theories to explain this unanticipated transsocietal phenomenon. Among the more popular explanations have been (1) the theory of relative (economic, cultural, and/or political) deprivation; (2) anomie, resulting from a growing feeling of alienation from the depersonalized and dehumanizing modern mass society, leading, in turn, to what is alternately described as a reversion to "tribalism" or as a new, more relevant alternative; (3) a "center-periphery" series of relationships in which these newly assertive ethnic groups (the peripheral peoples) are viewed as having remained essentially outside or at the edge of the dominant society and have, therefore, been only marginally influenced by that society's principal currents;[8] and (4) the loss of global prestige suffered by individual European states, as contrasted with their eminence in the prewar period, and a corresponding loss of pride in being viewed as British rather than Scottish, or French rather than Breton.[9]

One explanation that has been overlooked is that the surge of ethnonationalism among Basques, Bretons, Welsh, and other such groups reflects a quite natural and perhaps even predictable stage in a process that has been underway for approximately two centuries. Ever since the abstract philosophical notion that the right to rule is vested in *the people* was first linked in popular fancy to a particular, ethnically defined people, a development which first occurred at the time of the French Revolution, the conviction that one's own people should *not*, by the very nature of things, be ruled by those deemed aliens has proved a potent challenger to the legitimacy of multinational structures. As a consequence of this wedding of popular sovereignty to ethnicity (a marriage that during its history would come to be known as national self-determination), the political legitimacy of any state falling short of actual nation-statehood would become suspect to a segment or segments of its population.[10] Since 1789, the dogma that "alien rule is illegitimate rule" has been infecting ethnically aware peoples in an ever-broadening pattern. Indeed, as far as Europe is concerned, the region's subsequent history has been largely a tale of national liberation movements.[11] Ethnonational sentiments undergirded the struggle of the Greeks for independence in the 1820s; the liberation struggle of the Walloons and Flemings in 1830; the abortive revolutions of 1848 (particularly among the Germans, Italians, and Hungarians); the political consolidation of Germany and of Italy in the 1860s and very early 1870s; and the creation of Romania (1878), Serbia (1878), Norway (1905), Bulgaria (1908), Albania (1912), Finland (1917), Czechoslovakia, Estonia, Hungary, Latvia, Lithuania, Poland, Yugoslavia (all in 1918), Ireland (1921), and Iceland (1944).[12] Thus, by the end of World War II, all but three of the states of Europe either were the result of ethnonational aspirations or had lost substantial territory because of them.[13]

Consonant with my earlier comments concerning the scarcity of true nation-states within Western Europe, it is clear that many of the entities created or modified in response to ethnonational aspirations did not represent a completion of the self-determination process. Multiethnic structures remained the rule both within and without Europe.[14] But just as a host of secessionist movements throughout Africa and Asia (including the aborted Ibo and the successful Bengali secessions) serve to remind us that attempts to stop short of fulfilling self-determination for all ethnically conscious elements are not apt to go long unchallenged, so too should developments in Eastern Europe.[15] Although the designers of the peace treaties following World War I believed that they could prescribe limits to ethnonational aspirations, stopping short of balkanization, unsatisfied ethnonational demands plague the area more than fifty years later. The case is little different in Western Europe. The rationale for the independence of Cyprus in 1960 and for that of Malta in 1964 was the illegitimacy of alien rule.[16] And the surge of nationalism among Basques, Catalans, Scots, and other ethnic groups can be viewed as merely the most recent step in a process that has been unfolding since the late eighteenth century.

Perceiving this recent surge as part of a long-range process does not preclude acknowledging catalytic roles for other phenomena. To return to the matter of modernization and the intensification of communications, for example, while it may trouble many whose lives straddle World War II to hear the prewar period characterized as "primitive," there does appear to be a substantial difference in the nature and intensity of contacts between groups during the prewar and postwar periods. As noted elsewhere:

> The recent upsurge in ethnic conflict within the more industrialized, multiethnic states of Europe and North America seriously challenges the contention that modernization dissipates ethnic consciousness. But does not this upsurge also run counter to the assertion that modernization increases ethnic consciousness? Given the fact that the Industrial Revolution was introduced into each of these states more than a century ago, should not the high-tide mark of ethnic consciousness have appeared long ago? Part of the answer may be found in what Marxists term "The Law of Transformation of Quantity into Quality," a paraphrase of which might read "enough of a quantitative difference makes a qualitative difference." The processes of modernization prior to World War II did not necessitate or bring about the same measure of international contacts as have developments in the postwar period. With fewer and poorer roads, far fewer and less efficient private cars, local radio rather than state-wide television as the primary channel of non-written mass communications, lower levels of education and of knowledge of events beyond one's own experience, and lower general income levels that kept people close to home, ethnic complacency could be maintained: Brittany's culture appeared safe from French encroachment, Edinburgh felt remote and isolated from London, most Walloons and Flemings seldom came into contact (including artificial contact through media such as television) with members of the other group. In short, the situation of ethnic groups within these states was not totally dissimilar from that which was described earlier with regard to non-industrialized societies. The difference was only one of degree until that point was reached at which a qualitative change occurred. However, the point at which a significant number of people perceived that the cumulative impact of the quantitative increases in the intensity of intergroup

contacts now constituted a threat to their ethnicity represented, in political terms, a qualitative transformation.[17]

One author has noted with regard to the Bretons: "Indeed the sense of ethnic identity grew sharper as contacts and communications increased between Brittany and the rest of France. It was only after World War I, the first opportunity for most young Bretons to see 'France' and live among 'Frenchmen,' that regional ethnic organizations with political demands were created."[18] There is little question that mass support for these movements underwent a quantum jump during the late 1950s and 1960s.[19]

This perception of the impact of modernization upon social relations differs appreciably from Karl Deutsch's assimilationist model mentioned in note 3 above. The tendency to perceive contacts as encouraging assimilation apparently rests upon two situations in which at least one of the parties is not an ethnically conscious group. For example, Deutsch's model apparently does hold true for sectionalism. Indices to sectional attitudes within the United States have indicated a growing, countrywide uniformity as intersectional contacts increase. But while increased sectional contacts tend to dissipate sectional differences among a people, increased contacts among diverse ethnonationally conscious groups appear more apt to cement and reinforce the divisive sense of uniqueness.[20] Therefore, while "nationalism and social communication" may indeed be linked within a crucible containing only a single ethnonational element, "nationalism and *unsocial* communication" is a more apt description of the relationship when the crucible contains two or more ethnonational elements.

The second situation in which contacts have had an assimilationist impact occurred when one or both parties were still in a prenational state. Thus, prior to the Age of Nationalism, the trend was toward amalgamation into larger groups. Angles, Picts, Saxons, Vandals, and Visigoths were among those who traded group identities. Since the advent of the Age of Nationalism, however, contacts between groups, each of whom possesses even a dim sense of a separate ethnic heritage, have tended to cement and reinforce the sense of uniqueness. The quite common practice of employing cases of successful assimilation that were culminated prior to the eighteenth century as precedent for cases today involving self-conscious ethnic groups is therefore analogically spurious.

In yet another way, modernization and more effective communications have acted as catalysts for ethnonationally inspired demands. As formal education and globe-girdling communications have spread, the likelihood of people becoming cognizant of historic and contemporary self-determination movements has also spread. The quite common re-action to such cognition is, "If that people has a self-evident and in-alienable right of national self-determination, then why not we?" What social scientists term the "demonstration effect" has had a very discern-ible, chain-reaction impact upon the evolution of nationalism.[21] Each claim to national self-determination has tended to trigger still others. Through their cooperative efforts with one another and through spo-radic precedential references to peoples who have successfully ob-tained and retained political independence, the most recent leaders of self-determination movements within Europe have indicated a strong role for the demonstration effect. Needless to say, the intensity of the effect exerted by a particular model upon a given ethnic group will depend upon a number of variables, for example, (1) chronological time (in general the more recent the illustration, the more graphic its analogical impact).[22] (2) proximity,[23] (3) comparability of size of popu-lation and territorial extent, (4) myths involving ancestral relation-ships,[24] and (5) whether or not the two groups were once ruled from the same capital.[25] Such factors can, of course, overlap in a reinforcing pat-tern. Thus, the pertinence of an independent Ireland partakes of all five elements for the Scots and the Welsh, of all but the fifth for the Bretons, and of only the first and the second for the Basques.[26]

Two developments have proved to be particularly significant for the demonstration effect they exerted upon the postwar self-determination movements within Western Europe. One is the general, though irregu-lar, trend in the historical evolution of nationalism within Western Eu-rope from larger to smaller ethnic elements. The political independence of Norway in 1905, for example, represented an important milestone because the Norse number less than either the Catalans or the Scots.[27] Ireland's emancipation was a further step in this direction, and Ice-land's decision to acquire separate status during World War II offered existent proof that size was no barrier whatsoever to independence. The contrary notion that insubstantial size posed an insurmountable barrier to political independence had long been treated as a truism by scholars and statesmen and also must have exerted its impact upon the masses. Otherwise, it is difficult to account for the great stress that the leaders of the new movements have placed upon the examples of still smaller communities in their quest for converts.[28] In any event, there were few ethnic elements in Western Europe, which harbored potential leaders with dreams of independence, whose numbers did not exceed that of Icelanders. As late as 1944, Alfred Cobban, as a means of ridicul-ing the logical extension of the national self-determination principle, raised the image of an Iceland or a Malta someday achieving indepen-dence.[29] The fact that Iceland achieved independence the same year as the publication of Cobban's comments and that Malta followed suit in 1964 illustrates how the formerly potent psychological restraint of meager size had been effectively exorcised from political axioms inherited from an earlier age.

A second development of great import was the ending of the colonial era due to the infectious spread throughout the overseas possessions of the notion that "alien rule is illegitimate rule." As noted, the demonstration effect produced by the obtaining of political independence by a specific state varied in the impact that it exerted among different Western European ethnic groups. Thus, the freeing of India could be expected to have its maximal impact upon groups within the United Kingdom, and the freeing of Algeria, upon groups within France. But the total effect of this spectacle of a global parade toward independence could be expected to have a broad impact upon all ethnically conscious European peoples without regard to state borders. In the words of Pierre Fougeyrollas: "The decolonialization of Asia and Africa incites the oppressed minorities of Europe to subsequently undertake their own decolonialization. . . . Why should not the ideas and the inclinations which had asserted themselves at Dakar, Brazzaville, Algiers, and even Montreal, irresistibly develop at Brest, Strasbourg, Dunkirk?"[30] Even had decolonialization not occurred, there is no apparent reason to believe that the ethnonational virus would not in time have afflicted all of the ethnically distinct peoples of Western Europe, just as it had the Germans, the Norse, and the Irish at an earlier time. Indeed, the post–World War II movements did not, Athene-like, suddenly appear in fully developed form; their developmental history straddles World War II and, in many cases, World War I. But the manner in which so many movements suddenly became prominent in the late 1950s and 1960s indicates the presence of powerful catalysts, one of which unquestionably was the demonstration effect produced by global decolonialization. Ethnonationalism, which the post–World War I leaders of France, the United Kingdom, and the United States had believed they could quarantine within Eastern Europe, had spread to all non-European regions, from which it exerted a backlash effect upon Western Europe's nonindependent peoples.

Modernization and increased communications have indeed had an impact upon contemporary ethnonational movements, though not the type of impact perceived by the "modernization promotes assimilation" school. In an extraordinary anticipation of that school's erroneous thesis, Carlton Hayes warned nearly a half-century ago:

> Many optimists of the present day are convinced that the Industrial Revolution is fundamentally anti-nationalist. . . . The scope of communication

is beyond as well as within the frontiers of any particular nation. Each country, each nationality, is becoming more closely linked to others by railways, steamships, motor cars, automobiles, aircraft, postal service, telegraph, telephone, radio, and television. Travel is becoming more international. Information for the newspapers and the press is being gathered and distributed more internationally. Intellectual movements in one country ramify more and more speedily into other countries. . . . We do know that there has been an astounding improvement in the mechanical arts during the past hundred and forty years, involving a veritable industrial revolution. . . . But it is, or should be, apparent also that there have been during the same hundred and forty years . . . a parallel diffusion and intensification of nationalism. . . . It seems paradoxical that political nationalism should grow stronger and more virulent as economic internationalism increases. . . . For an understanding of the paradox, it is important to bear in mind that the Industrial Revolution is not necessarily an intellectual revolution. Of itself it is neither nationalist nor internationalist. It is essentially mechanical and material. It has merely provided improved means and greater opportunities for the dissemination of any ideas. . . . Now it so happened that when the Industrial Revolution began, nationalism was becoming a significant intellectual movement, even more significant than internationalism. Consequently, while the newer industrial machinery has been utilized for international ends, it has also been utilized, even more, for nationalist purposes. The obvious international fruits of the Industrial Revolution must not blind our eyes to its intensely nationalist contributions and implications.[31]

In short, the principal impact of modernization has been catalytic, rather than causal. It has held greater import for the tempo of nationalism than for its substance.[32] It helps to explain the ever-accelerating pace at which the idea of national self-determination has infected peoples. It has increased the impact of the demonstration effect. But while the media have undergone revolutionary changes, the disarmingly simple message that ethnicity and state legitimacy are linked has remained remarkably unembellished since put forth in the Declaration of the Rights of Man and of the Citizen in 1789: "The source of all sovereignty resides essentially in the nation; no group, no individual, may exercise authority not emanating expressly therefrom."

But if the emergence of national sentiment among the still dependent ethnic groups of Western Europe represented a sequential step in a historical evolution, why did it occasion so much surprise among scholars, particularly among scholars of nationalism? For many, one suspects, the answer is a general disregard for historical perspective. If, for example, one credits the rise of nationalism within a particular ethnic community solely to economic discrimination (the theory of relative economic deprivation), then there is little need to search history for antecedents or for the germination and development of an abstract notion of a kindred people. Similarly, what has been earlier described as the first pillar of conventional postwar scholarship on Western Europe (the image of the region's inhabitants as sophisticated cosmopolites who had come to recognize that nationalism is a dangerous anachronism in the current era) reflected a view of nationalism as an ephemeral, easily discarded phenomenon. This view is quite at odds with both political and intellectual history since the late eighteenth century.

For others, the total lack of anticipation of recent events is not so much a case of no history as of poor history. Those who perceived the surge of ethnonational demands throughout Western Europe in the late 1960s as without forerunners were overlooking numerous, well-advertised portents. Among them were the previously mentioned autonomy voted by the Basques, Catalans, and Galicians of Spain during the 1930s; the unrest among South Tyrolean Germans almost from the commencement of their incorporation into Italy after World War I, the well-publicized plebiscite ordered by Hitler to protect the Rome-Berlin Axis from the reverberations of this unrest (and in which an astonishing number indicated their willingness to leave their homes and settle within the Third Reich rather than to become Italian citizens), and the very early resumption of antistate activities within South Tyrol following World War II; Hitler's successes in appealing to the ethnonationalism of the Flemings and Bretons in order to get their collaboration; Mussolini's similar appeal to the Corsicans; and the separatist movements that were active in Sardinia and Sicily during World War II and among French-speaking Val D'Aostans both during and immediately following that same struggle.[33] Considering the historical pattern of the national *idea*—its infection, beginning with the French, of an ever-greater number of peoples—it is particularly perplexing to encounter Konstantin Symons-Symonolewicz's statement that "one can hardly discern any clear evolutionary trend with respect to the growth of the principle of nationality—to claim that it is steadily advancing would be no less foolhardy than to conclude that its dynamics had been spent completely."[34] Moreover, considering the path of ethnonationalism throughout Europe traced above (a path that has left the borders of only three states unaltered in its wake), it is disquieting to read in Arnold Toynbee's monumental work:

> Nationalism was comparatively innocuous in its West European birthplace, where, for the most part, it took the political map as it found it, and was content to utilize the existing parochial states, within their established

frontiers, as its crucibles for the decoction of its intoxicating political brew of psychic energy. Its noxious potentialities revealed themselves where, so far from consecrating the frontiers which it found on the map, this aggressive exotic political ideology denounced them in the name of the explosive political proposition that all persons who happened to be speakers of this or that vernacular language had a natural right to be united politically with one another in a single sovereign independent national state and therefore had a moral obligation to sacrifice their own and their neighbors' welfare, happiness, and life itself in the pursuit of this pedantic political programme. This linguistic interpretation—or caricature—of the West European ideology of Nationalism was never taken on pied de la lettre in the West European countries themselves, since here the external bond provided by community of speech was always recognized as being merely one among divers outward signs of an inward sense of political solidarity springing from common political experiences, institutions, and ideals.[35]

All of the foregoing is not to deny that praiseworthy histories of a number of these ethnic movements existed prior to the 1960s.[36] Nor is it to deny that country specialists have often shown awareness of ethnic diversity within their respective countries.[37] All too frequently, however, these histories and specialists have suffered from too narrow a focus: the tendency to see the movement as sui generis, to look only within the state for the source of its nourishment, and not to perceive it as part of a broader intellectual movement. As Hans Kohn has opined: "A study of nationalism must follow a comparative method, it cannot remain confined to one of its manifestations; only the comparison of the different nationalisms all over the earth will enable the student to see what they have in common and what is peculiar to each, and thus allow a just evaluation. An understanding of nationalism can be gained only by a world history of the age of nationalism."[38] Elsewhere, Kohn again underlined this need for both historic perspective and a broad comparative framework: "Only a study of the historical growth of nationalism and a comparative study of its different forms can make us understand the impact of nationalism today."[39] Kohn was not arguing against the necessity for case studies. During his lifetime, he produced several monographs dealing with the rise of ethnonationalism within a single environment. Rather, his contention was that the student of a particular movement or movements should first observe the manner in which nationalism evolved in a number of other societies.[40]

His advice would appear to be relevant to much of the recent scholarly work on Western Europe. It is likely, for example, that the theory of relative economic deprivation is less compelling to those who are aware that the Basques and Catalans are financially better off than the Castilians; that Croats and Slovenes are financially ahead of Serbs; that Flanders received a disproportionately large share of Belgium-wide investments between 1958 and 1968, a period of growing Flemish intransigence; that ethnic movements in Western Europe and Canada have not received their major support from the poor, but, while cutting across income lines, have tended to attract a disproportionately large number of professional people; that during 1974 more than one-third of the voters of Switzerland voted yes on a referendum drawn up by the National Movement against Foreign Domination of People and Homeland, which would have deported huge numbers of foreign workers, despite popular awareness that implementation would have caused serious economic dislocation and a drop in living standards; and that a number of ethnic groups within the Soviet Union have indicated opposition to additional investment within their ethnic homeland because of the conviction that greater industrialization brings with it more Russians, a price deemed too high to pay for increased living standards.

Similarly, those who feel that the explanation for the recent surge in nationalism is to be found in cultural deprivation should be aware that the Basques, who have been the most militantly nationalist element within Spain, are also the *least* interested in using their own language in everyday conversation, as well as the least interested in having their children taught to speak it;[41] that one of the factors that animated Flemish nationalists was *not* cultural deprivation but cultural freedom under which Flemish parents had been increasingly opting to have their children learn French as their primary tongue;[42] that Plaid Cymru (the National party of Wales) acknowledges that a majority of its members cannot speak Welsh and indirectly acknowledges that many have no interest in doing so, by promising that learning the language will not become compulsory; that polls have quite consistently indicated that a higher percentage of Scots than of Welsh are desirous of "going it alone," despite the fact that very few can speak the Scottish language and that the resuscitation of the language has not been a prominent element in the Scottish nationalist movement; and that the Irish vernacular, whose revitalization and reinstitution once occupied a prominent place in the programs of Irish liberation movements, has little support for its adoption (or even its learning as a secondary language) in the postindependence period. Those who maintain that the surge of nationalism is due to alienation from the modern, mass society should be perplexed by its concomitant vitality in such less modernized societies as those of Baluchistan, Kurdistan, Mizoland, or Nagaland.

There are several other elements, in addition to a lack of historical and comparative perspective, which help to account for the surprise engendered by the recent surge of ethnonationalism within Europe. Elsewhere. I have suggested twelve possible pitfalls in the study of nationalism, four of which would seem to have particular application to the European experience:[43]

1. *Confusing terminology leading to a tendency not to recognize ethnonationalism for what it is.* The literature on Western Europe, as elsewhere, has tended to employ the terms *nation* and *state* interchangeably. By extension, *nationalism* is employed (and is therefore perceived) as describing loyalty to the state, rather than to the ethnonational group. The need to find a term other than nationalism to describe loyalty to a Basque, Breton, or Flemish nation has led to a number of substitutes, for example, *subnational loyalties, ethnic pluralism, regionalism,* and the like. Such terminology can naturally hamper analysis. Since nationalism is perceived as in the service of the state, it is assumed that these other phenomena pose no serious, long-term competition for the loyalty of citizens; the newer movements are not seen as analogous to the nationalist movements of such state-controlling nations as the Germans, Poles, or Norse.[44] The description of ethnonational movements as "regionalism" is particularly pernicious because, as we have noted, regionalism (in the sense of sectionalism) has tended to disappear as modernization has linked the segments of a state more closely.[45] He who views the ethnonationalism of a people as regionalism is therefore preconditioned to perceive its demise as modernization progresses; but modernization tends to exert an opposite reaction where ethnonational groups are involved.[46] Moreover, *region* and *section* imply the existence of a larger whole; thus, even prior to its demise, regionalism is not mutually incompatible with loyalty to the state. By contrast, the ethnonational presumption that state legitimacy and ethnicity are linked is incompatible with loyalty to a state viewed as dominated by non-members of the group.

2. *The tendency to discern national strife as predicated principally upon language, religion, customs, economic inequity, or some other tangible element.* The classic contemporary case of this tendency is the strife in Northern Ireland, regularly depicted as a religious struggle. The compulsion to perceive and to report the struggle in terms of the handy, readily discernible element of religion, rather than to probe or to try to convey to one's audience the abstract notion of Irish identity on the one side versus the various national identities on the other is reflected in the following two illustrations. In an article in the *New York Times* reporting on an interview with Glenn Barr, a member of the non-Irish community, Barr is quoted as noting: "I don't know what I am. People

say I'm British. The British treat me as a second class citizen. I am not Irish. I am an Ulsterman."[47] Despite this colloquy, Barr is introduced to the reader as a "Protestant leader" (though he holds no religious office), and the entire article discusses the conflict in terms of a religious struggle. Similarly, an Associated Press dispatch dated 30 January 1975 indicates that arms are being shipped to the Irish Republican Army "by Breton separatist Catholics who want to free Brittany from France." Why the need to draw attention to the Catholic faith of the Bretons who are citizens of an overwhelmingly Catholic state? Reference to the Celtic dimension would, of course, have introduced abstract notions of ancestral ties and ethnonational consciousness, notions extremely difficult to convey to both readers and editors. However, the tendency to describe the nature of the struggle as religious is encountering an increasing amount of contrary evidence. For example, a statement of policy released by the Social Democratic and Labour party of Northern Ireland (a somewhat moderate party whose base of support is in the Irish segment of the community) employs such expressions as "more than one-third of [Northern Ireland's] population regard themselves as part of the wider Irish Community. . . . [The government] must take account of the divisions within Northern Ireland, the conflicting *national identities* and the special relations that Northern Ireland will always have with Great Britain and the Republic of Ireland. . . . *The two national identities* must be recognized in Northern Ireland's relations with Great Britain and the Republic of Ireland."[48] References to religion are noteworthy by their absence.

While the most dramatic illustration of the tendency to mistake tangible characteristics for essence, Northern Ireland is not the only Western European illustration of this phenomenon. As my earlier comments concerning theories of relative deprivation make clear, there have been many who have perceived ethnic restiveness in terms of a group's choice of battlefields, that is, in terms of economic statistics or an aspect of culture such as language.[49]

3. An unwarranted exaggeration of the influence of materialism upon human affairs.   Enough has previously been said concerning the theory of relative economic deprivation to document the prevalence of this tendency in the pertinent scholarship on Western Europe.

4. The tendency to interpret the absence of ethnic strife as evidence of the presence of a single nation.   With the South Tyroleans constituting the most noteworthy exception, the years immediately following World War II constituted a period of relative quiescence as far as ethnonationalism is concerned. The reasons for this respite are understandable. The area was still recuperating from a holocaust whose principal cause was ethnonationalism in its most extreme form. The extravagant activities carried out in the name of the *Volksdeutsch* (the German people) and the *razza italica* (the Italian race), made ethnonationalism per se suspect. This period of ethnonational apathy temporarily interrupted the continuity of a number of movements which antedated the war. Interruption was interpreted as demise, and reappearance was therefore viewed as something startling, if not totally original. Latent attitudes had been ignored, as scholars concentrated on the more overt opinions of the day.

A number of movements faced particular problems, in addition to the general fear of the destructive capacity of ethnonationalism, which had been engendered by the excesses of ethnic fascism. The recent equating of German nationalism and Nazism caused the feeling of a German heritage, in particular, to lose much of its luster. The impact of this phenomenon upon Germanic people such as the Alsatians was evident. Whereas the three political parties who favored autonomy for Alsace had garnered more than 40 percent of the Alsatian vote in 1928, ethnonationalism apparently declined among these people after the rise to power of Adolph Hitler, and seemingly disappeared during the immediate postwar era. Nevertheless, the resiliency of ethnonational motivation was indicated by the creation in 1970 of a Regional Movement of Alsace-Lorraine.[50] In a somewhat similar vein, the Flemish and Breton movements had become tainted by the collaboration of some of their leaders with the Nazis. In addition to needing time to permit memories of such activities and associations to fade, the movements also needed time to find new leaders to replace the tainted elite, many of whom had fled, been killed by the underground, or incarcerated in the postwar period.

The postwar reaction to ethnic fascism was not restricted to minorities. Its behavioral impact upon Frenchmen, Dutchmen, Danes, and others in the war's immediate afterglow lulled scholars into believing that Europeans had left nationalism behind (that syndrome which we have labeled the first pillar of conventional postwar thinking on Western Europe). Reaction could be expected to be most intense in the case of the people who had been most fanatically caught up in the ethnonational, nightmarish crusade, the Germans. Armed by the fresh memories of the unbridled passions proved to lurk in that Pandora's box of German nationalism, embarrassed by if not remorseful for the excesses carried out in its name, realistically appraising postwar power realities and aware that all non-German Europeans were vigilantly watching for the slightest symptom of a revitalization of German nationalism,

Germans held their ethnonational proclivities in tight rein. But as memories recede, as the realization grows that Nazism and German nationalism are not inevitably synonymous, as pride of postwar material and cultural achievements takes on the hue of pride in German achievements, as older Germans come to believe that Germany's period of atonement and parole has lasted long enough, and as a postwar generation that believes it cannot be held in any way culpable for the mistakes of its parents comes into power, German nationalism manifests commensurate signs of recovery.[51] Throughout Europe, then, the obituaries for ethnonationalism have proved premature.

.   .   .

The theme of this essay has been that recent ethnonational developments within Western Europe can be viewed as a sequential, evolutionary step in the extension or the force field of nationalism. Recalling again the surprise occasioned by the factual undermining of those two postwar pillars of scholarship on Western Europe (the obsolescence of nationalism and the absence of multinational states), consider the following passage by Carlton Hayes: "One striking feature of the period's nationalist agitation, obviously, was that it affected and widely publicized a number of European peoples that had not previously been supposed to have national consciousness or political aspirations. Another of its features, even more startling, was its quickened tempo and fiercer manifestation among . . . peoples already known to be nationalist." By peoples "not previously been supposed to have national consciousness," Hayes was indeed referring to Basques, Bretons, Catalans, Flemish, and the like. The passage, however, was written not in the 1970s but in 1941; not to describe Western Europe of the 1960s and 1970s, but of the 1870s, 1880s, and 1890s.[52] The point is that the more sensitive literature on nationalism written in the prewar period did contain valuable clues to what might be expected to occur within Western Europe as nationalism further evolved. As early as 1926, for example, Hayes warned of troubles between ethnonational groups within Belgium and Switzerland, "despite the artificial attempts to promote a sense of social solidarity, akin to nationality, among all the Swiss and among all the Belgians."[53] He also referred to "the budding little nationalisms" of Icelanders, Catalans, Provençals, Basques, Wends, White Russians (Belorussians), Manx, and Maltese.[54] Similarly, the famous 1939 report on nationalism by the Royal Institute of International Affairs painted a more insightful portrait of the Northern Ireland conflict than do most current works:

But in the minds of the Irish nationalists independence had become bound up with the idea of the geographical unity of Ireland, the territory which had formed the free, though slightly legendary, Kingdom of Ireland before the Anglo-Saxon invaders made their appearance. Not only must those who feel themselves to be members of the Irish nation be free to govern themselves, but the whole of Ireland must be united. The Irish question has thus created a second clash between the claims of two rival nationalisms.[55]

Elsewhere the report warned that "Great Britain herself is not immune from this problem, as it may be rash to assume that the present solution of the relationship between the English, Scottish, and Welsh must necessarily be permanent."[56]

Sensitive and perspicacious though these works are, many of their predictions proved fallacious.[57] The past need not be prologue. History—including the history of nationalism—does not operate independently of the whims and caprices of events and individuals. Even a proper regard for the historical development of nationalism does not, therefore, eliminate the hazards inherent in predicting future political developments. But, as the cited passages by Hayes and the Royal Institute indicate, an appreciation of the pattern of nationalism's development will perhaps increase the chances of making accurate predictions; at least it will reduce the likelihood of being totally surprised when confronted with nationalism's most recent manifestations.

Notes

1. Stanley Hoffmann, "Obstinate or Obsolete? The Fate of The Nation-State," in *Conditions of World Order*, ed. Stanley Hoffmann (New York, 1966), 110. See also Charles Lerche and Abdul Said, *Concepts of International Politics*, 2d ed. (Englewood Cliffs, N.J., 1970), 274. "Postwar Europe provided a particularly fertile field for experimentation with new forms of international organization. The European peoples needed to escape from the destructive nationalism which had led to the devastation of two world wars within a half-century." The broad acceptance this view received is also indicated by its endorsement in Dankwart Rustow's essay "Nation" in the *International Encyclopedia of the Social Sciences* (New York, 1968), 11. See p. 10: "Since World War II, common European loyalties have begun to compete with the national allegiances of the past, and to that extent the European countries are losing their character as nations; if the process should continue, our descendants may one day be able to speak of a European nation."

2. The states said to have assimilated their populations quite evidently displayed two distinct methods for attaining this end. While all were seen as pursuing (and achieving) psychological assimilation, some, such as Britain, France, and Spain, had fostered cultural assimilation, while others, such as Belgium

and Switzerland (and Canada) had tolerated cultural, particularly linguistic, diversity.

3. Easily the most prominent and influential member of the nation-building school has been Karl Deutsch. For a relatively early exposition of this thesis, see his "Nation-Building and National Development" in *Nation-Building*, ed. Karl Deutsch and William Foltz (New York, 1966), particularly 1–8. For a later statement concerning the successful assimilation experience of Western Europe, see his *Nationalism and Its Alternatives* (New York, 1969), chap. 1, entitled "The Experience of Western Europe." In this chapter, Italy, Spain, and Switzerland (as well as Canada and the United States) are cited as examples of states with a single national consciousness. Specific references to the successful assimilation of Bretons, Cornishmen, and Scots are also made. In both editions of his earlier *Nationalism and Social Communication: An Inquiry into the Foundations of Nationality* (Cambridge, 1953, 1956), Deutsch cites Bretons, Flemings, French Canadians, the French- and German-speaking Swiss, Scots, and Welsh as examples of totally assimilated peoples. The impact that this image of successful assimilation had upon Deutsch's vision of the future of the Afro-Asian states is apparent in his description of a four-stage process leading to successful assimilation. After enumerating the four stages, he inquires: "How long might it take for tribes or other ethnic groups in a developing country to pass through such a sequence of stages? We do not know but European history offers at least a few suggestions." See "Nation-Building and National Development," 324.

Another example of the linking of Europe's "assimilationist" experience with the future of the Afro-Asian states is offered by Benjamin Akzin, *State and Nation* (London, 1964). Having noted the dissolving political significance of groups such as the "Welsh, Scots, Lapps, Frisians, Bretons, Savoyards, [and] Corsicans" (p. 63), the author continues: "If we look at the modern nation-states of Europe we shall see that except perhaps for those of the Scandinavian peninsula, the population of each of them is largely the product of pre-existing ethnic groups which have integrated into the nations we know today. This is true of the French nation, consolidated from fairly heterogeneous elements between the seventh and the twelfth centuries. . . . Germans, Italians, Poles, Russians, and Spaniards have all become the well defined nations we know within a century or two of one another. . . . Under pre-modern conditions the process required a fairly long period of gestation. . . . Put into the pot of physical proximity, covered by the lid of a common political system, exposed to the heat of cultural and social interchange, the various elements will change after a fairly long time—it took a few centuries in the past, but may take less in the future— into a brew. The brew will not be quite homogeneous. You can still point to a grain of rice, to a leaf of onion, to a chunk of meat, to a splinter of bone. But it will manifestly be one brew, with its distinct flavor and taste" (pp. 83–84). A more succinct avowal of this same linkage doctrine is offered by Donald Puchala, *International Politics Today* (New York, 1972), 200–201. After defining the nation-state as one in which "the political perimeters of the state and the ethnic perimeters of the nation coincide," he concludes that "processes similar to those that produced nation-states in Europe during the last two centuries, are producing new nation-states in Africa and Asia today."

4. The First World here refers to the industrialized states of Canada and the United States, as well as to those of Western Europe. Though unquestionably also a member of the First World, Japan was usually ignored in the general, theoretic treatises on nation building, perhaps because of its ethnic homogeneity, which long antedated modernization.

5. A well-known American sociologist, Arnold Rose, tested the strength of supranational sentiment ("Europeanness") by studying the willingness of host populations to accept the alien workers as compatriots. Although noting some variations among host populations, he recorded a high incidence of xenophobia throughout Western Europe and failed to find substantial willingness anywhere to accept the foreigner as a fellow citizen. See his *Migrants in Europe* (Minneapolis, 1969). Since publication of the book, ethnic prejudice and attempts to expel foreigners have become more flagrant.

6. The lack of publicity accorded to some of these movements is, in turn, reflected in a low level of public awareness concerning their existence. For example, at the annual meeting of the Northeastern Political Science Association in November 1973, I was criticized for a reference to ethnonational stirrings within France and particularly for references to the Bretons. The critic (a specialist in French affairs) insisted that his many sojourns in Brittany had failed to uncover any such sentiment. Yet, only two months later, the French government felt compelled to outlaw four national liberation movements, two of which were Breton (the others being Basque and Corsican). See also Collette Guillaumin, "The Popular Press and Ethnic Pluralism: The Situation in France," *International Social Sciences Journal* 22 (1971): 576–93. The author presumably believes that ethnic minorities within France are limited to Jews, Gypsies, and people from overseas departments; she is apparently oblivious to the Alsatian, Basque, Breton, Catalan, Flemish, and Occitanian communities within her own state.

7. The mid-1970s witnessed a series of conferences of European minority groups. One held at Trieste in July 1974 was attended by representatives of, among others, Alsatians, Basques, Bretons, Catalans, Corsicans, Croats, Flemings, Frisians (of the Netherlands), Galicians, Irish, Occitanians, Piedmontese (of Italy), Sardinians, Scots, and Welsh. The Celtic League Conference held on the Isle of Man during September 1975 included representatives from "Alba," "Breizh," "Cymru," "Eire," "Kernow," and "Manin" (i.e., Scotland, Brittany, Wales, Ireland, Cornwall, and the Isle of Man).

8. The center-periphery model can vary among devotees. In some hands, it is essentially a spatial or geographic concept, connoting that a Brittany or Scotland has been physically remote from the state's sociopolitical ecumene and is, as a result, not part of the state's intensive communication and transportation network. In other hands, the notion of a peripheral people is essentially social, denoting those who are least socially mobilized and who are, for example, among those on the lowest income and education levels.

9. Further reference to some of these explanations is made below. It is worth noting here, however, that while some explanations overlap and reinforce one another, others appear to be at least somewhat contradictory (e.g., Denmark and Spain were hardly world powers in the prewar period).

10. This notion of popular sovereignty should be seen as a principle of state legitimacy rather than of governmental legitimacy. As such, it does not presuppose democracy, but only that the political elites acknowledge that they rule in the name of the people. Thus, spake the Emperor Napoleon, "We have been guided at all times by this great truth: that the sovereignty resides in the French people in the sense that everything, everything without exception, must be done for its best interests, for its well being, and for its glory." *Message to the Senate, 1804,* as reprinted in *The Mind of Napoleon: A Selection from His Written and Spoken Words,* ed. and trans. J. Christopher Herold (New York, 1955), 72. In a similar vein, Hitler described his "folkish state": "We, as Aryans, are therefore able to imagine a State only to be the living organism of a nationality which not only safeguards the preservation of that nationality, but which, by a further training of its spiritual and ideal abilities, leads it to the highest freedom." *Mein Kampf* (New York, 1940), 595.

11. For a more detailed account of the historic growth of ethnonationalism within Europe, see Walker Connor, "The Politics of Ethnonationalism," *Journal of International Affairs* 27, no. 1 (1973): 5–11 particularly.

12. In addition to the Finns, Estonians, Letts, and Lithuanians, at least nine other groups seceded from Russia during 1917 and 1918 and created separate states. With the exception of the above four, and the peoples of Bessarabia and what had been Russian Poland, the Soviet government succeeded in reabsorbing all the groups within a few years. Moreover, as a result of World War II, it reabsorbed all the remaining peoples with the exception of the Finns and Poles.

13. Of the three exceptions (Portugal, Spain, and Switzerland), one (Portugal) was an ethnically homogeneous state. Technically, Spain was not an exception, for during the short-lived Spanish Republic of the 1930s, the Basques, Catalans, and Galicians had voted themselves very abbreviated periods of autonomy before being reincorporated by Franco's forces. Switzerland too was not without its ethnic problems during the Franco-Prussian War (1871) and World Wars I and II. See chapter 1 in this volume.

14. From the Serbian viewpoint, the formation in 1918 of the Kingdom of Serbs, Croats, and Slovenes, later renamed Yugoslavia, might even be seen as a stride in the other direction. However, it brought the Croats and Slovenes a step closer to self-determination than they had been as part of the larger Austro-Hungarian Empire.

15. The tensions between Croat and Serb, Slovak and Czech, Magyar and Romanian have been most publicized, but numerous other groups (Albanians, Slovenes, Macedonians, Bulgars, and Bessarabian Romanians) are also involved. For a recent broad-brush treatment of many of these ethnic struggles, see Robert King, *Minorities Under Communism: Nationalities as a Source of Tension among Balkan Communist States* (Cambridge, 1973).

16. The subsequent de facto division of Cyprus into Turkish and Greek territories during 1974 can be seen as analogous to the Biafran and Bangla Desh movements, i.e., a further step toward national self-determination.

17. See chapter 2 in this volume.

18. Suzanne Berger, "Bretons, Basques, Scots, and Other European Nations,"

Journal of Interdisciplinary History 3 (Summer 1972): 170–71. A bit farther on (p. 174), the author notes, "Once conscious only of belonging to their own small region and to their administrative unit, the department, many Bretons discovered from radio and television that they were part of Brittany."

19. For a concise history of the Breton movement, see David Fortier, "Between Nationalism and Modern France: The Permanent Revolution," in *The Limits of Integration: Ethnicity and Nationalism in Modern Europe*, ed. Oriol Pi-Sunyer (Amherst, 1971), 77–109.

20. I first expressed this position in "Self-Determination: The New Phase," and Arend Lijphart, after citing it with favor in his stimulating and influential article "Consociational Democracy," *World Politics* 21 (January 1969): 220, went on to add: "This proposition can be refined further by stating both the degree of homogeneity and the extent of mutual contacts in terms of continua rather than dichotomies." From what has been said above concerning the difference in intensity of contacts between the prewar and postwar eras, it is evident that we agree that both the intensity *and the nature* of contacts can affect the level of conflict among ethnic groups. The matter of relative cultural similarity between two groups may be another matter, however. One of the oddities of our period (in large part a response to increases in the quantity and quality of communications networks) is that the cultures of various groups are becoming more resemblant of one another, while the saliency of feelings of ethnic distinction is also growing. What would seem to be involved here, then, is not the degree of cultural similarity. It is psychological and not cultural assimilation with which we are dealing, and whether or not one intuitively feels that he is a member of this or that ethnonational group is, for the mass of mankind, ultimately a matter of yes or no, rather than more or less.

21. The leaders of multiethnic states have quite consistently indicated their fear of this phenomenon. African political leaders, for example, have adamantly refused to recognize the legitimacy of secessionist ethnic movements within any of the black African states. India's intractability on the Kashmiri issue is also inspired in part by the fissiparous impact that Kashmiri independence might exert upon other ethnic segments of the population.

22. A noteworthy exception is the case where a prosecessionist is arguing against the often-heard statement that the proposed state could not become an economically viable entity. In such a case, the longevity of the selected model may be the key to its utility.

23. To take some non-Western European examples, the Biafran episode was clearly seen as a greater threat by African leaders than by those of Asia. Similarly, the creation of Bangla Desh was viewed by the leaders of India and Pakistan, quite rightly as it turned out, to hold the greatest significance for the subcontinent itself. And, one of the reasons underlying the Soviet decision to intervene in Czechoslovakia in 1968 was the fear of the effect that the Slovak movement for autonomy would have upon the already restive Ukrainians residing immediately across the Soviet border.

24. It is perhaps to risk accentuating the apparent to note that the closer the relationship is perceived to be, the more vivid the demonstration effect is apt to be. Thus, the creation of each independent Arab state incited demands that *all*

Arabs be free. While less poignant, the notion of common Slavism made the creation of each Slavic state a matter of special interest to those Slavic peoples still under alien rule.

25. For example, when an overseas possession gains its freedom, the event is of greater significance to minorities within the mother country than would be the case had the overseas territory been owned by another state. Still more significance would be attached to the successful severance of part of the "home territory," that is, of a portion of the state itself.

26. See, for example, Kenneth Morgan, "Welsh Nationalism: The Historical Background," *Contemporary History* 6 (1971): 172, in which it is noted that the Welsh national movement "clearly owed a little to nationalism everywhere, to Hungarian nationalism, and most of all to Irish." The common Celtic ancestry is what principally accounts for the influence of the Irish upon the Bretons; there are no common historic or political bonds. The influence of common celticity is more problematic in the case of the Scots and the Irish because traditional animosities exist between the two due to the predominance of people of Scottish ancestry among the non-Irish of Northern Ireland. George Malcolm Thomas, after first noting that the Scots "are nearer to the Irish in race and temperament than they like to admit," went on to note that "the truth is that Ulster is both Irish (geographically) and British. Or to be more exact, Scottish (culturally)." *Christian Science Monitor*, 6 July 1974. But see Owen Dudley Edwards et al., *Celtic Nationalism* (London, 1968), for contributions by Irish, Scottish, and Welsh nationalists, each of whom stresses the Celtic bond. See also the Scottish National Party's publication *100 Home Rule Questions Answered by Sandy M'Intosh*, 2d rev. ed. (Forfar, 1968), 15: "Where there is compulsory integration and discontent in one or more of the integrated countries, there is no real unity, as Irish history has well shown." And on p. 28, there is a reference to "proud and patriotic nations like Eire." Contemporary pan-Celtic organizations, such as the Celtic Congress and the Celtic League, though of unknown influence at the grass-roots level, are recent indications of political consequences flowing from pan-ethnicities.

27. The Scottish National Party often makes use of Norway for comparative purposes when insisting that Scotland can "go it alone." See, for example, *100 Home Rule Questions Answered by Sandy M'Intosh*, particularly 27 and 45.

28. Welsh nationalists, for example, point out that thirty-nine states have fewer people than Wales, and they particularly emphasize that Iceland, Luxembourg, and New Zealand are included among them. See the *Christian Science Monitor*, 2 August 1974.

29. Alfred Cobban, *National Self-Determination* (London, 1944), 131–32. On p. 173, the author makes similar comments concerning Wales, White Russia (Belorussia), Alsace, Flanders, and French Canada.

30. Pierre Fougeyrollas, *Pour une France fédérale: Vers l'unité européenne par la révolution régionale* (Paris, 1968), 12.

31. Carlton Hayes, *The Historical Evolution of Modern Nationalism* (New York, 1931), 234–37. Hayes's analysis of the relationship between industrial modernization and nationalism was markedly different from that of Karl Marx and

Friedrich Engels, as witnessed by the following passage from the Communist Manifesto: "National differences and antagonisms between peoples are daily more and more vanishing, owing to the development of the bourgeoisie, to freedom of commerce, to the world market, to uniformity in the mode of production and in condition of life corresponding thereto."

32. Tempo itself can, of course, exert a substantive impact: the more intense the contacts among groups, the more likely a militant ethnonational response. See chapter 2 in this volume.

33. A Canadian analogy would be the reaction of the French Canadians to proposals to draft them during World War I and World War II to fight what they perceived as "English wars." Little different is the case of Eastern Europe where Hitler gained a measure of Slovak and Croatian collaboration by offering them autonomy from the Czechs and the Serbs, respectively. The early positive response of Ukrainians, Crimean Tatars, and other non-Russian ethnic elements to the German invasion of the Soviet Union has also been heavily publicized.

34. Konstantin Symons-Symonolowicz, *Nationalist-Movements: A Comparative View* (Meadville, 1970), 4.

35. Arnold Toynbee, *A Study of History* (London, 1954), 8: 536.

36. Two noteworthy illustrations in the English language are Shepard Clough, *A History of the Flemish Movement in Belgium: A Study in Nationalism* (New York, 1930); and Reginald Coupland, *Welsh and Scottish Nationalism: A Study* (London, 1954).

37. It should not, however, be assumed that country specialists have been more attuned to such diversity than have generalists. Specialists on the United Kingdom, for example, had long emphasized the unusually high degree of homogeneity of what was called the British (or even the English) society. Richard Rose lists L. S. Amery, Samuel Beer, Harry Eckstein, Jean Blondel, and S. E. Finer as examples of some of the many authorities on the United Kingdom who have slighted ethnic considerations; see Richard Rose, *The United Kingdom as a Multi-National State* (Glasgow, 1970). He might have added himself to the list, for in his own work he has stated: "Today politics in the United Kingdom is greatly simplified by the absence of major cleavages along the lines of ethnic groups, language, or religion." *Politics in England* (Boston, 1964), 10. Monographs on France also indicate an amazing disregard of ethnic cleavages.

38. Hans Kohn, *The Idea of Nationalism: A Study of Its Origins and Background* (New York, 1944), ix–x. For an interesting discussion of the strengths and limitations of the comparative method (though not specifically applied to the study of nationalism), see Arend Lijphart, "Comparative Politics and the Comparative Method," *American Political Science Review* 65 (September 1971): 682–93.

39. Hans Kohn, *Nationalism: Its Meaning and History*, rev. ed. (Princeton, 1965), 4.

40. In a most stimulating essay, Milton da Silva used the Basque movement to illustrate weaknesses in several theories concerning the nature and causes of ethnonationalism. In doing so, he evidenced a remarkable breadth of knowl-

edge. See his "Modernization and Ethnic Conflict: The Case of the Basques," *Comparative Politics* 7 (January 1975): 227–51.

41. See Juan Linz, "Early State-Building and Late Peripheral Nationalisms against the State: The Case of Spain" (Paper presented at the UNESCO Conference on Nation-Building, Cérisy, Normandy, August 1970), 85–86.

42. Joseph Rudolph, "The Belgian Front Democratique des Bruxellois Francophones-Rassemblant Wallon (F.D.F.-R.W.) and the Politics of Sub-National Institution-Building" (Paper presented at the Annual Meeting of the Northeastern Political Science Association, 9 November 1973), 3.

43. For a fuller explanation and examples of each of the four categories, see chapter 2 in this volume. Subject to the omission of eight categories listed in the above-mentioned text, the four categories listed here are in the order in which they were first presented.

44. See, for example, the quote from Dankwart Rustow in note 1 above, in which "nation" clearly refers to "state." In the previous sentence, he links the experiences of the German nation to a "British" (and an also questionable "Italian") nation, noting that "in Britain today no serious conflict is generally felt between a wider British and a more particular English, Welsh, or Scottish nationality."

45. *Regionalism* is also an unfortunate term in that it can mean either intrastate sectionalism or suprastate integration within a major area, such as Western Europe or Latin America.

46. For an article grouping ethnonational movements (such as those in Brittany, Corsica, Scotland, and Wales) with localism (such as that evidenced within a number of German Laender) under the single rubric of "subnational regionalism," see Werner Feld, "Subnational Regionalism and the European Community" in *Orbis* 18 (Winter 1975): 1176–92. The result is a confusing comparison of different phenomena. For a description of Scottish nationalism as regionalism (and a corresponding undervaluation of its potency), see John Schwartz, "The Scottish National Party," *World Politics* 22 (July 1970): 496–517, and particularly p. 515, where the author speaks of a "regional identity." See also Jack Haywood, *The One and Indivisible French Republic* (New York, 1973), 38, 56, where the movement within Brittany is referred to as regionalism. No reference to ethnonationalism is made, nor are there any references to France's other ethnic minorities. Since the term *region* implies a larger whole, the indivisibility of France (as indicated by the title) is assured. The propensity to refer to ethnonational movements within France and Italy as regionalism has probably been heightened in recent years by "regionalization" plans to decentralize authority. In both cases, the borders of the new regions often closely correspond with the distribution of ethnic groups. For more details, see my chapter on Western Europe in *Ethnicity in an International Context*, ed. Abdul Said and Luiz Simmons (Edison, N.J., 1976). *Periphery*, as used in the center-periphery concept, often means region, and as a result the above reservations concerning the use of *regionalism* to connote ethnonationalism would pertain to a like use of *periphery* as well.

47. *New York Times*, 16 November 1974.

48. *Keesing's Contemporary Archives*, 23–29 September 1974, 26,732, emphasis added.

49. After repeatedly encountering the religious explanation for the strife in Northern Ireland, I was gratified to hear Professor John White of Queen's University (Belfast) say in a conversation at the Harvard Center for International Affairs (October 1974) that the conflict was certainly ethnic and not religious. A few minutes later, however, my comment to a representative of the Belgian government to the effect that I should enjoy the opportunity to speak with him concerning his country's ethnic problem brought forth the rejoinder that the issue was definitely not ethnic but linguistic.

50. *Le Figaro*, 5 July 1971. The selection of Strasbourg as the seat of the Council of Europe unquestionably has had significant, if immeasurable, impact upon recent Alsatian ethnonationalism. The international role of this Alsatian city serves as a constant reminder that the Franco-German border no longer represents the same barrier to relations with transborder Germans that it did in the prewar era.

51. In the 1972 elections, for example, the victorious Social Democratic party phrased its appeals in terms of national pride and consciousness. See, for example, the *New York Times*, 17 November 1972. Basing their case principally upon the interpretation of opinion surveys, several individuals have recently contended that the notion of a single German nation is a thing of the past, having been replaced by a coalescence of identity around the notions of Austria, East Germany, and West Germany, respectively. See, for example, William Bluhm, *Building an Austrian Nation* (New Haven, 1973); Gordon Munro, "Two Germanies: A Lasting Solution to the German Question" (Ph.D. diss., Claremont Graduate School, 1972); and Gebhard Schweigler, "National Consciousness in Divided Germany" (Ph.D. diss., Harvard University, 1972). The survey data are not uncontradictory, however, and run counter to other data (e.g., the decision of the East German authorities in early 1975 to backtrack temporarily on their attempt to purge the notion that the peoples of East and West Germany are part of the same German nation). Moreover, given the many psychological and political forces at work in postwar Germany (as described above), it is at least questionable whether a valid opinion survey on nationalism can be conducted in that environment. There is also the matter of latent attitudes versus overt opinions. Finally, there is the question of whether, even under the best of circumstances, an opinion survey is an effective vehicle for determining ethnic attitudes. For two studies that contend it is not, see Arnold Rose, *Migrants in Europe*, 100, and John Wahlke and Milton Lodge, "Psychological Measures of Change in Political Attitudes" (Paper presented at the Annual Meeting of the Midwest Political Science Association, 1971), particularly 2–3.

52. Carlton Hayes, *A Generation of Materialism: 1870–1900* (New York, 1941), 280.

53. Carlton Hayes, *Essays on Nationalism* (New York, 1926), 15.

54. Ibid., 59.

55. *Nationalism: A Report by a Study Group of Members of the Royal Institute of International Affairs* (London, 1939), 111.

56. Ibid., 137.

57. See, for example, Hayes's overly optimistic comments concerning the ability of Switzerland, Canada, the Republic of South Africa, and the British Empire to accommodate divergent nationalisms, in his *Essays on Nationalism*, 21, 22, 270. The report of the Royal Institute is the work of nine scholars, and inconsistencies, therefore, abound. While some of the essays indicate a keen understanding of the national phenomena, others do not.

PART THREE

Scholars in the Mythic World of National Identity

Chapter Eight

MAN IS A ᴺRATIONAL ANIMAL

In chapter 3, we noted a persisting tendency among scholars to badly underestimate the emotional depth of ethnonational identity, and we linked this failing to a lack of understanding concerning the nature of that identity. We suggested that one potentially fruitful avenue for probing its murky nature might be a comparative study of the speeches and written propaganda of those who had successfully appealed to nationalist sentiments. The following piece is an initial, exploratory attempt to do just that. It was designed in 1991 as a speech to inaugurate a series of annual lectures jointly sponsored by the journal *Ethnic and Racial Studies* and the London School of Economics and Political Science.

Beyond Reason: The Nature of the Ethnonational Bond[*]

FOR THE SAKE OF clarity, we begin by noting that nationalism and patriotism refer to two quite distinct loyalties: the former to one's national group; the latter to one's state (country) and its institutions. For people, such as the Japanese, who possess their own ethnically homogeneous *nation-state* and for *staatvolk*, such as the French, who are culturally and politically preeminent in a state, even though other groups are present in significant numbers, the fact that nationalism and patriotism are two different phenomena is usually of little consequence. For such people, the two loyalties tend to blur into a seamless whole. But in a world containing thousands of ethnonational groups and less than two hundred states, it is evident that for most people the sense of loyalty to one's nation and to one's state do not coincide. And they often compete for the allegiance of the individual.

For example, a Basque or Catalan nationalism has often been in conflict with a Spanish patriotism, a Tibetan nationalism with a Chinese patriotism, a Flemish nationalism with a Belgian patriotism, a Corsican nationalism with a French patriotism, a Kashmiri nationalism with an Indian patriotism, a Québèc nationalism with a Canadian patriotism. The list could be lengthened several times over. Nationalism and patriotism are vitally different phenomena and should not be confused through the careless use of language.

We know from the comparative study of nationalism that when the two loyalties are perceived as being in irreconcilable conflict—that is to say, when people feel they must choose between them—nationalism customarily proves the more potent. You have been privileged in your lifetime to witness one of history's most vivid illustrations of the relative strength of these two loyalties: the very recent case of the Soviet Union, wherein a beleaguered Soviet President Gorbachev only belatedly discovered that a sense of loyalty to the Union of Soviet Socialist

[*] Originally delivered as the inaugural *Ethnic and Racial Studies* / London School of Economics Lecture in the Old Theatre at LSE on 27 February 1992 and first published in *ETHNIC AND RACIAL STUDIES* 16, no. 3, (July 1993). Reproduced with permission of the Editors and Publishers of *ERS*.

Republics (what, for seventy years had been termed *Soviet patriotism*) was no match for the sense of nationalism demonstrated by nearly all of the peoples of the Soviet Union, including even the Russian nation. And obviously, events within what, until recently, was known as the Federal Republic of Yugoslavia certify that Albanian, Bosnian, Croatian, and Slovene nationalism has each proven itself far more potent than a Yugoslav patriotism.

To understand why nationalism customarily proves to be a far more powerful force than patriotism, it is necessary to take a closer look at national consciousness and national sentiment. What, for example, is the nature of the bond that both unites all Poles and differentiates them from the remainder of humanity? Until quite recently it was the vogue among prominent writers on nationalism to stress the tangible characteristics of a nation. The nation was defined as a community of people characterized by a common language, territory, religion, and the like. Probing the nation would be a far easier task if it could be explained in terms of such tangible criteria. How much simpler it would be if adopting the Polish language, living within Poland, and adhering to Catholicism were sufficient to define membership in the Polish nation—were sufficient to make one a Pole. But there are Germans, Lithuanians, and Ukrainians who meet these criteria but who do not consider themselves Polish and are not considered Polish by their Polish fellow citizens.

Objective criteria, in and by themselves, are therefore insufficient to determine whether or not a group constitutes a nation. The essence of the nation is a psychological bond that joins a people and differentiates it, in the subconscious conviction of its members, from all nonmembers in a most vital way.

With but very few exceptions, authorities have shied from describing the nation as a kinship group and have usually explicitly denied any kinship basis to it. These denials are customarily supported by data showing that most nations do in fact contain several genetic strains. But this line of reasoning ignores the dictum that it is not *what is* but *what people perceive as is* which influences attitudes and behavior. And a subconscious belief in the group's separate origin and evolution is an important ingredient of national psychology.

In ignoring or denying the sense of kinship that infuses the nation, scholars have been blind to that which has been thoroughly apparent to nationalist leaders. In sharpest contrast with most academic analysts of nationalism, those who have successfully mobilized nations have understood that at the core of ethnopsychology is the sense of shared blood, and they have not hesitated to appeal to it. Consequently, nationalistic speeches and proclamations tend to be more fruitful areas for research into the emotional/psychological nature of nationalism than are scholarly works. Too often such speeches and proclamations have been precipitously dismissed as propaganda in which the leadership did not truly believe. But nationalism is a mass phenomenon, and the degree to which its inciters are true believers does not affect its reality. The question is not the sincerity of the propagandist, but the nature of the mass instinct to which he or she appeals.

Consider, then, Bismarck's famous exhortation to the Germans, spread at the time throughout more than thirty sovereign entities, urging them to unite in a single state: "Germans, think with your blood!" Adolph Hitler's repeated appeals to the ethnic purity of the German nation (*Volk*) are notorious. To take but a single example: In a 1938 speech in Konigsburg (now Kaliningrad, part of the Russian Republic), Hitler declared:

> In Germany today we enjoy the consciousness of belonging to a community, a consciousness which is far stronger than that created by political or economic interests. That community is conditioned by the fact of a blood-relationship. Man today refuses any longer to be separated from the life of his national group; to that he clings with a resolute affection. He will bear extreme distress and misery, but he desires to remain with his national group. [It is this noble passion which alone can raise man above thoughts of gain and profit.] Blood binds more firmly than business.[1]

Although it may be tempting to pass off such allusions to the blood-bond as the exaggerations of a demagogue and zealot, what should not be forgotten is that it was precisely through such allusions that Hitler was able to gain the intense, unquestioning devotion of the best educated, the most literate nation in Europe. As earlier noted, it is not the leader but the mass instinct to which he or she appeals that interests us. And, by appealing to common blood, Hitler was able to wrap himself in the mantle of German nationalism—to become the personification of the nation in German eyes.

It is ironic that Benito Mussolini, to whom Hitler was indebted for the inspiration behind numerous nationalistic motifs, should have come to power in a state characterized by significant ethnic heterogeneity. His task was therefore far more difficult: if he were to mobilize all segments of the population through nationalistic appeals, he must first convince the Lombards, Venetians, Florentines, Neapolitans, Calabrians, Sardinians, Sicilians et al. of their consanguinity. To this end, the local vernaculars were outlawed, and state propaganda seldom passed up the opportunity to emphasize a common Italian ancestry. As but one example, the following is an extract from a manifesto promulgated throughout all of Italy in 1938:

The root of differences among peoples and nations is to be found in differences of race. If Italians differ from Frenchmen, Germans, Turks, Greeks, etc., this is not just because they possess a different language and different history, but because their racial development is different. . . . A pure 'Italian race' is already in existence. This pronouncement [rests] on the very pure blood tie that unites present-day Italians. . . . This ancient purity of blood is the Italian nation's greatest title of nobility.[2]

Nationalistic appeals to ethnic purity were fully consonant, of course, with fascist dogma. More surprising is that Marxist-Leninist leaders, despite the philosophical incompatibility between communism and nationalism, should feel compelled to resort to nationalistic appeals to gain the support of the masses. But both Marx and Lenin, while insisting that nationalism was a bourgeois ideology that must be anathema to all communists, nonetheless appreciated its influence over the masses. They not only condoned but recommended appealing to it as a means of taking power.[*] Even with this background, however, it appears strange to encounter Mao Tse-tung, when appealing for support from the Chinese masses, referring to the Chinese Communist Party *not* as "the vanguard of the proletariat," but as "the vanguard of the Chinese nation and the Chinese people."[3] The Chinese communists in Mao's propaganda became "part of the Great Chinese nation, flesh of its flesh and blood of its blood."[4]

In another proclamation, Mao appealed directly to the family ties deriving from a single common ancestor:

Beloved Compatriots! The Central Committee of the Chinese Communist Party respectfully and most sincerely issues the following manifesto to all fathers, brothers, aunts, and sisters throughout the country: We know that in order to transform this glorious future into a new China, independent, free, and happy, all our fellow countrymen, every single zealous descendent of Huang-ti [the legendary first emperor of China] must determinedly and relentlessly participate in the concerted struggle.[5]

Ho Chi Minh, the father of the Vietnamese communist movement, also appealed to common ancestors and made use of terms connoting familial relationships when courting the support of the masses. For example, in 1946 he stated: "Compatriots in the South and the Southern part of Central Viet-Nam! The North, Center, and South are part and parcel of Viet-Nam! . . . We have the same ancestors, we are of the same family, we are all brothers and sisters. . . . No one can divide the children of the same family. Likewise, no one can divide Viet-Nam."[6]

[*] For details, see this writer's *The National Question in Marxizt-Leninist Theory and Strategy* (Princeton, 1984), particularly chapters 1–3.

Democratic leaders have also appealed to a sense of shared blood in order to gain mass support for a course of action. Somewhat paradoxically, the early history of the American people—that human collectivity destined to form the polygenetic immigrant society par excellence—offers two noteworthy examples, one involving the decision to separate from Britain and the other the decision to form a federal union. The explanation for the seeming paradox lies in *staatvolk* psychology. The political elite of the period did not believe that they were leading an ethnically heterogeneous people. Despite the presence of settlers of Dutch, French, German, Irish, Scottish, and Welsh extraction—as well as the presence of native Americans and peoples from Africa (the latter accounted for one of every five persons at the time)—the prevalent elite-held and mass-held self-perception of the American people was that of an ethnically homogeneous people of English descent. As perceived by would-be revolutionary leaders of the time, if popular support for separation from Britain was to be propagated, a major problem to be overcome was the colonists' sense of belonging to a larger English family. Therefore, the framers of the Declaration of Independence apparently concluded that the feeling of transatlantic kinship should be directly confronted and countered in order to ensure popular support for the separation. After itemizing the grievances against the king, the Declaration turned to the transgressions of the branch of the family still in Britain:

> Nor have We been wanting in attention to our British brethren. . . . We have appealed to their native justice and magnanimity, *and we have conjured them by the ties of our common kindred to disavow these usurpations,* which, would inevitably interrupt our connections and correspondence. *They too have been deaf to the voice of justice and of consanguinity.* We must, therefore . . . hold them, as we hold the rest of mankind, Enemies in War, in Peace Friends.

In sum, from the American viewpoint, the apostates were "they," not "we." It was "they" who had destroyed the family through faithlessness to the sacred bond between kindred, through having been "deaf to the voice of consanguinity."

Eleven years later, political reformers were trying to entice the population, now spread throughout thirteen essentially independent countries, to adopt a federal constitution. The situation was therefore not unlike that which, as we earlier noted, would face Bismarck nearly a century later: How to appeal to people, strewn throughout a number of states, to join together. And, just as Bismarck, one of the authors of the *Federalist Papers* (which were designed to elicit popular support for union) appealed to the popularly held self-perception of the society as an ancestrally related nation. In the second of the eighty-five papers, John Jay wrote:

> With equal pleasure I have as often taken notice, that Providence has been pleased to give this one connected country to one united people—*a people descended from the same ancestors, speaking the same language, professing the same religion*, attached to the same principles of government, very similar in their manners and customs. . . .
>
> This country and this people seem to have been made for each other, *and it appears as if it was the design of Providence, that an inheritance so proper and convenient for a band of brethren, united to each other by the strongest ties*, should never be split into a number of unsocial, jealous, and alien sovereignties.[7]

Jay was saying in effect, we are members of one family and the family should be reunited. And so, in the case of the United States, charges of betrayal of an ancestral bond were first used to gain popular support for politically dividing the family, and this was followed years later by appeals to the ancestral bond to bring about the political union of the American section of the family.

Parenthetically, it may be of interest to note that Americans of Anglo-Saxon ancestry (the so-called WASPS) continued to manifest the *staatvolk* perception that all Americans—or rather "all true Americans"—were blood relatives of the English. For example, in a mid–nineteenth-century poem, entitled "ᴛᴏ ᴇɴɢʟɪsʜᴍᴇɴ," John Greenleaf Whittier wrote:

> O Englishmen!—in hope and creed,
> In blood and tongue our brothers!
> We too are heirs of Runnymede;
> And Shakespeare's fame and Cromwell's deed
> Are not alone our mother's.

> 'Thicker than water,' in one rill
> Through centuries of story
> Our Saxon blood has flowed, and still
> We share with you its good and ill,
> The shadow and the glory.

Paeans to the greatness of the Anglo-Saxon strain said to be inherited by the true Americans were plentiful well into the twentieth century. Fear of diluting or polluting that strain with immigrants of inferior ethnic background undergirded the country's immigration policy until after World War II.

We have thus far confined our illustrations mainly to in-state situations. But because political and ethnic borders seldom coincide, appeals in the name of the nation have often jumped state borders. A shared sense of ancestral ties can become intermeshed in foreign policy and raise the issue of divided loyalties if important segments of the group are separated by political borders. Hitler's appeals in the name of the *Volksdeutsche* to all Germans living within Austria, the Sudetenland, and Poland are well known. More recently, Albania has claimed the right to act as the protector of Albanians within Yugoslavia on the ground that "the same mother that gave birth to us gave birth to the Albanians in Kosovo, Montenegro, and Macedonia";[8] China has proclaimed its right to Taiwan on the ground that "the people of Taiwan are our kith and kin";[9] the leader of North Korea, Kim Il Sung, has declared the need to unify Korea in order to bring about the "integration of our race."[10] And in 1990, those who advised Germans in the Federal Republic of Germany and in the German Democratic Republic to approach most cautiously the question of reuniting the family in one state were no match for the kinship-evoking strategy of Chancellor Helmut Kohl, who appealed successfully for support of immediate unification by employing the disarmingly simple slogan: *Wir sind ein Volk!* We are one nation!

Unlike most writers on nationalism, then, political leaders of the most diverse ideological strains have been mindful of the common blood component of ethnonational psychology and have not hesitated to appeal to it when seeking popular support. Both the frequency and the record of success of such appeals attest to the fact that nations are indeed characterized by a sense—a feeling—of consanguinity.

Our answer, then, to that often asked question, "What is a nation?" is that it is a group of people who feel that they are ancestrally related. It is the largest group that can command a person's loyalty because of felt kinship ties; it is, from this perspective, the fully extended family.

The sense of unique descent, of course, need not, and *in nearly all* cases *will not*, accord with factual history. Nearly all nations are the variegated offsprings of numerous ethnic strains. It is not chronological or factual history that is the key to the nation, but sentient or felt history. All that is irreducibly required for the existence of a nation is that the members share an intuitive conviction of the group's separate origin and evolution. To aver that one is a member of the Japanese, German, or Thai nation is not merely to identify oneself with the Japanese, German, or Thai people of today, but with that people throughout time. Or rather—given the intuitive conviction that one's nation is unique in its origin—perhaps we should say not *throughout time* but *beyond time*. Logically, such a sense of one's nation's origin must rest upon a presumption that somewhere in a hazy, prerecorded era there existed a Japanese, German, or Thai Adam and Eve. But logic operates

in the realm of the conscious and the rational; convictions concerning
the singular origin and evolution of one's nation belong to the realm of
the subconscious and the nonrational (note: not *ir*rational but nonrational).

This distinction between reason and the emotional essence of the nation was expressed in a tract written a few years back by a person in
solitary confinement within the Soviet Union. He had just been found
guilty of antistate activities in the name of Ukrainian nationalism. He
wrote:

> A nation can exist only where there are people who are prepared
>   to die for it;. . .
> Only when its sons believe that their nation is chosen by God and
>   regard their people as His highest creation.
> I know that all people are equal.
> My reason tells me that.
> But at the same time I know that my nation is unique . . .
> My heart tells me so.
> It is not wise to bring the voices of reason and of emotion to a
>   common denominator.[11]

The dichotomy between the realm of national identity and that of
reason has proven vexing to students of nationalism. With the exception of psychologists, people trained in the social sciences tend to be
uncomfortable in confronting the nonrational. They are inclined to seek
rational explanations for the nation in economic and other "real"
forces. But national consciousness resists explication in such terms. Indeed, in a strong testament to the difficulty of explicating national consciousness in any terms, Sigmund Freud, who spent so many years
exploring and describing what he termed "the unconscious," acknowledged that the emotional wellsprings of national identity defied articulation. After noting that he was Jewish, Freud made clear that his own
sense of Jewishness had nothing to do with either religion or national
pride. He went on to note that he was "irresistibly" bonded to Jews and
Jewishness by "many obscure and emotional forces, *which were the more
powerful the less they could be expressed in words*, as well as by a clear
consciousness of inner identity, a deep realization of sharing the same
psychic structure."[12]

Having noted that national identity defied articulation in rational
terms, Freud made no attempt to further describe the national bond
and the feelings to which it gives rise, but there is no mistaking that the
sentiments he was trying to express are the same as those more
concisely and enigmatically summed up in the German maxim, "Blut
will zu Blut!"—a loose translation of which might be "People of the

same blood attract!" A nineteenth-century author, Adolph Stocker, expanded on this sentiment: "German blood flows in every German body, and the soul is in the blood. When one meets a German brother and not merely a brother from common humanity, there is a certain reaction that does not take place if the brother is not German."[13] "German" in this passage could, of course, be replaced by English, Russian, Lithuanian, etc. without affecting the passage's validity. Indeed, the thrust of the passage is remarkably similar to the sentiment expressed by a young Chinese nationalist revolutionary (Chen Tiannua) around 1900:

> As the saying goes, a man is not close to people of another family. When two families fight each other, one surely assists one's own family, one definitely does not help the "exterior" family. Common families all descend from one original family: the Han race is one big family. The Yellow Emperor is a great ancestor, all those who are not of the Han race are not the descendants of the Yellow Emperor, they are exterior families. One should definitely not assist them; if one assists them, one lacks a sense of ancestry.[14]

No matter how described—Freud's interior identity and psychic structure, or blood-ties, or chemistry, or soul—it is worth repeating that the national bond is subconscious and emotional rather than conscious and rational in its inspiration. It can be analyzed but not explained rationally.

How can we analyze it? It can be at least obliquely analyzed by examining the type of catalysts to which it responds, that is to say, by examining the proven techniques for reaching and triggering national responses. And how has the nonrational core of the nation been reached and triggered? As we have seen in the case of numerous successful nationalist leaders, not *through* appeals to reason but *through* appeals to the emotions (appeals not to the mind but to the blood).

The nonrational core of the nation has been reached and triggered *through* national symbols, as historically varied as the rising sun, the swastika, and Brittania. Such symbols can speak messages without words to members of the nation, because, as one author has noted, "there is something about such symbols, especially visual ones, which reach the parts rational explanation cannot reach."

The nonrational core has been reached and triggered *through* nationalist poetry because the poet is far more adept than the writer of learned tracts at expressing deeply felt emotion, as witness the following words written in 1848 by a Romanian poet to describe the Romanian nation:

It is in it that we were born, it is our mother;
We are men because it reared us;
We are free because we move in it;
If we are angered, it soothes our pain with national songs.
Through it we talk today to our parents who lived thousands of
    years back;
Through it our descendents and posterity thousands of years later
    will know us.

The nonrational core has been reached and triggered *through* music popularly perceived as reflecting the nation's particular past or genius; the music may vary in sophistication, embracing the work of composers such as Richard Wagner, as well as folk music.

The core of the nation has been reached and triggered *through* the use of familial metaphors which can magically transform the mundanely tangible into emotion-laden phantasma: which can, for example, mystically convert what the outsider sees as merely the territory populated by a nation into a motherland or fatherland, the ancestral land, land of our fathers, this sacred soil, land where our fathers died, the native land, the cradle of the nation, and, most commonly, the *home*—the *home*land of our particular people—a "Mother Russia," an Armenia, a Deutschland, an England (Engla land: land of the Angles), or a Kurdistan (literally, land of the Kurds). Here is an Uzbek poet referring to Uzbekistan:

So that my generation would comprehend the Homeland's worth,
Men were always transformed to dust, it seems.
The Homeland is the remains of our forefathers
Who turned into dust for this precious soil.[15]

A spiritual bond between nation and territory is thus touched. As concisely stated in the nineteenth-century German couplet, "*Blut und Boden*," blood and soil become mixed in national perceptions.

It is, then, the character of appeals made through and to the senses, not through and to reason, which permit us some knowledge of the subconscious convictions that people tend to harbor concerning their nation. The near universality with which certain images and phrases appear—blood, family, brothers, sisters, mother, forefathers, ancestors, home—and the proven success of such invocations in eliciting massive, popular responses tell us much about the nature of national identity. But, again, this line of research does not provide a rational explanation for it.

Rational would-be explanations have abounded: relative economic deprivation; elite ambitions; rational choice theory; intense transaction flows; the desire of the intelligentsia to convert a "low," subordinate culture into a "high," dominant one; cost-benefit considerations; internal colonialism; a ploy of the bourgeoisie to undermine the class consciousness of the proletariat by obscuring the conflicting class interests within each nation, and by encouraging rivalry among the proletariat of various nations; a somewhat spontaneous mass response to competition for scarce resources. All such theories can be criticized on empirical grounds. But they can be faulted principally for their failure to reflect the emotional depth of national identity: the passions at either extreme end of the hate-love continuum which the nation often inspires, and the countless fanatical sacrifices which have been made in its name. As Chateaubriand expressed it nearly 200 years ago: "Men don't allow themselves to be killed for their interests; they allow themselves to be killed for their passions."[16] To phrase it differently: people do not voluntarily die for things that are rational.

The sense of kinship, which lies at the heart of national consciousness, helps to account for the ugly manifestations of inhumanity that often erupt in the relations among national groups. A chain of such eruptions in the late 1980s found Soviet authorities totally unprepared for the scale of the brutality that surfaced in the wake of *perestroika* and *glasnost*, as national groups across the entire southern USSR gave vent to their previously pent-up ethnic enmities.

Such behavior patterns are hardly unusual. The annual reports of organizations such as Amnesty International offer a dismal recitation of officially condoned oppression of national minorities: Tibetans by Han Chinese; West Bank Arabs by Jews; Kurds by Iraqi Arabs, by Persians, and by Turks; Dinkas and other Nilotic peoples by Sudanese Arabs; Xhosas, Zulus, and other black peoples by Afrikaners; Quechuans by Peruvian mestizos; Ndebele by Shonas; Turks by Bulgars; Mayan peoples by Guatemalan mestizos; Kachins, Karens, Mons, and Shans by Burmese. The list could be lengthened. Moreover, as suggested by earlier described events in the Soviet Union, genocidal tendencies toward members of another nation have often surfaced without governmental approval. Recent non-Soviet illustrations of sets of nations who have manifested such tendencies are Xhosa and Zulu, Serb and Croat, Serb and Albanian, Irishman and "Orangeman," Greek and Turk, Sikh and Hindi, Punjabi and Sindhi, Sindhi and Pushtun, Hutu and Tutsi, Ovambo and Herero, Corsican and Frenchman, Vietnamese and Han, Khmer and Vietnamese, Assamese and Bengali, Malay and Han. Again, the list could be lengthened.

Not all relations among nations are so hate-filled. Popular attitudes held by one nation toward another are often quite positive. But while attitudes toward various other nations may vary across a broad spectrum, the national bond, because it is based upon belief in common descent, ultimately bifurcates humanity into "us" and "them." And this propensity toward bifurcating the human race has a long history. Notice the simple cause-and-effect relationship between ethnic purity and hatred of all outsiders that Plato has Menexos ascribe to that most cultured and sophisticated of ancient peoples, the Athenians:

> The mind of this city is so noble and free and so powerful and healthy *and by nature hating the barbarians because we are pure Hellenes* and not commingled with barbarians. No Pelops or Cadmus or Aegyptus or Danaus or others who are barbarians by nature and Hellenes only by law dwell with us, but we live here as pure Hellenes who are not mixed with barbarians. *Therefore, the city has acquired a real hate of alien nature.*

Because the sense of common kinship does not extend beyond the nation, that sense of compassion to which kinship usually—not always—but usually gives rise is lacking in the relations among national groups. The fault lines that separate nations are deeper and broader than those separating nonkindred groups, and the tremors that follow those fault lines more potentially cataclysmic. What underlies the now commonplace phrase, "man's inhumanity to man" is all too often "nation's inhumanity to nation."

Failure on the part of scholars to appreciate the psychological wellsprings of the nation most certainly contributes to the tendency to undervalue the potency of nationalism. As earlier noted, when nationalism and patriotism are perceived as in conflict, it is nationalism that customarily proves the more powerful allegiance.

This is not to deny that patriotism can be a very powerful sentiment. The state has many effective means for inculcating love of country and love of political institutions—what social scientists collectively term "political socialization." Not the least effective of these is control of public education and particularly control over the content of history courses.

Moreover, even governments of complex multiethnic states are free to—and often do—adopt the idiom of nationalism when attempting to inculcate loyalty to the state. From my own primary school education, a century or so ago, I recall how we students—many, probably most, of whom were first-, second-, or third-generation Americans from highly diverse national backgrounds—were told we shared a common ancestry. We were programmed to consider Washington, Jefferson, et al. as our common, "founding fathers." We memorized Lincoln's reminder in the Gettysburg Address that four score and seven years earlier, it

208 MYTHIC WORLD OF NATIONAL IDENTITY

was "our Fathers [who had] brought forth upon this continent a new nation." We repetitively sang that very short song—"America"—one of whose seven lines reads "land where my fathers died."

But despite the many advantages that the state has for politically socializing its citizens in patriotic values, patriotism—as evident from the multitude of separatist movements pockmarking the globe—cannot muster the level of emotional commitment that nationalism can. Loyalty to state and loyalty to nation are not always in conflict. But when they are perceived as being in irreconcilable conflict, nationalism customarily proves the more potent.

Again, perhaps the most instructive recent case is that of the Soviet Union—wherein a most comprehensive, intensive, and multigenerational program to exorcise nationalism and exalt Soviet patriotism has proven remarkably ineffective. Similar programs throughout Eastern Europe also clearly failed—most glaringly in Yugoslavia. As noted in a piece written twenty-five years ago: "Political developments since World War II clearly establish that national consciousness is not on the wane as a political force, but is quite definitely in the ascendency."[17]

NOTES

1. Adolph Hitler, *The Speeches of Adolph Hitler, April 1922–August 1939* (London, 1942) 2: 1438.
2. As cited in Charles Delzell, *Mediterranean Fascism* (New York, 1970), 193–94.
3. Conrad Brandt et al., *A Documentary History of Chinese Communism* (London, 1952), 260.
4. Mao Tse-tung, *Selected Works of Mao Tse-tung, Vol. 2* (Peking, 1975), 209.
5. Brandt, *A Documentary History*, 245.
6. Ho Chi Minh, *On Revolution: Selected Writings 1920–1966*, ed. Bernard Fall (New York, 1967), 158.
7. Alexander Hamilton, John Jay, James Madison, *The Federalist: A Commentary on the Constitution of the United States* (New York, 1937), 9.
8. Robert King, *Minorities Under Communism* (Cambridge, 1973), 144.
9. *New York Times*, 1 September 1975.
10. *Atlas*, February 1976, 19.
11. Valentine Moroz, *Report from the Beria Reserve* (Chicago, 1974), 54.
12. The quotation interutilizes translated extracts in Leon Poloakov, *The Aryan Myth* (London, 1974), 287, and the more clumsy translation in *The Standard Edition of the Complete Psychological Works of Sigmund Freud, Vol. 20 (1925–26)* (London, 1959), 273–74.
13. Carlton Hayes, *A Generation of Materialism, 1871–1900* (New York, 1941), 258.
14. Frank Dikötter, "Group Definition and the Idea of 'Race' in Modern China (1793–1949)," *Ethnic and Racial Studies* 13 (July 1990): 427.

15. Walker Connor, "The Impact of Homelands upon Diasporas," in *Modern Diasporas in International Politics*, ed. Gabriel Sheffer (London, 1985).

16. Cited in Walter Sulzbach, *National Consciousness* (Washington, D.C., 1943), 62.

17. See chapter 1 in this volume.

Chapter Nine

WHEN IS A NATION?

The following article, written in 1988, recounts how leading scholars have often badly miscalculated the date of creation of a nation, sometimes by hundreds of years. There are two reasons for the article's inclusion in a section entitled *Scholars in the Mythic World of National Identity*. First, it attests to the difficulties that scholars have experienced in grappling with the phenomenon of ethnonational identity: in this case with the problem of determining when—or even if—national consciousness has surfaced among one or another people. Second, it further emphasizes the division between the realm of national identity and the realm of fact. It examines the ethnic history of a number of peoples, broadly perceived as nations, in order to confirm that national identity is based upon sentient or mythical rather than factual history and that it is capable of overcoming flagrantly contradictory, factual data.

The article is therefore an appropriate closing piece, serving (1) as a last reminder to students of nationalism of the subject's inherent complexity and (2) as a warning to treat as suspect "rational" explanations of its nature. Presumably influenced by the careless confusion of nation and state, the British poet Swinburne (1837–1909) wrote in "A Word for the Country":

> Not with dreams but with blood and with iron,
> Shall a nation be moulded to last.

To the contrary, nations, national identity, and nationalism are "the stuff that dreams are made of," and this helps to account both for their emotional appeal and for their resistance to rational inquiry. And resist they certainly have. The quest for understanding is far from fulfillment.

From Tribe to Nation?*

DESPITE THE EXTENSIVE effort that generations of chroniclers and analysts have devoted to the history of Europe and its peoples, assigning
dates to the acquisition of national consciousness by any of Europe's
roughly fifty national groups remains a most contentious undertaking.
Disagreement is very conspicuous in the writings of some of the last
generation's distinguished historians. To the French medieval authority, Marc Bloch, for example, "the texts make it plain that so far as
France and Germany were concerned this national consciousness was
already highly developed about the year 1100"; Bloch felt the same
could be said of the English.[1] Others placed the rise of national consciousness among the major peoples of Western Europe at only a
slightly later date. The Dutch scholar, Johan Huizinga, perceived national consciousness evolving throughout the Middle Ages, and considered French and English nationalism to be "in full flower" by the
fourteenth century.[2] The British historian, George Coulton, agreed; basing his analysis on the foreign alignments of the Italian states, France,
England, Scotland, Germany, Hungary, Flanders, and Spain during the
late 1300s, he concluded that "by this time, the nationalism towards
which Europe had been evolving for three centuries past was accepted
not only as a social fact but as a fundamental factor in European politics."[3] Another British scholar, Sydney Herbert, concurred that "the
idea of nationality [began to] appear in real force [as] medieval society
was dying"; he asserted that the Scottish thirteenth-century "fierce resistance to an English overlord, provides one of the first examples of
nationalism in action," and he added that "if the Hundred Years War
[1337–1453] between France and England is as far as possible from
being a national war in its origins, yet toward its close genuine nationality appears, splendid and triumphant, with Jeanne d'Arc."[4] In an article dedicated to the early stirring of national consciousness among the
English, the American scholar, Barnaby Keeney, concluded: "The English of the fourteenth century liked to think of themselves as one people with a fanciful common origin and a vague sort of destiny. They

* Reprinted from Walker Connor, "From Tribe to Nation?" *History of European
Ideas* 13, no. 1/2 (1991): 5–18. Copyright © 1991 Pergamon Press. Used by permission of the publisher, Pergamon Press.

were thoroughly aware that they were Englishmen as well as York-shiremen; they disliked foreign foreigners more than they disliked the man from the next county."[5] In a similar, although somewhat more cautious vein, a British authority on French history, Dorothy Kirkland, wrote that "some kind of national spirit was stirring in France in the last quarter of the thirteenth century."[6]

Other, equally respected authorities have denied any role to national consciousness during the Middle Ages. Austria-Hungary-born Hans Kohn wrote of this period: "People looked upon everything not from the point of view of their nationality or race but from the point of view of religion. Mankind was divided not into Germans and French and Slavs and Italians, but into Christian and Infidels, and within Christianity into faithful sons of the Church and heretics."[7] One of the United States' foremost authorities on nationalism, Carlton Hayes, agreed with Kohn's timetable. Allowing for the single possible exception of the English, he asserted:

> There can be little question that in the first half of the eighteenth century the masses of Europe, as well as of Asia and America, whilst possessing some consciousness of nationality, thought of themselves chiefly as belonging to a province or a town or an empire, rather than to a national state, and made no serious or effective protest against being transferred from one political domain to another.[8]

Thomas Tout, the British historian, would not even exclude the English. In his view, a medieval person "could be a Londoner, a Parisian, a Florentine: he could be a West-Saxon, a Norman, a Breton, or a Bavarian. But he found it hard to feel that he had any obligations as an Englishman, a Frenchman, or a German."[9]

Such vast disagreement among eminent authorities has been made possible by the near absence of conclusive evidence. Nationalism is a mass phenomenon. The fact that members of the ruling elite or intelligentsia manifest national sentiment is not sufficient to establish that national consciousness has permeated the value-system of the masses. And the masses, until recent times totally or semi-illiterate, furnished few hints concerning their view of group-self.

When used pristinely, *nation* refers to a group of people who *believe* they are ancestrally related.[10] It is the largest grouping that shares such a belief. Still larger associations, such as citizenship in a multinational state are, of course, extant and may well be the object of powerful emotional attachments. But common Britishness, Belgianness, or Yugoslavianness does not involve the ultimate sense of blood affiliation; the sense of having evolved from common ancestors does not extend beyond the Welsh, Fleming, or Croatian nation. And, as attested to by the numerous separatist movements that have recently affected states in all sectors of the globe, if and when loyalty to nation and loyalty to an association not predicated upon a belief in common ancestry are perceived as being in irreconcilable conflict, loyalty to the nation can be expected to prove the more potent.

Although the nation can be defined as the largest grouping predicated upon a myth of common descent, its relationship to other kinship groups is far from clear. Some cultural anthropologists postulate a five-tiered hierarchy of such groups beginning with the family. A number of families constitute a *band*, several of whom ultimately join to form a *clan*. *Clans*, in turn, unite to form a *tribe*, and tribes over time join together to form a *nation*.[11]

In reality, however, this pattern has certainly not proved to be an iron law of evolution. Many a people, who were assigned the role of tribe or some other componential status, and who for a time appeared to accept that designation, subsequently became convinced that they constituted a thoroughly fulfilled nation in their own right. The present state of Yugoslavia, for example, was created in 1919 on the presumption that all southern Slavs (Yugo-Slavs) constituted a single nation; Croats, Serbs, and Slovenes were explicitly described as "tribes."[12] At the time, the masses (though definitely not all of the intellectuals) apparently took no exception to their group being described as only a component part of a nation, but the 1930s witnessed growing demands for greater autonomy or independence for their nation on the part of both Croats and Slovenes. Similarly, at the time of the creation of the state of Czechoslovakia in 1920, the Slovak masses passively accepted their status, set forth in the Constitution, as a branch of a single "Czechoslovak nation." But by the late 1930s, the concept of a Slovak nation had germinated sufficiently for it to be used as a divide-and-rule implement by the German Third Reich.[13]

In some cases, popular opinion is still divided over whether a group of people constitute a nation by themselves or are merely a subdivision of a larger national group. There are Montenegrins, as well as Serbs, who consider Montenegrins part of the Serbian nation.[14] Even more complex is the case of the Macedonians. Bulgaria has traditionally maintained that the Macedonians are Bulgars; Greece has claimed that at least a significant portion of them are Greeks; they have also historically been claimed by the Serbs; since World War II, the Yugoslavian government has insisted that they constitute a separate nation. At least until quite recently, Macedonian opinion has been divided. Majority opinion agreed with Sofia that Macedonians were a branch of the Bulgar nation, while others considered themselves to be either Serb or Greek. There was scant indication of any conviction that Macedonians considered themselves a separate nation. There is little reason to question Belgrade's recent success in encouraging a sense of nationhood among most Macedonians, although the 1981 census data, which indicated a total absence of people within Macedonia who claimed either Bulgar or Greek identity, were unquestionably fraudulent and, in their unrestrained exaggeration, underscore the seriousness with which Belgrade continues to view the self-identity and loyalty of Macedonia's population.[15]

Our list of examples of groups, who were once considered componential or subnational but who subsequently came to perceive themselves as national, could be lengthened.[16] The histories of both those peoples who have vanished through assimilation into larger groups and those who developed and retained a separate sense of nationhood reveal no common evolutionary path. Dante (1265–1321) once wrote of the "Slavs, the Hungarians, the Germans, the Saxons, the English, and other nations" and identified himself as "Florentine by nation."[17] History ultimately vindicated his terminology with regard to "Hungarians," "Germans," and "English." But even with hindsight, it is difficult to understand why his terminology should not have been totally vindicated. There was no predictable reason why the Slavic "tribes" did not evolve into a single nation, rather than fragmenting into the some fifteen Slavic peoples today asserting nationhood. And if the assimilation of the continental Saxons into the German nation should have been anticipated, then how are we to account for the survival of the equally Germanic Dutch, Fleming, Frisian, and Luxembourger peoples?[18] Since the nation is a self-defined entity, popular opinion could at any stage come to feel that the nation had been realized. Thus, Little Russians (Ukrainians), though related to the Great Russians, came increasingly in this century to feel that that relationship was not sufficiently close so as to represent a national bond.

The Ukrainian and Dutch examples raise the question: Given our earlier definition of the nation as the largest human grouping predicated upon a myth of common ancestry, is it not contradictory that a number of contemporary nations are splinters from a larger ethnic element—Slavic, Germanic, and so on? This seeming paradox is due to the fact that the myth of common ancestry is the product of sensory or intuitive, rather than rational knowledge. Most, if not all nations are the product of diverse ethnic elements. The English nation, for example, is an ethnically complex compound: those Celtic Britons who were not forced by the Germanic Angle, Saxon, and Jute invaders of the fifth century into the western reaches of Great Britain were absorbed by them; to this amalgamation were later added the Germanic Danes who arrived in large numbers in the ninth century, and, still later, the Germanic Normans who came as conquerors in the eleventh century.[19]

Somewhat similarly in the case of the French, the indigenous Celtic Gauls became heavily suffused with Germanic Franks, Burgundians, and Normans. Nor are the Germans a purely Teutonic people, as we are reminded by the following passage:

> Although the French are popularly believed to be of Celtic descent and the Germans of Teutonic origin there are scientists, like M. Jean Finot, who maintain that if it is absolutely necessary to attribute Celtic descent to any European people that people must be not the French but the Germans, while the French, on the other hand, are more Teutonic in blood than the Germans. According to another authoritative student of race problems, Ripley, the northeastern third of France and one half of Belgium are to-day more Germanic than is South Germany. This seemingly startling view will cease to surprise when it is remembered that France was the abode of the Franks, the Burgundians, the Visigoths and the Normans, all of whom were of Germanic race. . . . One is reminded of the apt remark made by Israel Zangwill: "Turn Time's Cinematograph back far enough, and the Germans are found to be French and the French Germans."[20]

At one level of consciousness, the English, French, and German peoples are aware of their ethnic heterogeneity. Their history books record it. But at a more intuitive or sensory level, they "know" their nation is ethnically, hermetically pure. Thus, the English, French, and Germans feel no sense of familial relationship to one another, despite the Celtic and Teutonic strains in all three peoples. The famous British scholar of nationalism, G. P. Gooch, aptly and succinctly described this division between national perception of self and reality: "With the discovery that racial unity is a myth, race in its biological sense loses much of its significance [as an explanation for national consciousness] though racial self-consciousness remains virtually unaffected."[21]

Gooch's use of the word race was not considered inappropriate in 1929, for until quite recently it was the fashion to employ it as a synonym for nation, references to an English race, a French race, and the like being extremely common. Nor is this terminology totally passé. In 1982, in a book broadly viewed as biased against recent immigrants from Asia and the West Indies, a prominent British jurist noted with obvious displeasure that "the English are no longer a homogeneous race."[22] As the justice made explicit, the use of race as an acceptable substitute for nation conveyed the notion that each nation was homogeneous and therefore complete in itself.

As the examples of the English, French, and German nations suggest, the myth of a common and exclusive descent can overcome a battery of contrary fact. The Greeks, for example, are convinced that they are the direct, pure descendants of the Greeks of ancient Hellas. Panslavic appeals have no audience here. In fact, however, commencing with the sixth century, the region was subjected to massive migrations of Slavs who so overwhelmed the indigenous population that continental Greece was often referred to during the Middle Ages as Slavinia (Slavland).[23]

The Bulgars offer something of a mirror image of the Greek case. They were an Asian people who migrated to Eastern Europe during the seventh century. There they encountered and conquered the Slavic peoples who, as noted in the case of next-door Greece, had been pushing southward since the sixth century. But whereas the Greek culture and identity remained virtually untouched by the Slavs, who in time became fully assimilated, the Bulgars became thoroughly Slavicized, retaining only their name. In the words of one authority: "The original Bulgars were so completely absorbed by their Slavonic subjects that not a single word survives in the modern Bulgarian language which can be traced back to the people which first bore the name."[24]

Romanian identity also demonstrates the power of myth over fact. It is the official position of the zealously nationalist, albeit communist, government that the Romanians are the otherwise unadulterated product of the fusion of Latins with the Dacians (a Thracian people) during the days of the Roman Empire.[25] The Daco-Romans disappeared from history following the withdrawal of Roman forces in the third century, but it is the contention of current Romanian historiography that they had retreated into the mountains in the face of a series of Teutonic, Slavic, Magyar, and Tatari invasions, to reappear in the eleventh century as the Vlachs, a Latin-speaking people. More certain is that having arrived or rearrived in the Romanian lowlands, the Vlachs over time fused with a population that had earlier assimilated strong Slavic and Tatari strains. In the early days of communist rule (the late 1940s), the government stressed that all things that were Russian/Slavic were good and deserving of emulation. This campaign extended to a rewriting of the ethnic history of the Romanians, which introduced the novel proposition that the Dacians had been a Slavic tribe.[26] There is, as noted, a Slavic strain among Romanians, but it was introduced after the sixth century. In any case, this pan-Slavic posture was soon dropped in favor of the unadulterated Daco-Roman theory, and it is most unlikely that pan-Slavism ever enjoyed any significant popularity among the masses. The "Latinist" movement, with its stress on Roman heritage, the Latin alphabet, and purity of blood had been promoted by intellectuals (including many clerics) beginning in the late eighteenth century, so the present position of the government is in full accord with this tradition. It is generally agreed that this more traditional view has found favor among the people and that an image of the Romanian nation as a Latin isolate surrounded by Slavs to north and south and Magyars to the west has by now deeply penetrated the popular psyche.

Although a factual foundation is therefore far from indispensable to a myth of unique origin and development, nationalists can be expected to warmly embrace all scientific evidence of such uniqueness. Thus, the Basque claim to purity of blood is substantiated by statistical evidence of a remarkably high percentage of people whose blood samples test Rh negative. Moreover, the fact that linguists are unable to attribute the Basque language to any larger linguistic family figures prominently today in Basque claims to ethnic uniqueness. Such claims, however, antedate this evidence. In the sixteenth through eighteenth centuries, it was argued that the Basques were direct descendants of Tubal, grandson of Noah. Even today there are those who maintain that the Basques are descendants of the survivors of the lost continent, Atlantis. Others claim they are the long lost tribe of Israel, a claim that has been made in the name of many other national groups throughout the globe. Some hold the Basques to be the only direct descendants of the Cro-Magnon people who dwelled in the general area some thirty to forty thousand years ago; others hold that they descend from a people who migrated from the Caucasus; still others maintain the Basques came originally from northern Africa. All of these theories rest more on imagination than on science.[27] But on one thesis all Basque nationalists agree: the Basques are a distinct people, completely unrelated to all those around them.

Given the subjective nature of national consciousness, it is not only enormously difficult to tell when, but sometimes even *if*, a nation has emerged. We earlier noted the controversy surrounding the existence of both a Montenegrin and a Macedonian nation. There are also grounds for questioning the degree to which a sense of an Italian nation has permeated the people of Italy. The independent state of Italy is customarily viewed as having been created in the nineteenth century to fulfill the desire of Italians for national self-determination. However, the oft-cited words of a member of the Risorgimento, Massimo d'Azeglio, delivered in 1860, are not without significance even today: "Having made Italy, we must now make Italians." One of the barriers to achieving that end is a popularly perceived Alpine/Mediterranean racial division between the northern and southern peoples. The northerners have traditionally looked with disdain upon the inhabitants of the south. As Mussolini well understood, such a biracial myth is anathema to the notion of a single nation, and he attempted to dispel it by a so-called *Manifesto of the Racist Scientists*, which was publicized throughout every city and village of Italy in 1938. More an article of faith than a scientific treatise, part of its credo read:

> If Italians differ from Frenchmen, Germans, Turks, Greeks, etc., this is not just because they possess a different language and different history, but

because their racial development is different. . . . A pure "Italian race" is already in existence. This pronouncement [rests] on the very pure blood tie that unites present day Italians.[28]

It is interesting to contrast this proclamation with the comment of an authority on Italy written just two years earlier:

From the earliest times the Italians have been a mixture of races, and successive invasions have added so many strains to their blood that there is no danger of a racial theory of Italian nationality. In physical characteristics they differ widely, from the tall, red-haired types found in Lombardy and Venetia and the Celts of Romagna, to the Mediterranean type prevailing in the South.[29]

Mussolini's desire to weld the peoples of Italy into a single nation faced other obstructions in addition to the north-south divide. On either side of this division, group designations, such as Neapolitan or Calabrian in the south or Florentine or Venetian in the north, convey not only the geographic area of one's ancestral home but also stereotypical attributes of a genetically distinct people.[30] Although Mussolini had pressed to eradicate these identities and their for the most part mutually unintelligible vernaculars, both retain vitality. Nearly half of the country's population still discourse in the local tongue within the home.[31] As to the relative vitality of the local identities compared to Italianness, this is how one British observer of the Italian scene characterized it:

Most Italians will tell you, sooner or later, that there is no such place as Italy. Oh yes, no doubt, as a geographical expression or a legal and diplomatic entity, capable of entering into treaties and voting at the United Nations and suchlike unimportant things. But as a nation—a coherent, homogeneous, more or less likeminded collection of people with a shared sense of pride and patriotism—as that, they will say, Italy remains an invention of you foreigners. We Italians are not really Italians at all—or anyway, not often. We are Florentines, Venetians, Neapolitans, Bolognese. But Italians? Oh dear, no![32]

To accentuate the obvious: it would be quixotic to search for the birthdate of the Italian nation, if such a sentiment has not materialized.[*]

---

[*] Despite all this, appearance of separatist-leaning parties in a number of the northern regions and their performance in the 1990 elections was, in the words of one correspondent, "wholly unpredicted." *Lega Lombarda* provided the greatest surprise, garnering 20 percent of the Lombardy vote. See the *Independent* (London), 9 May and 21 May 1990.

Uncertainty also prevails in the case of Albanianism. Political leaders have long insisted that the existence of an Albanian nation is incontestible. However, the country remains sharply bifurcated—geographically, culturally, and *ethnically*—by the Shkumbin River. To the north are the highland dwelling Gegs, while the Tosks live in the less rugged terrain to the south. Differences in culture, including social organization, are pronounced, although becoming less so. Far more consequential are readily perceptible physical differences between the two peoples,[33] a formidable barrier to the inculcation of the myth of common ancestry which the government so assiduously cultivates.

The Scottish case suggests a few parallels. The highlanders are the descendants of fifth- and sixth-century emigres from Ireland (Ireland was then called Scotia and its inhabitants Scoti) who fused with the indigenous Picts. By contrast, the Teutonic lineage of the lowlanders in the south and east of Scotland is the same as that which was earlier described in the case of the English. As we have seen, the myth of common ancestry is capable of overcoming contrary historical fact, but it is problematic whether the two identities, for which *highlander* and *lowlander* are the popular cognomina, have totally lost their ethnic vitality. Scottish history books do not dispel this ambiguity. Indeed, history books specifically designed to inculcate a transcendent Scottish nationalism in young minds often appear to be combining the histories of two distinct and often violently antagonistic peoples. Their authors are forced to record that in the numerous wars and uprisings against England, which continued until the mid-eighteenth century, highlander and lowlander often opposed or failed to support one another. Highlanders and lowlanders may have subsequently fought for the British Empire, but London's tactical decision to create highland regiments perpetuated the image of the highlanders as a distinct people. Unsurprising, then, that those histories designed to instill national consciousness should resemble uncomfortable composites of the histories of two peoples: sometimes relating highlander history; in other places describing lowlander history; but seldom appearing to describe the history of a single Scottish people.[34]

The murkiness surrounding the national identity of, inter alia, the Albanians, Italians, Macedonians, Montenegrins, and Scots reminds us that nation-formation is a process, not an occurrence. And, as we have seen in the case of the Croats, Dutch, Slovaks, and others, it is a process that can terminate at any time. Moreover, until the process is fulfilled, it is capable of reversing itself, as witness the post–World War II reinvigoration of nationalism among many European minorities who were generally perceived as nearly or totally assimilated. As far back as 1866, the perspicacious Frederick Engels mistakenly perceived the "Highland Gaels, the Welsh, Manxmen, Serbs, Croats, Ruthenes, Slovaks, and Czechs" as "relics of people," "people without a history," and "an absurdity."[35] And as recently as 1970, the prevailing view among scholars was that substate national minorities were no longer a consequential fact. Recent nationalist-inspired activity among the Albanians (of Yugoslavia), Armenians, Azerbaijani, Basques, Bretons, Catalans, Corsicans, Croats, Estonians, Flemings, Irish (of Northern Ireland), Latvians, Lithuanians, Magyars (within Romania), Sardinians, Scots (both highlander and lowlander), Serbs, Sicilians, Slovaks, Slovenes, Sorbs, (South) Tyroleans, Walloons, Welsh, and others was totally unanticipated.[36]

The fact that *nation-formation* is a process—and one that is unculminated for a few of Europe's peoples—does not absolve us from addressing the issue posed by those historians who were cited at the outset of this essay: Approximately when was the process completed for those European peoples who have indisputably acquired national consciousness? The answer: Far later than is generally acknowledged.

In a most impressive piece of scholarship, Eugen Weber has recently established that most rural and small-town dwellers within France did not consider themselves members of the French nation in 1870 and that many retained this view until World War I.[37] His revelation is a particularly dramatic one because France has so often been referred to as the earliest example of how the victory of monarchy over feudal barons led to effective centralization and integration—that is, to the creation of a nation-state. As we have seen, some historians have suggested that the French nation was a reality by the mid–Middle Ages. Others credit the Bourbon monarchs (1589–1793) with this accomplishment, although usually considering the process completed by the reign of Louis XIV (1643–1715). This is how an encyclopedic, matter-of-fact history has described the situation about the time of his accession: "France, at the middle of the seventeenth century, held the first rank among the powers of Europe. . . . For a time France alone in Europe was a consolidated unit of race and institutions, showing the spirit of nationality and employing the agencies and methods of a great modern state."[38]

Weber's disclosure that France had not approximated this level of integration more than two centuries later overturned even the most cautious estimates of when French national consciousness permeated the masses. A number of scholars had opined that the French Revolution had been necessary to complete the nation;[39] and others had noted the Jacobins' determination to eradicate local vernacular in the outlying areas, particularly among France's Alsatians, Basques, Bretons, Corsicans, and Flemings.[40] Some of Weber's supporting data are drawn from these areas, but his analysis indicates that the absence of French national consciousness characterized most of geographic France. He cites several nineteenth- and twentieth-century sources which uniformly emphasize the isolation—physical, political, and cultural—of the typical village. With the partial exception of the regions to the north and east of Paris, the integration of the countryside was still largely fanciful in the 1870s.[41] The famed road network was in essence an arterial system without branches, tying the cities to Paris but bypassing the villages. The vaunted school system was still inadequate to carry out the Jacobin scheme of a unilingual citizenry. Although the situation began to alter substantively after 1880, because of a vast improvement in the transportation and communication networks, as well as in the school system, Weber quotes a 1911 source as noting that "for peasants and workers, the mother tongue is patois, the foreign speech is French."[42]

To this writer's knowledge, no comparable study, aimed at probing the degree to which the masses identified themselves as members of their *ostensible* nation at the turn of this century, has been done on any other European nation. However, there is one important source of such data that covers a broad sampling of peoples. Between 1880 and 1910, there occurred a huge migration of peoples, principally from southern and eastern Europe, to the United States. For the most part, these migrants were from rural areas, and their education had been either minimal or nonexistent. The few intellectuals and those who came from major cities were often aware of their membership in one of the European groupings which today are incontrovertibly nations. But the peasants, who accounted for most of the population in the countries from which they had migrated, certainly were not. They regularly identified themselves in terms of locale, region, province, and the like. For example, those we would currently describe as Croats described themselves as Dalmatian, Istrian, Slavonian, and the like, but not as Croat; Czechs described themselves as Bohemian, but not as Czech; Italians as Neapolitan, Calabrian, and the like, but not as Italian; Poles as Gorali, Kashubi, Silesian, and so on, but not as Polish; Slovaks as Sarisania, Zemplincania, and the like, but not as Slovak.[43]

It would be inappropriate to presume that these late nineteenth- and early twentieth-century identities, although described in terms of locale or region, reflected essentially geographic rather than ethnic identities. We have seen how Florentine, Calabrian, and the like have a vital ethnic dimension. So too, there is little reason not to presume that Dalmatian, Silesian, and their like did not represent in 1900 the same type of identity as did Burgundian and Saxon in a not-too-much-earlier period.

Moreover, although the migrants who poured into the United States at the turn of the century were overwhelmingly from southern and eastern Europe, it would also be inappropriate to presume that, with the possible exception of France, national consciousness in northwestern Europe was operating on a dramatically different timetable. The Dutch who came to the United States in the 1840s and 1850s indicate the opposite. Despite the small size of the Netherlands and the general lack of serious geographic impedimenta to integration, the Netherlander migrants proved to be a remarkably diverse people whose local identities took precedence over a common identity as Dutch. In the United States, they attempted to recreate the same geosocial enclaves they had known at home.

> Immigrants carried this localism to America and frequently tried to create segregated enclaves within the larger Dutch communities. The pattern was particularly evident in the colony of Holland, Michigan. The central town, called simply *de stad*, was founded in 1847 largely by people from Geldeland and Overijssel provinces. Within two years, new arrivals founded villages within a 10-mile radius bearing the provincial names of Zeeland, Vriesland, Groningen, Overisel, North Holland, Drenthe, and Geldersche Buurt (Gelderland Neighborhood), or the municipal names Zutphen, Nordeloos, Hellendoorn, Harderwijk, and Staphorst. There was even a settlement called Graafschap, consisting of Dutch-speaking, Reformed Church Germans from Bentheim in Hanover. The majority of settlers in these villages originated in the place bearing the village name; they spoke the local dialect and perpetuated local customs of food and dress. The entire Michigan settlement was known as *de Kolonie*, but it required the passing of the first generation before the colony became a common community. The Pella, Iowa, and Chicago settlements, also founded in 1847, similarly had particular regional origins.[44]

Only after lengthy experience in North America would these identities begin to lose their paramountcy to an overarching identity as Dutch.

Norse migrants who came to the United States between 1840 and 1915, also brought with them powerful local identities that were reflected in settlement patterns. Moreover, to the degree that the Norwegians manifested any wider identity, it was more apt to be as Scandinavian rather than as Norse, a pan-Scandinavianism being somewhat popular in the United States during the very late nineteenth century.

Unfortunately, United States immigration tells us virtually nothing about English identity in the nineteenth century. It may well be that the insularity of homeland and the imperial adventure abroad may have produced a single national identity throughout the populace of "Engla land" long before one could speak with assurance of a French nation. Claims, however, to such a development during the Middle Ages do appear to ignore later developments. There is, for example, a certain incongruity between a fervid English nationalism and the lack of any notable resentment among the English populace when the foreign prince, William of Orange, was offered and accepted the English crown in 1689; to the highland Scots, by contrast, he remained "Dutch William." Nor did the English masses manifest overt resentment to the fact that George I (1714–1727) and George II (1727–1760) of England were German both by birth and inclination. (Indeed, George I never bothered to learn English so that he might speak to, or better understand, his subjects.) Yet, only a century later, Queen Victoria's consort, Albert, would be denied what would have been the largely empty title of king, ostensibly because of his foreignness. Clearly, something momentous occurred, albeit incrementally, in the interim.

Near the end of his analysis of French nationalism, Weber had this to say: "We have seen, in short, the nation not as a given reality but as a work-in-progress, a model of something at once to be built and to be treated for political reasons as already in existence."[45] The statement hints at why governments, intellectuals, and other elites have often anticipated national consciousness and treated it as a reality long before it was.

By Way of Summary

Although numerous authorities over the decades have addressed the question, "What is a Nation?" far less attention has been paid to the question "When is a Nation?" At what point in its development does a nation come into being? There is ample evidence that Europe's presently recognized nations emerged only very recently, in many cases centuries later than the dates customarily assigned for their emergence. In the matter of nation-formation, there has been far less difference in the timetables of Western and Eastern Europe than is customarily acknowledged, and the lag time between Europe and the Third World has also been greatly exaggerated. Indeed, in the case of a number of putative nations within Europe, it is problematic whether nationhood has even yet been achieved.

A key problem faced by scholars when dating the emergence of nations is that national consciousness is a mass, not an elite phenomenon, and the masses, until quite recently isolated in rural pockets and being semi or totally illiterate, were quite mute with regard to their sense of group identity(ies). Scholars have been necessarily largely dependent upon the written word for their evidence, yet it has been elites who have chronicled history. Seldom have their generalities about national consciousness been applicable to the masses, and very often the elites' conception of the nation did not even extend to the masses.

Another vexing problem is that nation-formation is a process, not an occurrence. The point in the process at which a sufficient portion of a people has internalized the national identity so as to cause nationalism to become an effective force for mobilizing the masses does not lend itself to precise calculation. In any event, claims that a nation existed prior to the late nineteenth century should be treated cautiously.

NOTES

1. Marc Bloch, *Feudal Society*, trans. L. A. Manyon, Vol. 2 (Chicago, 1964). The quotation is from p. 436; his statements concerning English national consciousness appear on p. 432.

2. Johan Huizinga, *Men and Ideas: History, the Middle Ages, the Renaissance* (New York, 1959), as republished in *Nationalism in the Middle Ages*, ed. Leon Triton (New York, 1972), 21.

3. George C. Coulton, "Nationalism in the Middle Ages," *Cambridge Historical Journal* (1935): 37.

4. Sydney Herbert, *Nationality and Its Problems* (New York, 1919), 66–67. Elsewhere (p. 72), Herbert described the sixteenth-century revolt of the Netherlands against Spain: "Originating in religious conflict, the Dutch rebellion passed into an assertion of national individuality on the one hand, and a demand for political liberty—what modern politicians would call 'self-determination'—on the other. In the same struggle with Spain, English nationality was not born, but brought to manhood." It is difficult to reconcile these and still other assessments with Herbert's later statement (p. 76): "To sum up: the world on which the French Revolution was about to break was one in which nationality played but a small part."

5. Barnaby Keeney, "Military Service and the Development of Nationalism in England, 1272–1327," *Speculum* 22 (1947): 549.

6. Dorothy Kirkland, "The Growth of National Sentiment in France before the Fifteenth Century," *History* 23 (1938–1939), reprinted in Triton, *Nationalism in the Middle Ages*. The citation is from p. 105.

7. Hans Kohn, *The Idea of Nationalism: A Study of Its Origins and Background* (New York, 1944), 78.

8. Carlton Hayes, *The Historical Evolution of Modern Nationalism* (New York, 1931), 293.

9. Thomas Tout, *France and England: Their Relations in the Middle Ages and Now* (Manchester, 1922), partially reprinted in Triton, *Nationalism in the Middle Ages*. The citation is from p. 61.

10. For a discussion of the confusion surrounding the term *nation*, see chapter 4 in this volume.

11. See Roger Pearson, *Introduction to Anthropology*, (New York, 1974), 175–90.

12. For details, see Walker Connor, *The National Question in Marxist-Leninist Theory and Strategy* (Princeton, 1984), 128 ff.

13. During World War II, the Nazis created a separate Slovak state. The Croats were also awarded their own polity.

14. For evidence that the Montenegrin view of group-self is not yet settled, see Connor, *The National Question*, 333–34, 381–82. [Given the tendency of many Montenegrins to view themselves as Serbs, it was not surprising that at the time

of the breakup of Yugoslavia in 1991, only the Montenegrins elected to retain the association with Serbia.]

15. According to the census, those identifying themselves as either Bulgar or Greek did not account for even one percent of the population in any of the thirty districts (*opstinas*) comprising Macedonia. By contrast, most emigrants from Macedonia now living in the United States (as well as their descendants) describe themselves as of Bulgar descent. And many from that section of Macedonia abutting Greece, declare themselves to be of Greek ancestry. See Stephan Thernstrom, ed., *Harvard Encyclopedia of American Ethnic Groups* (Cambridge, 1980), 691.

16. A number of such cases will emerge during our later discussion of immigrants in the United States.

17. Cited by Tout, *France and England*, 60.

18. The matter of a "Florentine nation" is addressed below.

19. It is intriguing that such terms as *Great Britain* and *British* should reflect the Briton heritage, while the name of the ethnic homeland, *England* (from Engla land, literally "land of the Angles"), should reflect the Angle strain.

20. Bernard Joseph, *Nationality: Its Nature and Problems* (New Haven, 1929), 41–42.

21. From G. P. Gooch's foreword in Joseph, *Nationality*, 14.

22. *New York Times*, 29 May 1982.

23. Rinn Shinn, ed., *Greece: A Country Study*, (Washington, D.C., 1986), 14–15.

24. C. A. Macartney, *National States and National Minorities* (London, 1934), 56.

25. For details, see Connor, *The National Question*, 561 ff.

26. Eugene Keefe et al., *Romania: A Country Study* (Washington, D.C., 1972), 2.

27. This listing of myths was extracted from William Douglass, "A Critique of Recent Trends in the Analysis of Nationalism" (Paper presented at the Second World Basque Congress, Vitoria-Gasteiz, Spain, 21–25 September 1987).

28. Reprinted in Charles Delzell, ed., *Mediterranean Fascism* (New York, 1970), 193–94.

29. Herbert Schneider, *The Fascist Government of Italy* (New York, 1936), 2.

30. See, for example, John Adams and Paopa Barile, *The Government of Republican Italy* (Boston, 1961), 11–31; and Joseph La Palombara, "Italy: Fragmentation, Isolation, Alienation," in *Political Culture and Political Development*, ed. Lucien Pye and Sydney Verba, (Princeton, 1965).

31. George Armstrong, "Language of Dante Defeats the Dialect," *Guardian Newspaper*, 24 November 1983. Cited in Jim MacLaughlin, "Nationalism as an Autonomous Social Force: A Critique of Recent Scholarship on Ethnonationalism," *Canadian Review of Studies in Nationalism* 14 (Spring 1987): 10.

32. David Holden, "The Fall of Rome goes on and on," *The New York Times Magazine*, 9 March 1975, 80. The author, a correspondent for the *Sunday Times of London*, later explained the general unwillingness to pay taxes to the Italian state in these terms: "After all, if the nation doesn't really exist, why pay to support it?"

33. Eugene Keefe et al., *Area Handbook for Albania* (Washington, D.C., 1971), 53.

34. See, for example, *The Albany Reader: History* (Edinburgh, n.d.), whose

self-described purpose "is to supply a simple narrative of Scottish history, suitable for lower senior classes in Primary Schools" (from the Preface). See also, A. D. Cameron, *History for Young Scots*, 2 vols. (Edinburgh, 1963), intended for "the first two years of Senior Secondary School." "The guiding principle has been to select those facts that children ought to know about the history of their own country and its place in the world down the centuries" (from the Preface).

35. The quotations are extracted from three letters written by Engels to the editor of the British journal, *Commonwealth*.

36. For specifics, see chapters 1, 2, and 7, in this volume.

37. Eugen Weber, *Peasants into Frenchmen: The Modernization of Rural France, 1870–1914* (Stanford, 1976).

38. "France: Historical Outline," in *A Reference History of the World from the Earliest Times to the Present*, ed. Albert Bushnell Hart (Springfield, Mass., 1934), 131. This work was the coordinated effort of six of the United States' most distinguished scholars.

39. Weber, for example, cites the contemporary French historian, Albert Soboul: "The French Revolution completed the nation which became one and indivisible." See *Peasants into Frenchmen*, 95.

40. Maurice Barrés became particularly well known for his attacks on the continuing use of non-French languages within France and for statements such as "Citizens! the language of a free people ought to be one and the same for all. . . . It is treason to *la Patrie* to leave the citizens in ignorance of the national language." See the section, "Jacobin Nationalism," in Hayes, *Historical Evolution*, particularly 64–65.

41. It is intriguing that the most Francofied area should be the northeast, the area of heaviest settlement by the Teutonic Burgundians, Franks, and Normans. This pattern, however, was probably pure accident, a more compelling explanation being the more intensive road and water networks in this area.

42. Weber, *Peasants into Frenchmen*, 73.

43. All these examples, and many others, can be found in Thernstrom, *Harvard Encyclopedia of American Ethnic Groups*.

44. Ibid., 287.

45. Weber, *Peasants into Frenchmen*, 493.

INDEX

acculturation, 21, 51, 69, 79
Acton, Lord John, 6, 7, 8, 11, 13, 22, 25n.2
Adams, John Q., 120
Afghanistan, 17, 60n. 25, 82, 167
Afrikaners, 12, 43, 80, 206
Albania, 16, 169
Albanians, 15, 155, 185n. 15, 197, 202, 206;
    ethnic history of, 219
Algeria, 17, 23, 173
alienation, 177
Alliance for Progress, 46, 120, 121
Almond, Gabriel, 63n. 51, 71, 86n. 20
Alsace, 187n. 29
Alsatians, 95, 167, 168, 180, 190n. 50
American Revolution, 5
Americans, 43, 95
Amerindians, 79, 101, 134
Amery, L. S., 188n. 37
Amnesty International, 206
Angles, 171
Angola, 65n. 64
anomie, 168
Arabdom, 22, 80, 109, 186n. 24
Arabistan, 17
Arabness, 109
Arabs, 79–80, 101, 109, 110, 116n. 38, 133,
    206
Arab World. *See* Arabdom
Argentina, 119, 121
Armenia, 152
Armenians, 17, 63n. 39
Ashantis, 65n. 64, 108
Assam, 78
Assamese, 74
assimilation, 128, 167, 171, 183n. 3, 186n.
    20, 214
Athenians, 207
Attaturk, 135
Australia, 16
Austria, 90, 168
autonomy, 150, 151
Azerbaijani, 107

Bahutu, 10, 58n. 3, 63n. 39, 206
Balinese, 63n. 39

Baluchi, 22, 82, 152, 167
Baluchistan, 22, 77, 78, 177
Bangla Desh, 186n. 23
Bangsamoro, 78
Barbados, 20, 136
Barker, Ernest, 4, 6, 7, 11, 12, 14, 16, 17, 19,
    22, 104
Barrés, Maurice, 226n. 40
Basques, 16, 21, 35, 47, 51, 68, 74, 83, 95, 99,
    124, 139, 148, 152, 153, 167, 168, 169, 170,
    172, 175, 177, 181, 184n. 6, 185n. 13, 188n.
    40, 196; ethnic history of, 217
Bavarians, 109
Beer, Samuel, 188n. 37
Belgium, 12, 13, 14, 21, 30, 35, 43, 45, 47,
    64n. 57, 71, 84, 90, 113n. 7, 138, 140, 151,
    166, 177, 181, 182n. 2
Belize, 136
Belorussia, 187n. 29
Belorussians, 181
Bengal, 146
Bengali, 43, 74, 111, 167, 169
Benin, 65n. 64
Berbers, 17, 23
Bern, 14, 35, 168
Biafra, 186n. 23
Bismarck, Otto von, 93, 198, 200
Bloch, Marc, 211
Blondel, Jean, 188n. 37
Bolivia, 79
Bonaparte, Napoleon, 76, 185n. 10
Bosnia, 155
Bosnians, 197
Brazil, 119
Bretons, 35, 95, 167, 168, 169, 171, 172, 175,
    179, 180, 181, 183n. 3, 184nn. 6 and 7,
    186n. 18, 187n. 26
Brittany, 38, 65n. 61, 146, 171, 184n. 8, 186n.
    18
Bromley, Yu., 74
Buganda, 10
Bulgaria, 16, 28, 169
Bulgars, 18, 185n. 15, 206, 213; ethnic his-
    tory of, 216
Burma. *See* Myanmar